GRIEVOUS ENTANGLEMENT

THE CARTER G. WOODSON INSTITUTE SERIES
Black Studies at Work in the World
Deborah E. McDowell, Shawn Leigh Alexander,
and Robert T. Vinson, Editors

GRIEVOUS ENTANGLEMENT

CONSUMPTION, CONNECTION, AND
SLAVERY IN THE ATLANTIC WORLD

ERIN PEARSON

UNIVERSITY OF VIRGINIA PRESS
Charlottesville and London
Published in association with the
UNIVERSITY OF VIRGINIA'S CARTER G. WOODSON INSTITUTE

The University of Virginia Press is situated on the traditional lands of the Monacan Nation, and the Commonwealth of Virginia was and is home to many other Indigenous people. We pay our respect to all of them, past and present. We also honor the enslaved African and African American people who built the University of Virginia, and we recognize their descendants. We commit to fostering voices from these communities through our publications and to deepening our collective understanding of their histories and contributions.

University of Virginia Press
© 2025 by the Rector and Visitors of the University of Virginia
All rights reserved
Printed in the United States of America on acid-free paper

First published 2025

1 3 5 7 9 8 6 4 2

ISBN 978-0-8139-5387-8 (hardback)
ISBN 978-0-8139-5388-5 (paperback)
ISBN 978-0-8139-5389-2 (ebook)

Library of Congress Cataloging-in-Publication Data
is available for this title.

Cover art: Tangled lines, MalyskaStudio/Envato
Cover design: Elke Barter

To Ian, Kai, and Asher

CONTENTS

Acknowledgments | *ix*

Introduction   1

PART ONE
The Aversive Connections of Tangible Commodities

1. Blood-Sugar Metaphors in British Abolitionism   19

2. Ambivalent Connections in Free Produce Abolitionism   44

3. Blackface Minstrelsy and the Disavowal of Consumption's Connections   72

PART TWO
Metaphoric Consumption in the Discourse on Slavery

4. Feeding the Body Politic: Slavery, Cannibalism, and Identity in the United States   99

5. Consuming Monsters: Hungry Animals
   in the Discourse on Slavery   126

Conclusion   151

Notes | *159*

Works Cited | *191*

Index | *213*

ACKNOWLEDGMENTS

I am grateful to the many people who made the long path to this book easier. At UC Irvine, I benefited enormously from the guidance and mentorship of many faculty members, including Arlene R. Keizer, Brook Thomas, Jayne Lewis, Rachel Sarah O'Toole, and Virginia Jackson. Richard Godden has offered both inspiration and encouragement at pivotal moments then and since. I am especially thankful for Rodrigo Lazo, whose early recommendation to "get into the archives!" proved pivotal to everything that followed. His clear-eyed pragmatism and sharp insights, not to mention his generous and ongoing guidance, have improved this project and many others besides. I was also lucky enough to find a community both intellectually stimulating and supremely fun at UC Irvine. To Angela Beckett, Brian Garcia, Terry Pawlowski, Bowen Slate-Greene, John Nieman, Leah Kaminski, Cailin O'Connor, and Jim Weatherall: Our conversations shaped this book and continue to shape the ways I see the world. Cristina Rodriguez has offered feedback on drafts, moral support, and well-timed drinks every step of the way.

Once I followed Rodrigo's advice to get into the archives, I benefited from the patience and generosity of archivists and librarians at the following institutions: the Library of Congress Prints and Photographs Division, the American Antiquarian Society (especially Paul Erickson and Elizabeth Watts Pope), the Houghton Library, the Autry Library, the Braun Research Library, and the

Huntington Library. I am also grateful for Elon University's interlibrary loan service, and the fact that the library at the University of North Carolina at Chapel Hill extends borrowing privileges to North Carolina residents, a true public good.

This project's long development spanned a number of institutions from which I have been lucky to receive financial and intellectual support. Generous fellowships from the University of California Humanities Network, the UC Irvine School of Humanities, and the UC Irvine Humanities Center supported my earliest archival research. A postdoctoral fellowship at the Frederick Douglass Institute for African and African-American Studies at the University of Rochester provided both time to write and the invaluable opportunity to discuss the project with interlocutors like Ezra Tawil and John Michael. The 2015 NEH Summer Institute "Slavery in the American Republic," organized by Paul Benson, introduced vital historical contexts and facilitated enlightening conversations. During my time in the History and Literature Concentration at Harvard, my project was immeasurably improved by the insights of colleagues including Jennifer Brady, Angela Allan, Daniel Loss, Lauren Kaminsky, and Robin Bernstein. I am particularly grateful to Amanda Claybaugh, whose incisive advice proved transformative. At Elon University, I have received important support in the form of a Hultquist Summer Fellowship, release time, and publication support. I am fortunate to have an exceptional community of scholars and friends at Elon, including Kevin Bourque, Megan Isaac, Deandra Little, Margaret Chapman, Dinidu Karunanayake, Ben Murphy, Lina Kuhn, Dan Burns, Scott Proudfit, Drew Perry, Tita Ramírez, Greg Hlavaty, and Jeana Schickedantz. I benefited from both the historical expertise and camaraderie of Amanda Laury Kleintop. Jean Schwind, who read every word of the manuscript, offered me not only indefatigable support but also painstaking and insightful feedback. Heather Lindenman provided the coworking opportunities, resiliency walks, and sustaining friendship without which I would have been lost.

I wish to thank the many people in the broader C19 community whose questions, suggestions, and feedback helped me hone my argument and broaden my scope, including Janet Neary, Lori Merish, Bridget Bennett, Sarah Juliet Lauro, and Teresa A. Goddu. Michele Currie Navakas and Kelly Ross offered exceptionally helpful guidance. Sharon Kunde both read drafts and introduced me to the writing group that provided crucial insights and timely community—special thanks to AJ Baginski, Rachel Lim, Julia Havard,

Caitlin Cawley, and Garrett Gilmore. Sarah Dempsey offered cowriting and welcome encouragement.

This project is much better for the expertise of dedicated readers. In addition to many of the people listed above, I wish to thank the two anonymous readers of this manuscript for their critical acuity and generosity. I have been immensely lucky to work with everyone at the University of Virginia Press. Beth Colón Pizzini's astute suggestions have sharpened my argument, and her calm command of every aspect of this potentially bewildering process has made for unexpectedly smooth sailing. I am grateful to Deborah E. McDowell, Shawn Leigh Alexander, and Robert T. Vinson for believing in my vision and including this work in the Carter G. Woodson Institute Series: Black Studies at Work in the World. An earlier version of chapter 1 appeared in *ELH* (volume 83, issue 3, Fall 2016, pages 741–69), while an earlier version of chapter 5 appeared in *Arizona Quarterly* (volume 77, issue 2, Summer 2021, pages 25–53). I thank Johns Hopkins University Press for the permission to reprint this material.

This project, like every aspect of my life, has been enriched by friends and family. Jill O'Brien, Rick Lutjens, and Laura Johnson remind me constantly how extraordinarily lucky it was to find so many of my favorite people so early on. Early drafts of this book were written across the table from Lauren Goins, whose curiosity, love, and cooking have sustained me. My sister Brenda Anthony provided a well-timed break from writing. Although they did not live to see the final result, my grandparents Dolly and Karl Kilpatrick and Alice Pearson supported the early stages of this project. My childhood conversations with Grandad sowed the seeds of this book. Karen and Bruce Jackson have cheered me on every step of the way, and I'm thankful for their help and good company. My dad, David Pearson, used to come to every single school play performance and applaud wildly, a fitting embodiment of the encouragement that set me on this path. I'm grateful to him and Tara Pearson for their support. My mom, Kathleen Kilpatrick, with her steady presence, love, and gentle (and much-needed) reminders to take care of myself, has made my day-to-day life better in innumerable ways. My kids, Kai and Asher, inject fun, chaos, and unbridled affection into days that might otherwise be overly devoted to work. Finally, to Ian Jackson: Quite simply, your unwavering support, intellect, and humor have made all of this possible. I dedicate this book to Ian, Asher, and Kai, with love.

GRIEVOUS ENTANGLEMENT

INTRODUCTION

In May 1770, shortly after recovering from a life-threatening illness, John Woolman recorded a remarkable nightmare in his journal. He dreamed that a hunter had captured a strange animal—part cat, part fox—that was brandishing its teeth and claws. In the dream, Woolman soon learns that his fellow white townspeople had just murdered an elderly and likely enslaved Black man so they could feed his flesh to the monstrous creature as well as to some hunting dogs.[1] The white residents thus simultaneously satisfied the appetites of various hungry animals while also ridding themselves of the cost of supporting a man who could no longer work. Despite Woolman's horror, the perpetrators express no remorse, though one woman admits that watching the killing has put her off her tea. The dream is ripe for interpretation, and Woolman himself added the following comment in the margin: "A fox is cunning; a cat is often idle; hunting represents vain delights; tea drinking with which there is sugar points out the slavery of the Negroes, with which many are oppressed to the shortening of their days."[2] As Woolman's own gloss notes, his dream figures slavery in terms of consumption: A monster born of indulgence and carrying the threat of physical violence, it is only satiated through the destruction of Black life. Its belly is filled not by self-exertion, but by white people viciously pursuing their own financial interests.[3] Voracious appetites perpetuate this system. In a detail that foreshadows nineteenth-century abolitionist portrayals of dogs pursuing fugitives, the hunting dogs are fed with human flesh, maintaining their energy to guide more hunts in pursuit of more strange animals, the appetites of which may well demand more blood. Lest the connection to everyday commodities be too subtle, the dream includes (as Woolman remarks) a woman at her tea table, emphasizing that quotidian actions mirror the horrific consumption in which personal taste drives human suffering.

In his seminal history of the sources of antislavery sentiment in Europe and North America, David Brion Davis argues that Woolman's writings appeared at a "turning point in the history of Western culture," epitomized by Woolman's "sense of personal involvement, his ability to see Negro slavery as something more than an abstract institution, his conviction that he shared the profound guilt of all America."[4] In his travels throughout the American colonies and England, Woolman advocated that his fellow Quakers stop directly participating in slavery, but he also urged avoiding less obvious means of participation, including (as he came to recognize in the years directly preceding his nightmare) the sale or consumption of slave-grown sugar.[5] He lamented the difficulty of convincing people to reject slavery and the immoral luxuries it perpetuated, a condition he repeatedly characterized as entanglement. Whether enslaving others or financially supporting slavery, such actions left people "grievously entangled in the spirit of this world" and in need of being "disentangled from connections in interest with known oppressors."[6] The ability to understand oneself as not only linked but entangled—disturbingly implicated in slavery even at a distance—was, as Davis notes, a crucial development in the rise of widespread antislavery activism. Taking its title from Woolman's formulation, *Grievous Entanglement* reveals why these imagined connections so often assumed the form of consumption, whether the symbolic consumption in Woolman's dream or the economic consumption of the slave-grown commodities he refused to sell or purchase.

The historical turning point represented by Woolman resulted from multiple factors that made it newly possible for people who were seemingly removed from the system—geographically distant and not themselves enslaved or enslavers—to understand themselves as connected to slavery. The peak of the transatlantic slave trade in the second half of the eighteenth century coincided with the "consumer revolution."[7] This radical expansion of consumer commodities brought previously unattainable luxuries within reach of even low-income consumers, a process emblematized by the sugar that rapidly transformed from an exotic rarity into an everyday necessity for consumers in Europe and colonial America.[8] Beyond changing diets and social rituals, newly ubiquitous sugar also provided material connections between quotidian personal habits and the Atlantic slave system. As Sidney Mintz observes, "The West Indian plantations had been profitable from the first because of the desire for sugar (and like products) in Europe. . . . Sugar, then, was a cornerstone of British West Indian slavery and the slave trade, and the enslaved Africans who produced the sugar were linked in clear economic relationships to the British laboring people who were learning to eat it."[9]

The same period in which sugar connected ever more British and American homes with Caribbean plantations also saw increased attention to the linkages created by sympathy. Eighteenth-century moral philosophers like David Hume and Adam Smith questioned how and why people came to feel imaginative bonds with those in different circumstances, and eighteenth-century novelists and poets attracted wide audiences with sentimental literature designed to cultivate sympathetic connection to other people.[10] As with the sugar that was more widely available than ever before, ideas about sympathy and sensibility reached unprecedented numbers of Britons and Anglo-Americans by the late eighteenth century.[11] Markman Ellis notes that, in the late eighteenth century, sentimental novels gained a larger readership than had previously existed in literature, extending to women and the middle class and forging "a new political role for literature."[12]

Sympathy represented a vital means by which people came to feel imaginatively connected to distant others, but new forms of market relations offered novel opportunities to enact actual change. In this period, global trade and markets were increasingly understood as channels through which moral influence could flow, and modern historians have identified direct links between economic development and antislavery sentiment.[13] Thomas Haskell has influentially argued that capitalism and abolitionism arose in the same period because market relations facilitated new forms of perception that allowed people to understand themselves as morally implicated and able to effect change at great distances. According to Haskell's thesis, the market "taught" people how to keep promises and recognize the far-reaching consequences of local actions, thereby "expand[ing] a person's horizons of causal involvement" and creating a "precondition" for, though not a guarantee of, new forms of humanitarian understanding.[14] Charlotte Sussman, Lawrence B. Glickman, and Mimi Sheller extend Haskell's observations to underscore the specific role of consumption in generating activism, arguing that the late eighteenth century marked the beginning of a sense of what Glickman calls "long-distance solidarity through acts of consumption" in which "[c]onsumer activists . . . proposed a new physics of time and space, highlighting the real-time effects of consumption and suggesting that in an increasingly global market economy, the moral impact of one's actions was not determined by physical propinquity but by the market-based effects of one's economic actions."[15]

Grievous Entanglement expands on these important insights by showing that the shifting semantics of "consume" in this period transformed consumption into a conceptual vehicle with profound and multifaceted relevance to slavery. At the same moment that the transatlantic slave trade built toward its abominable peak and the products of Caribbean slavery insinuated themselves ever more prominently into the daily lives of Britons and Anglo-Americans, "consume" increasingly indexed both everyday behavior and the economic forces that underpinned global systems. In addition to older (largely negative) meanings like "use up," "destroy," "eat," and "waste away," the meaning of "consume" evolved in the eighteenth century to include what Raymond Williams refers to as "a neutral sense in descriptions of bourgeois political economy."[16] According to Williams, "In the new predominance of an organized market, the acts of making and of using goods and services were newly defined in the increasingly abstract pairings of *producer* and *consumer, production* and *consumption*."[17] The coexistence of negative destructive and more neutral economic connotations provided the connective tissue between seemingly innocuous consumer behavior, the depredations of enslavement, and the economic logic that drove the entire system. Enslaved people were economically consumed (via the slave trade) and physically consumed (via grueling labor regimes and violent punishment), all so that the products of their labor could become objects of consumption (via purchase and, in the case of commodities like sugar, eating).

From eighteenth-century Britain to the antebellum United States, consumption encapsulated both economics and destruction in the discourse on slavery. Published in Manchester in 1787, Thomas Cooper's *Letters on the Slave Trade* captures the economic sense of the term when describing nine million Africans enslaved and transported across the Atlantic as having been "consumed by the Europeans."[18] A half century later, an antislavery book uses the same economic terminology in its condemnation of the U.S. domestic slave trade, referring repeatedly to the *"breeding* states" of the Upper South and the *"buying* or *consuming* states" of the Lower South.[19] Even as "consume" was used to refer to the purchase of enslaved people, its usage often shaded into noneconomic senses as well. A few lines below his reference to the "nine millions of slaves . . . consumed by the Europeans," for instance, Cooper estimates a staggering number of overall deaths resulting from the transatlantic slave trade, claiming that they are the murders with which "the infernal voracity of European avarice has been glutted."[20] Within one paragraph, Cooper moves between consumption as a descriptor for global trade and the specter of consumption's earlier (negative) associations with both excessive appetites and hellish destruction. Frederick Douglass similarly bundles multiple connotations of "consume" in "What to the Slave Is the Fourth of July?" (1852) when he declares that enslaved people being forcibly transported via the internal slave trade "are food for the cotton-field, and the deadly sugar-mill. . . . Heat and sorrow have nearly consumed their strength."[21] By evoking the cotton and sugar that his Northern audience certainly purchased, Douglass connects the trade in and destruction of enslaved bodies with national habits of consumption, implicitly rebuking listeners for their own role in the larger system.

I use "consumption-as-connection" to describe formulations in which the multivalence of consumption allowed people to conceptualize their everyday habits as entangled with slavery. Consumption-as-connection was more than just the recognition that slave-grown commodities represented tangible links to slavery; it encapsulated the way buying those commodities unlocked a range of associations, from the economics of purchasing both goods and enslaved people to the metaphors that captured the destruction those purchases financed. *Grievous Entanglement* reveals how consumption-as-connection enabled geographically distant people to understand themselves as intimately tied to slavery, but it also reveals that such understandings did not elicit a singular response. While it spurred the world's first mass grassroots abolitionist campaign, in which hundreds of thousands of Britons abstained from slave-grown sugar, it also became a means for white working-class Americans to forcefully reject any connection to Black Americans.[22] While it offered both Black and white antislavery activists a powerful metaphor for denouncing slavery's violence, it also incited anti-Black racism, undermining humanitarian principles and fueling white supremacist humor and politics. From the late eighteenth century to the mid-nineteenth century, consumption-as-connection inspired consumer activism in Britain and the

United States, shaped the content of blackface minstrelsy (the most popular cultural form in the antebellum U.S.), and forged tropes that would permeate transatlantic literature, political speech, visual culture, and popular performance long after emancipation.

The few scholars who have considered how consumption shaped perceptions of slavery and enslaved people have focused on either antislavery consumer activism or metaphors of eating that conveyed racial dynamics. Sussman, Glickman, and Sheller compellingly illustrate the way commodities facilitated the sense that people could create change, even at a great remove, through their buying habits. As Sheller observes, consumer activist movements sought to imaginatively bring the bodies of producers and consumers "into closer proximity, even solidarity, by reflecting on how they directly touch each other through the commodity."[23] Conversely, Kyla Wazana Tompkins and Vincent Woodard do not emphasize tangible commodities, but rather uncover how the widespread trope of the "edible black body" played out complexities of race, enslavement, desire, and aversion in U.S. culture.[24] *Grievous Entanglement* builds on, combines, and moves beyond these approaches by showing that, for commentators in this era, consumption as both material practice and imaginative metaphor was inextricably tied to slavery's economic logic.[25] Sussman and Sheller astutely analyze how metaphors attached to sugar, and Tompkins and Woodard briefly and rightly note that depictions of edible Black bodies were related to the commodification of those bodies in slavery.[26] I extend their work by establishing how the overlapping economic and metaphoric senses of "consume" resonated with the fundamental logic of chattel slavery, and how that resonance in turn enabled people to simultaneously grasp multiple aspects of enslavement. While other scholars offer insightful accounts of cannibalism metaphors in relation to specific aspects of slavery, for instance, I argue that cannibalism metaphors pervade the discourse on slavery not just because they express unspeakable violence or reconfigure the significance of familiar consumer goods, but also because they recapitulate precisely what distinguishes chattel slavery from other forms of exploitation: It is a system that renders one human (economically) consumable by another.[27]

By uncovering what it meant to feel "grievously entangled" in slavery, this project expands our understanding of the discourse on slavery in two primary ways. First, it reveals that the ability to understand oneself as painfully connected to slavery through everyday actions was not limited to abolitionists, despite the prevailing scholarly focus on antislavery consumer activism.²⁸ Consumption's associative network was both potent and unwieldy, and it could easily slip between motivating active abolitionism, reinforcing white supremacy, or doing both at the same time. Although scholars have long noted that humanitarianism and sympathy can also promote narratives of difference, attending to consumption-as-connection moves past simple diagnosis of white abolitionist racism to demonstrate that the very basis of the construction's efficacy in inspiring antislavery action was also the source of its frequent anti-Blackness. Second, recognizing the prevalence of consumption-as-connection reveals its broad cultural relevance. In addition to extending its focus beyond abolitionism, *Grievous Entanglement* expands the geographic scope of previous studies to show that, because these semantic and economic conditions existed throughout the Anglophone Atlantic, these new understandings circulated throughout the Atlantic world (frequently alongside the writers and performers who promulgated them). Although this book pays more sustained attention to the antebellum United States, it is impossible to fully grasp how consumption shaped ideas about slavery without situating those ideas in a broader transatlantic context.

The establishment and expansion of slavery was inescapably transatlantic, from the slave trade that forcibly displaced millions of enslaved Africans to the Americas, to the international shipments of slave-grown commodities like sugar and especially cotton, which drove the explosive growth of slavery, the U.S. economy, and British manufacturing alike.²⁹ Starting in the eighteenth century, opponents of slavery formed their own transatlantic links, exchanging ideas and strategies through a "transnational abolitionist network" that was especially strong between Britain and America.³⁰ Antislavery consumer activism, for instance, started with American Quakers like Woolman, who spread his radical ideas in England as well as colonial America. Those ideas, in turn, helped ignite the massive grassroots sugar-abstention campaign in late eighteenth-century Britain.³¹ In the 1820s, British Quaker Elizabeth Heyrick's tract *Immediate, Not Gradual Abolition*, which was printed in Britain and the United States, inaugurated a new era of mass British abstention, extensive U.S. literary output, and numerous organizations dedicated to sourcing free labor products in both countries.³² The movement of enslaved people, commodities, and ideas about consumption facilitated new understandings of slavery throughout the Atlantic world. Even as *Grievous Entanglement* examines antebellum U.S. texts in more depth, I take opportunities throughout the book to note the many connections (and disconnections) between the U.S.

and British contexts, which are essential to recognizing how a wide range of people combined abstract economic logic and daily material practice to ethically orient themselves within vast national and international systems.

Despite important scholarship on consumption as an economic and symbolic means of connection to slavery, far more scholarly attention has been paid to a different means of imagined connection: sympathy, especially in relation to sentimentalism (its primary cultural vehicle). In fact, consumption-as-connection and sentimentalism share many key features and frequently work in tandem.[33] As with consumption-as-connection, sentimentalism forges imaginative connections that traverse distance and difference, whether geographic separation, disparate experiences or identities, or even the divide between real life and fictional worlds.[34] Both sentimentalism and consumption-as-connection emphasize intimate physical contact: The commodities that underpin consumption-as-connection enter and physiologically alter the body (sugar, tobacco) or rest against the body (cotton), while sentimental literature triggers bodily reactions like tears and heartbeats that, according to Karen Sánchez-Eppler, "radically contract[] the distance between narrated events and the moment of their reading, as the feelings in the story are made tangibly present in the flesh of the reader."[35] Both modes were historically tied to consumerism: Whether through the purchase of books, branded merchandise, or specific commodities, everyday purchases offered a mechanism by which stories and systems became personal.[36] Both modes also evince a remarkable ideological elasticity. Even though scholarship has largely focused on sentimental abolitionism, for instance, multiple scholars have noted that both pro- and antislavery activists deployed sentimentalism, much as I will demonstrate that consumption-as-connection did not preordain a specific political position.[37] Finally, both sentimentalism and consumption-as-connection blur lines between the figurative and literal. Chattel slavery was a global system in which consumption represented an economic metaphor as well as the concrete facts of bodily destruction and the ingestion of goods. Sentimentalism, as Naomi Greyser asserts, surfaced in "appeals to sympathy as a meeting ground of the narrated and the embodied, the psychic and the material."[38]

The key difference between the imagined relationships facilitated by sentimentalism and consumption-as-connection is their affective charge. Scholars widely agree that, whatever its actual effects, sentimentalism purports to extend lines of care and kinship through the mobilization of sympathy.[39] As Joanne Dobson writes, "The principal theme of the sentimental text is the desire for bonding, and it is affiliation on the plane of emotion, sympathy, nurturance, or similar moral or spiritual inclination for which sentimental writers and readers yearn."[40] While sentimentalism prioritizes what Dobson calls "affectional ties," consumption-as-connection engenders aversive ties: temporary linkages that encourage their own dissolution at the very moment they are discerned.[41] As with the monstrous eating of human flesh in Woolman's dream, or the antislavery activists who claimed that using sugar effectively meant sweetening tea with the blood of enslaved people, consumption-as-connection formulations rely on disgust, guilt, and the threat of contamination. If the sentimental bond represents a warm embrace, then consumption-as-connection suggests horrifying contact that triggers an urgent pushing away. Despite linking people across many of the same gulfs as sentimental formulations, consumption's imagined ties do not seek to permanently bridge those gulfs so much as sever the linkage that briefly shimmered into view. As I will show, the target of that pushing away varied depending on the formulation: Sometimes the connection to be broken was to the system of slavery or ill-gotten luxury; often, it was to enslaved people themselves.

Aversion's double-edged impact is central to the history of consumption-as-connection. Proclaiming disgust "the most embodied and visceral of emotions," William Ian Miller argues that it "differs from other emotions by having a unique aversive style. The idiom of disgust consistently invokes the sensory experience of what it feels like to be put in danger by the disgusting."[42] Disgust is more than just being revolted; it includes a sense of physical threat that stokes fear. That combination of fear and revulsion, in turn, facilitates clarity. Sianne Ngai observes that "disgust is never ambivalent about its object," echoing Miller's claim that disgust "marks out moral matters for which we can have no compromise."[43] As a result, disgust can galvanize action. Both Miller and Ngai assert that disgust holds special power to enforce moral limits and motivate political action, even as they also note the ways in which disgust can reinforce hierarchies, police boundaries, and buttress racism, classism, and misogyny.[44] On the one hand, consumption-as-connection used disgust to generate moral clarity alongside a physical immediacy that spurred direct antislavery action. On the other hand, the aversion and fear it produced threatened to attach to enslaved people as much as to the institution of slavery. In the hands of many white abolitionists, consumption-as-connection did both, and yet the frequency with which Black abolitionists continued to use it suggests they deemed its efficacy worth its risks.

Despite their affective opposition, consumption-as-connection actually serves as a gothic double to sympathetic connection by laying bare what critics identify as sentimentalism's tacit shortcomings.[45] Scholars have extensively debated the ethics and political efficacy of sentimental fiction, especially in regards to issues like slavery, poverty, and gender.[46] While some scholars have argued that the sympathy sparked by sentimentalism transforms readers and the world, expanding dominant perspectives on who counts as "human" and redefining the ethical grounds on which individuals should act, others have criticized sympathy (and sentimentalism more broadly) for reinforcing asymmetrical power dynamics, offering voyeuristic titillation rather than true fellow feeling, and displacing the experience of the sufferer with that of the sympathizer.[47] Perhaps the most vociferous debates have centered on whether and how sentimentalism uses sympathy to create change in the world. Critics have charged that sentimentalism saps the drive toward effective change by focusing on personal emotional transformation rather than tangible action.[48] Even the scholars who defend sentimentalism's ability to change the world frequently struggle to offer evidence of concrete results, tending instead to focus on the way it lays the foundation for political consequences by influencing hearts and minds.[49]

Shifting attention from the affectional links imaginatively facilitated by sentimentalism to the aversive links of consumption-as-connection opens a new direction in the decades-long debate over sympathy, power, and political action. The links implied by consumption provide a test case for many of sympathy's alleged flaws by explicitly embracing them. Where critics argue that sympathy covertly enforces power differentials while claiming to facilitate identification, consumption-as-connection overtly positions consumers as the powerful causes and selfish beneficiaries of the suffering of enslaved people. Where critics claim that sympathy downplays the experiences of the sufferer by overemphasizing the feelings of the sympathizer, consumption-as-connection unapologetically centers the physical and emotional reactions of consumers. Where critics see sentimental sympathy as false kindness, what James Baldwin calls "the mask of cruelty," consumption-as-connection is unabashedly aversive, rooted in guilt and disgust.[50]

Consumption-as-connection diverges from sentimentalism's supposed flaws in one crucial way, however. It has a track record of not only influencing hearts and minds, but also triggering action in the form of consumer activism. Marshaling disgust and guilt was undoubtedly a valuable means of inspiring action, but the mechanics of aversion proved difficult to control, frequently fomenting racism and defensive disavowal in addition to consumer activism. By investigating the imaginative mechanics of consumption-as-connection, *Grievous Entanglement* reveals that sentimentalism's desire for human kinship may indeed have limited its effectiveness in generating direct antislavery action, but it also exposes the significant risks of a more aversive approach.

Throughout this study I practice a kind of cultural close reading that applies the tools of literary criticism to both literary and archival materials to analyze how small details constellate into larger cultural patterns.[51] In this approach I follow Jacqueline Goldsby's method of "reading history *out* of literary texts instead of *into* them" and Peter Coviello's "insistence on close reading as a way of doing history," sharing their conviction that careful attention to form uncovers broader trends in thinking and feeling.[52] This study starts with what may seem a fundamentally literary concern—metaphors of consumption—and then traces those metaphors through a wide-ranging archive typical of cultural history.[53] Because metaphors depend on cultural associations to create the "system of ideas" that allows them to function, investigating the metaphors that underlay consumption-as-connection offers remarkable insight into the widely shared conceptual grounds that made such a system possible.[54] Beyond their power to disclose cultural patterns, these metaphors also replicate the mechanics of consumption-as-connection. As Paul Ricœur has argued, metaphors work by creating new "semantic proximity" between previously remote terms, initiating a "shift in the logical distance, from the far to the near" much as consumption-as-connection established new and startling contact between geographically distant consumers and enslaved laborers.[55] For Ricœur, metaphors can "reveal[]" or "unconceal[]," enabling "the emergence of a more radical way of looking at things."[56] Consumption-as-connection, I contend, emerged from a historically specific system of ideas and represented a new understanding of the intersections between economics, ethics, and feeling—a revelation with far-reaching consequences to histories of abolitionism and race in the Atlantic world.

Grievous Entanglement is divided into two sections. Comprising three chapters, the first section, "The Aversive Connections of Tangible Commodities," investigates cultural formations in which people grappled with their relationship to slavery through slave-grown commodities like sugar, cotton, and tobacco. In these cultural formations, everyday items transform into charged sites of reckoning or disavowal as consumers effectively defetishize the commodity to envision enslaved laborers instead. Through vivid depictions of bloodstained sugar and tearstained cotton, transatlantic antislavery activists urged consumers to avoid the products of slavery. Meanwhile, blackface minstrel performers repeatedly portrayed enslaved people as indistinguishable from slave crops, though such portrayals served to absolve rather than implicate white working-class audiences in slavery. Encompassing British and U.S. abolitionist consumer activism as well as white supremacist U.S. popular culture, the first section explores the material basis of consumption-as-connection, revealing how a range of far-reaching economic and ethical associations settled onto the tangible stuff of everyday life.

The book's final two chapters comprise its second section, "Metaphoric Consumption in the Discourse on Slavery." Whereas the first section considers actual commodities, the second section turns toward the pervasive metaphors of eating that structured how people wrote, spoke, and thought about slavery—namely, metaphors featuring cannibalism and voracious animals. This section emphasizes the difficulty of separating slavery's economic logic (human beings converted into saleable commodities in order to facilitate commodity consumption) from its more imaginative registers (visions of abject devouring). Failing to analyze metaphoric consumption in addition to slave-grown commodities would miss a crucial aspect of how consumption structured ideas about slavery: Both cannibalism and hungry animal metaphors capture a system that seeks to make human beings consumable. It is worth noting that, even though the second section focuses on them, these metaphors thread through the first section as well. The horror of cannibalism drove antislavery abstention campaigns, for instance, and Herman Melville used both cannibalism and depictions of ravenous sharks to express doubts that consumers would prioritize ethically sourced commodities. The overlaps between sections illustrate the book's larger point about how distant and disparate people and ideas became entangled in the system of slavery. In the same way that people and commodities circulated throughout the Atlantic world, and both antislavery and proslavery sentiment straddled the Atlantic, ideas about consumption reverberated in a number of overlapping formulations from a variety of perspectives and locations.

My first chapter, "Blood-Sugar Metaphors in British Abolitionism," begins with Samuel Taylor Coleridge's assertion that sentimentalism makes for ineffective abolitionism. In a 1795 lecture condemning the slave trade, Coleridge argues that, rather than eliciting tears of sympathy, writers should strive to make slavery immediately tangible to readers by revealing that their consumption directly connects them to enslaved people. For Coleridge and other commentators, metaphors of cannibalism offered a powerful means of defetishizing the commodity and spurring action: Depicting sugar soaked in the blood of enslaved people forced consumers to confront their implication in slavery by making their everyday sweetener symbolize the excruciating labor that produced it. This chapter analyzes blood-sugar metaphors in late eighteenth-century British poetry, fiction, and pamphlets to establish how white abolitionists deployed a mechanism of disgust to galvanize antislavery action. These attempts to make slavery tangible frequently reinforced a white abolitionist obsession with physicality, which in turn worked against the movement's purported humanitarian goals by reinforcing racial difference. The chapter concludes by showing how Afro-Caribbean abolitionists Olaudah Equiano and Mary Prince sought to capitalize on the power of cannibalistic metaphors to critique slavery while also avoiding dehumanizing enslaved people.

My second chapter, "Ambivalent Connections in Free Produce Abolitionism," turns to the antebellum United States and the free produce movement, which advocated buying commodities produced by free rather than enslaved labor, to investigate what happens when abolitionists attempted to use the disgust of consumption-as-connection without sacrificing the sympathetic bonds promoted by sentimentalism. While eighteenth-century British sugar abstainers emphasized an aversive physicality that worked against human kinship, the antebellum American free produce movement sought to strike a balance between the disgust that generated action and the sympathy that would make connection with enslaved people appealing rather than appalling. The abolitionist poetry of Frances Ellen Watkins Harper and Elizabeth Margaret Chandler indicates an ambivalence toward aversion that is, I argue, characteristic of the U.S. free produce movement. While Harper and Chandler still use disturbing tropes of bloodstained commodities, they also encourage readers to imagine slavery's products as imbued with the tears and sighs of enslaved people, an adjustment that aims to inculcate sympathetic identification instead of instinctual recoil. Their ambivalence toward revulsion is mirrored in Harriet Beecher Stowe's *Uncle Tom's Cabin* and Henry David Thoreau's *Walden*. Even though Stowe and Thoreau urge readers to recognize how financial networks could implicate them in slavery, they avoid depicting the more troubling (and more physical) contact suggested by consumption-as-connection. Alternatively, Herman Melville's *Moby-Dick* portrays consumers who are enticed rather than horrified by participating in exploitative global networks, demonstrating that perceiving direct connection through commodities hardly guaranteed altered consumer behavior. This chapter reveals that merely recognizing consumption-as-connection was insufficient to inspire action if it did not also marshal disgust.

The third chapter, "Blackface Minstrelsy and the Disavowal of Consumption's Connections," turns to a distinctly non-abolitionist context, blackface minstrelsy, to expand the previous chapter's argument that identifying links to slavery did not automatically trigger antislavery action. While other scholars have examined antislavery consumer activism, this chapter is the first to show that the same consumption-as-connection formulations underpinned the frequent moments in U.S. minstrel performances in which enslaved people are imagined as interchangeable with the fields they tended and the crops they produced. Although this metaphoric merging implies consumer complicity by suggesting that consuming sugar and tobacco also means consuming enslaved bodies, these moments did not result in antislavery declarations or actions. Instead, the songs repress the recognition of complicity by portraying enslaved people as driving market demand for such commodities themselves. Examining the fantasy that minstrel audiences were free of any real connection to slavery alongside the physical objects (songsters and sheet music) in which that fantasy appeared, this chapter uses material culture to show that consumption-as-connection helped white working-class consumers grapple with their ambivalence toward the middle class rather than confront their links to slavery. In the process, the chapter argues that scholars must consider at-home performances in addition to theatrical contexts to fully grasp the racial and class dynamics of blackface minstrelsy.

While the first three chapters focus on actual commodities and consumers, the fourth chapter, "Feeding the Body Politic: Slavery, Cannibalism, and Identity in the United States," turns to metaphoric consumption to assert that, in addition to helping people envision their personal connection to slavery through purchases, consumption also provided a widely used conceptual framework for defining regional and national identities in relation to slavery. As the first three chapters of this study indicate, cannibalistic metaphors expressed the horror of purchasing a commodity that was inseparable from the commodified laborer who produced it, but this chapter contends that the specific conditions of the antebellum United States also opened new ways of using cannibalism to think about slavery. In its ability to capture the fundamental ambivalence between identity (eating that which is the same as you) and difference (making humans into meat), cannibalism offered a powerful metaphor for debates about whether a nation could viably include multiple groups whom commentators assumed to be fundamentally different. The chapter begins by sketching the contours of the historical discourse on cannibalism to establish how these ideas informed the cannibalism metaphors applied to slavery. It then traces two major strands of those metaphors in the United States: images of a cannibalistic body politic used to grapple with the ultimate place of Black people and slavery within the nation, and evocations of cannibalism used to critique slavery's economic basis. Examining texts including Ralph Waldo Emerson's private journals, Frederick Douglass's autobiographies, and antebellum newspapers and political cartoons, this chapter demonstrates that antebellum cannibalism metaphors represent slavery as driven by greed and threatening to destroy the nation as a whole.

The fifth chapter, "Consuming Monsters: Hungry Animals in the Discourse on Slavery," pivots from metaphors of humans being consumed by other humans to humans being consumed by monstrous animals. On both sides of the Atlantic, abolitionists used depictions of sharks, birds, and dogs to capture the consumptive logic of chattel slavery. As with the cannibalistic metaphors in the first chapter, these tropes proved powerful in eliciting audience disgust but also hazardous in their tendency to bolster anti-Black racism. In white abolitionist broadsides, poetry, and illustrations, hungry animal imagery critiques the economic foundations of slavery, but it also frequently implies that enslaved people were "natural" prey and passive victims. Moreover, just as recognizing economic connections to slavery did not necessarily generate abolitionist action (as chapters 2 and 3 establish), this chapter argues that the prevalence of similar hungry animal tropes in antebellum racist kitsch proves that economic critique alone is insufficient for securing antislavery results. In response, Black abolitionists reworked hungry animal tropes to emphasize resistance and offer a more nuanced picture of the enslaver psyche in slave narratives, fiction, and traveling panoramas. Building on scholarship on animals in the discourse on slavery, this chapter reveals that the threat of consumption is a critical (and overlooked) aspect of these tropes, allowing commentators to show how the slave system fused abstract economics and lived experience, instinctive impulses and careful strategy.

The book's conclusion proposes that consumption-as-connection offers insight into what motivates people to act against apparently unchangeable systems. As *Grievous Entanglement* reveals, the answer may well be unwieldy or even perilous, as with the disgust that generated antislavery action and anti-Black racism alike. I end by suggesting that the Black abolitionists who appear throughout this study offer a model for pragmatically deploying effective but imperfect strategies. Recognizing the potentially harmful aspects of consumption-as-connection, many Black antislavery activists nevertheless chose to rework rather than abandon it, prioritizing efficacy without acquiescing to its propensity for harm.

PART ONE
THE AVERSIVE CONNECTIONS OF TANGIBLE COMMODITIES

ONE

BLOOD-SUGAR METAPHORS IN BRITISH ABOLITIONISM

In Samuel Taylor Coleridge's view, the transatlantic slave trade would be stopped by action, not sympathy. Performative feelings—stoked by sentimental literature and the desire to appear virtuous—risked distracting Britons with futile outpourings of emotion instead of promoting the behavior that would create real change. "If only one tenth part among you who profess yourselves Christians, if one half only of the Petitioners," Coleridge admonishes in a 1796 essay based on a lecture he gave the previous year, "instead of bustling about with ostentatious sensibility, were to leave off—not *all* the West-India commodities—but only Sugar and Rum . . .—all this misery might be stopped."[1] The problem, in Coleridge's opinion, is that knowledge of calamity is insufficient to produce action if that calamity does not seem proximate and tangible: "[T]he citizen at the crouded feast is not nauseated by the stench and filth of the slave-vessel—the fine lady's nerves are not shattered by the shrieks! She sips a beverage sweetened with human blood, even while she is weeping over the refined sorrows of Werter or of Clementina. Sensibility is not Benevolence. . . . Benevolence impels to action, and is accompanied by self-denial."[2] In an illustration of what Simon Gikandi has called the "culture of taste," the lady's comfortable surroundings insulate her from the economies of violence that have facilitated her lifestyle, allowing her to ignore the actual human suffering behind her sugar even as she sympathizes with fictional characters. Rather than maintain the "censoring mechanisms" on which the culture of taste depended, Coleridge strives to break through the fog of ineffectual sympathy by replacing it with a more visceral (and action-producing) feeling: disgust.[3] In the revolting image of a blood-sweetened beverage, Coleridge seeks to render slavery appallingly immediate and thereby impel the antislavery action that sentimentalism alone fails to achieve.

Cannibalism metaphors encapsulate consumption-as-connection: They express the economic logic and interpersonal violence of slavery while also inspiring a visceral response that spurs action. If cannibalism means human beings made into meat, chattel slavery means something similar: human beings treated as commodities to be consumed. Building on abstentionist ideas from American Quakers like Benjamin Lay and John Woolman, white British abolitionists used the cannibalistic image of blood-soaked sugar to catalyze the world's first major consumer boycott: After a 1791 bill abolishing the slave trade failed to pass, hundreds of thousands of British consumers refused to buy slave-grown sugar.[4] William Fox, whose pamphlet urging abstention went through twenty-six editions in London alone, proclaimed sugar to be "steeped in the blood of our fellow-creatures," while a poem by Robert Merry wonders, "Are Drops of Blood the Horrible Manure / That fills with luscious juice the teeming Cane?"[5] Imagining the physical body of the laborer composing or adhering to the product allowed abolitionists to establish a chain of relation between consumers and enslaved people an ocean apart. In the attempt to inspire action, however, it was not enough to establish the metaphoric connection; it was imperative to make that connection as immediate (and uncomfortable) as possible. By replacing the commodity with the laborer who produced it, blood-sugar metaphors figure enslaved people and consumers not only in direct relation, but also in intimate contact. Coleridge tries to make the metaphoric more material by combining the intellectual recognition of complicity with the affective gut punch of primal disgust.

Critics have seen the cannibalistic implications of blood-sugar metaphors in two ways: as an act of racial reversal and/or as an indication of racist disgust. The metaphors stage a reversal in which the presumably white British consumer is made to assume the imagined position of the cannibalistic dark-skinned Other. Charlotte Sussman, who has shown that colonial commodities generated anxiety about how British bodies (and the body politic) were being transformed by foreign goods, notes the long-standing fantasy about the Caribbean being populated by cannibals before arguing that "[t]he abolitionist accusation of English cannibalism enacts a kind of paranoid reversal of this fantasy; as a result of their improper consumption of colonial products, British consumers are themselves transformed into the savage cannibals they had once fantasized about as existing only on the colonial periphery."[6] In addition to the racist horror of an eroded distinction between white European and cannibalistic Other, the prospect of ingesting taboo items like human blood, sweat, and flesh would have inspired disgust in most readers. According to Timothy Morton, the "'blood-sugar' topos" is "a particularly aversive topos," in which "[t]he sweetened drinks of tea, coffee and chocolate are rendered suddenly nauseating by the notion that they are full of the blood of slaves."[7] Together, the reversal and disgust explanations reveal how these metaphors created a double imperative for consumers to refuse the product: to avoid assuming the racialized label of cannibal and to escape contamination by bodily fluids. In both cases, white abolitionist rhetoric uses cannibalistic metaphors to create new proximity between British consumers and enslaved people in the Caribbean while simultaneously working to make that proximity horrifying.

My account goes beyond reversal and disgust to demonstrate that the same features that provoked anti-Black racism were also key to prompting widespread action. When white abolitionists expressed consumption-as-connection through cannibalistic imagery, they made slavery feel tangible through reference to abhorrent physicality. That focus on physicality, in turn, exemplified a pervasive fixation on the physical in white British abolitionist writing about people of African descent. Resonant and revolting, blood-sugar metaphors unleashed antislavery consumer activism even as they reinforced racial difference. Multiple critics have rightly noted the way these formulations frequently contradicted the humanitarian goals of abolitionists; as Deirdre Coleman observes, "The belief in a common humanity, the sentimental identification of the African as brother: these recuperative features of abolitionism always coexist with a panicky and contradictory need to preserve essential boundaries and distinctions."[8] Scholarly accounts characterize the combination of inclusive ideals and dehumanizing racism in blood-sugar metaphors as incongruous, but I maintain that, even as it worked against inclusion, the disgust generated by consumption-as-connection was a crucial factor in the ability of these formulations to inspire action.[9] Blood-sugar imagery embraced the aversion it produced, offering double-edged metaphors that were simultaneously problematic and powerful.

This is the first of two chapters on antislavery consumer activism, each of which considers a major geographic and chronological node in the movement. In this chapter, I focus on the first significant outpouring of abolitionist abstention, which was centered in late eighteenth-century Britain even as it also attracted a small number of U.S. adherents.[10] I examine a range of works from the final two decades of the eighteenth century, a period in which an isolated initiative among dedicated supporters blossomed into a mass movement in which hundreds of thousands signed petitions, abstained from sugar, and distributed pamphlets and poetry for the cause. I begin by analyzing Coleridge's "On the Slave Trade" to show how blood-sugar metaphors insist on a kind of bodily incarnation with troubling implications for universal kinship. I then orient those metaphors within the larger abolitionist tradition, including poems, a firsthand account from a slave ship's surgeon, and a didactic novel for children, to establish the obsessive focus on the physical realm in white British abolitionist writing. The abstention pamphlet in which Andrew Burn contends that British consumers literally ingest the bodily fluids of enslaved people is far from the oddity other critics have declared it. His literalizing impulse represents the logical culmination of blood-sugar metaphors within the context of the white abolitionist emphasis on physicality. Robert Southey's rarely studied antislavery sonnet sequence offers a literary version of Burn's literalizing impulse; it vividly exposes how both consumption-as-connection and the focus on physicality ultimately undermine rather than maintain connection.[11] Finally, the autobiographies of Olaudah Equiano and Mary Prince demonstrate that Afro-Caribbean abolitionists embraced the antislavery potential of cannibalism metaphors while also seeking to circumvent their tendency toward dehumanizing physicality.

CANNIBALISTIC METAPHORS AS INCARNATION

In Coleridge's estimation, successfully catalyzing real action rather than mere emotion requires revealing the normally hidden relations between producers and consumers. In his essay "On the Slave Trade," he declares, "Surely if the inspired Philanthropist of Galilee were to revisit Earth, and be among the Feasters as at Cana, he would not now change water into wine, but convert the produce into the things producing, the occasion into the things occasioned. Then with our fleshly eye should we behold what even now Imagination ought to paint to us; instead of conserves, tears and blood, and for music, groanings and the loud peals of the lash."[12] Coleridge reimagines the miracle at Cana as transformation in reverse; instead of making something more luxurious, he strips sugar products and genteel table manners of their luxury to uncover the human suffering at their core. He thus stages a remarkable dismantling of the commodity fetish, the conditions under which, as Karl Marx puts it, "the definite social relation between men themselves . . . assumes here, for them, the fantastic form of a relation between things."[13] By disguising the actual labor that created the product, the commodity fetish makes value appear as an inherent property of the commodity rather than a function of the labor that produced it.

The commodity fetish has particular relevance to chattel slavery. William Pietz has argued that the idea of the fetish emerged alongside the commodity form during sixteenth- and seventeenth-century interactions between Africans and Europeans—interactions that also helped spawn the transatlantic slave trade. In Pietz's view, the fetish as a concept depends upon "the fetish object's irreducible materiality," even as that material object nevertheless embodies ineffable "religious, commercial, aesthetic, and sexual values."[14] Given that chattel slavery was a system that attempted to reduce people to tradeable property, the tension between materiality and human meaning is significant. As Stephen M. Best has shown, fugitive slave laws were designed to resolve the "paradox of the commodity form" by "manag[ing] the slave's coeval status as material property and willing self."[15] When Coleridge refuses to let a fine meal distract from the conditions of its production, he re-centers human laborers in an effort to redress the failure of imagination that normally prevents consumers from recognizing their direct relationship to slavery.[16]

Coleridge's desire to place these scenes before the "fleshly eye" implies incarnation. It is not just the conditions of labor he wants to render in the flesh, but also flesh itself—the "tears and blood" of the bodies of enslaved people. This attachment to the consumed body in turn raises the specters of both communion and cannibalism in a crux that demonstrates the fundamentally double-edged nature of the blood-sugar trope, which simultaneously promotes humanitarianism and aversion. Immediately before his vision of Cana, Coleridge evokes communion: "A part of that food among most of you, is sweetened with Brother's Blood. 'Lord! bless the food which thou hast given us!' O Blasphemy! Did God give food mingled with the blood of the Murdered? Will God bless the food which is polluted with the Blood of his own innocent children?."[17] At first glance, Coleridge's rhetoric seems almost tongue-in-cheek. In the sacrament of communion, God indeed gives and blesses food "mingled with the blood of the Murdered," though that blood is more precisely that of His own innocent child rather than children. And yet the statement evokes the Protestant critique of the fatal misinterpretation Catholics supposedly make about the Eucharist.[18]

When early Protestants latched onto the idea that the Catholic doctrine of transubstantiation rendered communion a cannibalistic rite, they were, according to Maggie Kilgour, anxiously rejecting a doctrine that seemed troublingly worldly as opposed to spiritual. By misrepresenting Catholic communion, Protestants "made the other extreme, their own position, appear as the only alternative for those who did not wish to be cannibals."[19] In this light, the subtext of Coleridge's blasphemous dinner table might be paraphrased as "To think that God would bless a table laden with the fruit of slavery would be as fallacious as the Catholic belief that the literal body of Christ is present in communion, and just as cannibalistic." This subtext is even stronger in the manuscript of the lecture on which the essay was based, where Coleridge inserts an incredulous question after the line about "Brother's Blood": "Will the Father of all men bless the Food of Cannibals . . . ?"[20] This question illuminates one reason why the blood-sugar metaphor seemed so powerful to abolitionists: Just as Protestant reformers harnessed the horror generated by imagined Catholic cannibalism to garner support, abolitionists took advantage of the revulsion generated by cannibalistic consumption-as-connection to convince people of the appalling immorality of purchasing the products of slavery.

The mechanics of this revulsion depended on aversion not just to being a cannibal, however, but also to the distressing specter of bodily functions. Protestant condemnation of Catholic communion practices again proves illuminating by demonstrating how cannibalism taints even the most hallowed subjects with a troubling physicality. For John Milton in *On Christian Doctrine,* the cannibalistic overtones of Catholic communion are horrifying because they forced Christ back into the fleshly realm in the most ignominious of ways: "Finally the Mass brings down Christ's holy body from its supreme exaltation at the right hand of God. It drags it back to the earth . . . to be broken once more and crushed and ground, even by the fangs of brutes. Then, when it has been driven through all the stomach's filthy channels, it shoots it out—one shudders even to mention it—into the latrine."[21] Unlike debates over communion, in which the purportedly cannibalized flesh is the divine body of Christ, the victims of cannibalism in white abolitionist constructions are people of African descent—a distinction with great significance. For many Europeans, long-standing ideas about Blackness had already systematically associated darker skin with dirtiness and spiritual evils.[22] Even Coleridge's essay evokes contamination by grouping slavery within the human miseries that he presents as a dunghill: "Provided the dunghill be not before their parlour window, they are well content to know that it exists, and that it is the hot-bed of their pestilent luxuries."[23] In Protestant visions of communion, the problem is degrading the flesh; in white abolitionist evocations of cannibalistic sugar consumption, the problem is more often being degraded by it.

As the obsessive, even prurient focus on physical suffering in much of antislavery writing attests, many white abolitionists were invested at least as much in the spectacle of mutilated flesh as in the tragic denial of humanity. The fixation on debased and potentially dangerous bodies in turn worked against the stated goals of abolitionists. Perhaps best embodied by the "Am I Not a Man and a Brother?" seal of the London Committee of the Society for Effecting the Abolition of the Slave Trade (and, later, medallion by Josiah Wedgwood), but echoed in phrases like Coleridge's indignant "Brother's Blood," many abolitionists proposed a kinship that went beyond physical markers of difference—a connection beyond flesh, in the more spiritual sense of communion. The cannibalistic metaphor's emphatic physicality invariably pulls efforts at spiritual kinship back into the domain of bodies, bodies whose differing phenotypes have formed the basis of racist exploitation in the first place. As Saidiya Hartman has argued, the recognition of the humanity of enslaved people did not necessarily negate the logic of slavery. In fact, the circumscribed ways in which slavery allowed for that recognition resulted in a fixation on enslaved bodies in pain: "Bluntly stated, the violence of subjection concealed and extended itself through the outstretched hand of legislated concern. The slave was considered a subject only insofar as he was criminal(ized), wounded body, or mortified flesh."[24]

The power of blood-sugar metaphors lies in their ability not only to conjure disturbing physicality, but to make it immediate to readers. They collapsed the distance between suffering enslaved people and British consumers through the mechanics of metaphor. According to Paul Ricœur, metaphoric meaning depends on bringing disparate ideas closer together: "The *new* pertinence or congruence proper to a meaningful metaphoric utterance proceeds from the kind of semantic proximity which suddenly obtains between terms in spite of their distance. Things or ideas which were remote appear now as close. Resemblance ultimately is nothing else than this rapprochement which reveals a generic kinship between heterogeneous ideas."[25] The cannibalistic metaphor establishes proximity on two levels: at the level of the image, which envisions Britons in close bodily contact with enslaved people in the Caribbean, and at the level of the metaphor, which seeks to expose the "generic kinship" between the cannibal act and the institution of slavery (namely, that they represent conditions under which human beings are rendered consumable).

As with consumption-as-connection more broadly, blood-sugar metaphors represent an uncomfortable fusion of connection and separation: British consumers and enslaved people were imaginatively linked under conditions that encouraged the consumer to quickly reestablish distance. The aversive mechanism of these metaphors was not inevitably problematic, however. The intended humanitarian gesture was not subverted by the conceptual connection of slavery and cannibalism at the level of metaphor, but rather by the insistent physicality of the cannibalistic image itself. In the case of the new semantic proximity between slavery and cannibalism, the desire to create more distance between the terms dovetailed perfectly with abolitionist objectives without sacrificing the possibility for real communion. Abolishing the transatlantic slave trade would remove one system that worked to convert human beings into consumable commodities, while mandating better treatment of enslaved people would limit some of the physical and psychological depredations of a system in which human beings were treated more like meat. Either way, the actions would restore some breathing room between slavery and cannibalism and improve conditions for enslaved people. When it came to the imagined proximity between white British consumers and people of African descent, however, the desired distancing of terms would mean an anxious pushing away of the Afro-Caribbean bodies suddenly in close relation. Unfortunately, this second vein dominated white British abolitionist rhetoric, betraying an obsession with the physical realm that overwhelmed the less problematic possibilities suggested at the level of metaphor.

"THEIR WHOLE SOUL BLEEDS": THE WHITE BRITISH ABOLITIONIST OBSESSION WITH THE PHYSICAL

Close attention to the physical realm—the bodies of producers and consumers and the substance of sugar—allowed abolitionists to conceptualize the material connections between Afro-Caribbean enslaved people and the British public, paving the way for the cannibalistic metaphors that would collapse the distance between the newly connected bodies. Unfortunately, the obsessive focus on physical attributes also shared a primary pitfall of the cannibalistic metaphor, since the emphasis on the physical realm not only highlighted difference and encouraged disgust, but also downplayed the subjectivity of enslaved people. Even as it undermined humanitarian goals, this insistent physicality helped blood-sugar metaphors resonate within a white abolitionist tradition characterized by what Karen Sánchez-Eppler has called a "hyberbolic insistence on embodiment."[26] For all their touting of universal kinship beyond any superficial differences—as when the speaker of William Cowper's "Negro's Complaint" asserts,

> Fleecy locks and black complexion
> Cannot forfeit Nature's claim;
> Skins may differ, but Affection
> Dwells in White and Black the same[27]

—many white British abolitionists seemed thoroughly rooted in the physical realm.

A case in point is Dorothy Kilner's didactic novel *The Rotchfords; or, The Friendly Counsellor: Designed for the Instruction and Amusement of the Youth of Both Sexes* (1786). The titular family's efforts to instruct their white son about the soul shared by Africans and Europeans alike demonstrate how even the most well-intentioned antiracist advocates can get bogged down in the physical attributes that have been a primary focus of racist attention in the first place. The arrival of Pompey, an enslaved child who fled an abusive enslaver, gives the Rotchford children ample opportunities to learn about tolerance and human fellowship. When Pompey falls and cuts his face, the other children are surprised by the color of his blood: "*Harriot* and *George*, were not a little astonished to see the blood which flowed from the wound, of the same colour as that which on any accident came from their own fingers, or cheeks. Pray, mamma, said *George*, with an air of surprise, could you have supposed that that *inkey* looking boy would have had such red blood? Did not you expect to see it look like ink or mud?"[28] When it comes to people with darker skin, George assumes correlation between exterior and interior. It is interesting to note that the terms in which he codes the imagined interior are those of writing—ink—or dirt, almost as if the most obvious possibilities for white conceptualization of the Black body are through discourse or disgust.[29]

George's mother dutifully attempts to disabuse him of his misapprehensions. Her first example is not auspicious for its antiracism—she turns to livestock to make the point ("Do you suppose, *George*, the blood of your papa's horse, and that of *Charles*'s, would be very different, because one is black and the other white . . . ?")—and George refuses to acknowledge any merit to the argument, instead hewing to his shock.[30] It takes George's father to finally get the lesson across. To George's amazed exclamation "That a *black* boy should have *red* blood like ours!" Mr. Rotchford replies, "Aye, *very* like yours indeed . . . and was your skin and his to be stripped off, there would be no difference to be discovered between the black, and the white boy."[31] George, understanding at last, quickly asks if Pompey's bones are like his: "*Exactly*, replied his father, and not only his bones, but his *soul* too, is of the same immortal, never-dying nature."[32] Although the final lesson is about a shared humanity between Africans and Europeans, it is notable that the path to get there requires a figurative flaying (picturing the children's skin being "stripped off") to reach the soul, because one must first get beneath deceptive "black" surfaces to reveal blood and bones.

Mary Birkett's "A Poem on the African Slave Trade, Addressed to Her Own Sex" expresses a similar sense that, where enslaved (or perhaps just African) bodies are concerned, the physical realm takes precedence even in questions of the soul. Her poem passionately argues that women have a moral duty to "no more the blood-stain'd lux'ry choose" and thereby ease the suffering of fellow human beings.³³ She repeatedly proclaims a universal kinship with enslaved people that transcends superficial differences, arguing that "little boots a white or sable skin, / To prove a fair inhabitant within" and calling, as many white abolitionist poems do, on God's universal love as a model to be espoused here on earth:

> And how can you his blessing think to prove,
> Whose first, best law is *universal love*?
> Man was his fav'rite work—he form'd him free;
> His fav'rite work whate'er his colour be:
> And far more dark's the sinful soul within,
> Than the poor harmless Negro's sable skin.³⁴

Her choice of the loaded adjectives "fair" and "dark" hints that, professions of universal kinship notwithstanding, she struggles to relinquish physicality in her considerations of enslaved people. Countering arguments that deny the mistreatment of enslaved people, Birkett insists that the recognition of inherent similarity will necessarily lead to a sympathetic understanding of enslaved suffering:

> Ah, Sophist, vain thy subtle reas'nings aim!
> Look at the Negro's sun-burnt, grief-worn frame!
> Examine well each limb, each nerve, each bone,
> Each artery—and then observe *thy own*;
> The beating pulse, the heart that throbs within,
> All, (save the sable tincture of his skin,)
> Say, Christians, do they not resemble you?
> If so, their feelings and sensations too:
> One moment now with you his burthen rest,
> Then tell me, is he happy—is he blest?³⁵

It is not enough to proclaim that enslaved people have the same inner life as white Britons. Birkett must instead delve carefully into the physical being of the enslaved person, starting with an examination of the exterior and systematically cutting through to the beating heart, pointing out anatomical points of interest with the precision of a vivisectionist. She ends by connecting these qualities to the European body and then finally by relating them to spiritual qualities like "feelings and sensations," but it is only through the physicality of the Black body that she gets there.

Later in the poem, Birkett again evinces an inability to divorce the souls of enslaved people from their physical bodies:

> Now dead to hope they see resistance vain,
> They in their manly breasts conceal their pain;
> A silent grief to furious rage succeeds,
> And by resentment stung—their whole soul bleeds.[36]

The stoic slave is a stock figure of white British abolitionist poetry, allowing speakers to assign enslaved people a courageous dignity but also to place themselves in the role of privileged translator, peeling back the apparently unfeeling exterior to expose the pain bravely hidden underneath. Although Birkett's speaker purports to reveal the ineffable—pain, grief—that ineffable itself is linked to the physical reality that would accompany skin actually being "stripped off," to repeat Mr. Rotchford: It may be the soul, but the soul of the wronged enslaved person actually bleeds.

Nowhere is the obsession with the physicality of enslaved people clearer than in the catalogic profusion of bodily emissions that appears in white abolitionist writing. This is the body at its most abjectly and inescapably physical, far away from spiritual glory (recall that Milton evoked defecation to characterize the ignominy of the physical realm). In his *Account of the Slave Trade on the Coast of Africa* (1788), Alexander Falconbridge, a white surgeon who had practiced aboard slave ships and later testified against the trade, repeatedly describes the ravages caused by fluxes, a term meaning copiously flowing blood, excrement, or mucus: "The deck, that is, the floor of their rooms, was so covered with the blood and mucus which had proceeded from them in consequence of the flux, that it resembled a slaughter-house. It is not in the power of the human imagination to picture to itself a situation more dreadful or disgusting."[37] The proliferation of fluids conceptually links the captives to animals, not because of forced labor or the ability to be sold, but because their area of the ship is so covered in bodily fluids that it looks like they've been categorically broken down into edible joints. Imagery of bodily fluids dominated antislavery poetry and theater as well. The play *Furibond; or, Harlequin Negro* (1807) offers a typical example:

She heard the toil-bled father's shrieks,
While tears roll'd down their sable cheeks;
Saw mothers from their children torn,
Beneath the whip to waste and mourn.
The lash she heard, she saw the wound,
And human gore polute the ground[.][38]

In this vision, suffering is akin to gushing—the father has been bled by toil, tears run down cheeks, and whips open wounds that then allow human gore to pollute the ground. These bodily emissions manifest a variety of interior feelings—exhausted despair, inconsolable grief—on the body, as if its breach allows ineffable interior feelings to spill out in physical form. Reminiscent of Birkett's "bleeding soul," this imagery gives as much (or more) weight to the physical signs as to the nonphysical signified. Even when talking about interior emotions or the spiritual realm, such images insist on the physical bodies of enslaved people.

"DISAGREEABLE SENSATIONS": ANDREW BURN'S MECHANISM OF DISGUST

William Fox's extraordinarily popular pamphlet *An Address to the People of Great Britain, on the Propriety of Abstaining from West India Sugar and Rum*, first published in 1791, makes the terms of consumption-as-connection clear. At different points in the pamphlet, "consumption" encompasses use, purchase, and eating. Fox directly implicates British consumers ("[I]f we purchase the commodity we participate in the crime. The slave-dealer, the slave-holder, and the slave-driver, are virtually the agents of the consumer"); suggests that the market logic of buying commodities mirrors chattel slavery ("[T]he money paid, either for the slave, or for the produce of his labour, is paid to obtain that criminal possession"); and precisely quantifies the connection between consumers and slavery ("A family that uses 5 lb. of sugar per week . . . will, by abstaining from the consumption 21 months, prevent the slavery or murder of one fellow-creature").[39] Fox's active constructions place the British public (himself included) firmly in the subject position, thereby asserting that consumers have a straightforward impact on the well-being and even lives of enslaved people.

When Fox introduces cannibalistic imagery, however, his language shifts toward a more figurative account of the relation between sugar consumers and enslaved people. "Nay, so necessarily connected are our consumption of the commodity, and the misery resulting from it," he admonishes, "that in every pound of sugar used, (the produce of slaves imported from Africa) we may be considered as consuming two ounces of human flesh."[40] The "considered" implies an act of imagination. That same imaginative consideration characterizes Fox's subsequent appeal to outside authorities: "A French writer observes, 'That he cannot look on a piece of sugar without conceiving it stained with spots of human blood:' and Dr. Franklin adds, that had he taken in all the consequences, 'he might have seen the sugar not merely spotted, but thoroughly dyed scarlet in grain.'"[41] The "French writer" (actually Claude Adrien Helvétius) moves from tangible reality (looking at a piece of sugar) to the nightmare mental image ("conceiving it stained with spots of human blood"). Benjamin Franklin's vision of scarlet sugar further emphasizes that these are realities seen not with the eyes but with an imagination duly informed by the conditions of enslaved labor. For Fox, the cannibalism of sugar consumption remains resolutely figurative—an imaginative leap that builds upon a foundation of logically stated facts to conjure a more visceral (and hopefully more effective) emotional reaction.

The year after Fox published his pamphlet, Andrew Burn, a British marine officer and religious convert who wrote frequently about the duty of being humble before God, anonymously authored a pamphlet that explicitly follows Fox's footsteps. In *A Second Address to the People of Great Britain: Containing a New, and Most Powerful Argument to Abstain from the Use of West India Sugar*, Burn praises Fox's ability to "rous[e] to powerful exertions, those sentiments of humanity, which it is to be hoped, are more or less implanted in every breast" while announcing his own opposing strategy: "My design in the following pages, is to tread in a very different path from him; and to excit every opposite *emotions* in the breasts of my Readers; yet all tending, I hope, to promote the same sacred Cause of Humanity."[42] Burn seeks to bolster the "Cause of Humanity" not by inspiring his readers' "sentiments of humanity," but by inspiring the "opposite"—his readers' disgust.

Burn's essay literalizes the blood-sugar metaphor by arguing that, in consuming slave-grown products, Britons actually ingest the bodily effusions of enslaved people. Just as white abolitionists started with questions of the soul but ended by fixating on enslaved bodies, Burn starts with a conceptual framework (consuming slave-grown products is akin to consuming enslaved people) but quickly moves that framework into physical reality (consumers of slave-grown products literally cannibalize enslaved people). Both cases betray the perception that focusing on the physical realm was more likely to help the abolitionist cause, and both starkly demonstrate how that focus could work against a larger goal of kinship and connection. In forsaking the metaphor, Burn also relinquishes the political move made available by the metaphor—namely, bringing slavery and cannibalism together in the minds of readers and forcing them to see the resonance between the exploitation of one and the consumptive violence of the other. Burn abandons political commentary on the institution of slavery itself (and the moral indignation it would inspire) to focus on engendering the physical aversion that would motivate consumers to refuse sugar out of revulsion. It mines the rhetorical efficacy in cannibalistic disgust, but it simultaneously courts racist repugnance.

The rare critics who have analyzed Burn's pamphlet have identified its literalizing impulse as aberrant within abolitionist discourse, but I contend that such an impulse actually represents the logical result of the general abolitionist obsession with the physical on the one hand, and the incarnation suggested by cannibalistic metaphors (as we saw in Coleridge's essay) on the other.[43] Burn's pamphlet may provide an extreme instance, but it nonetheless illuminates what abolitionists sought to achieve when they relied on physical imagery to advance metaphysical ideas. By creating disgust in his readers, he hopes to rewire their physiological response to sugar, effectively changing their minds by first altering their bodies.

Burn's preface explains why he prioritizes aversive physical reactions over intellectual or sympathetic responses. He describes a discussion with friends in which "neither motives of humanity nor conscience" can convince them to refuse sugar.[44] Some of the women present ask Burn to describe his personal experiences on West Indian plantations, and his description of the process by which enslaved people packed sugar into hogsheads with their feet elicits a notable response among his listeners—"knit Brows, distorted Features, and disgustful Emotions" followed by an emphatic declaration to never eat sugar again.[45] The lesson is not lost on Burn, who recounts his dawning realization of the rhetorical power of visceral disgust: "It immediately struck the Author, that some such powerful motive, that would affect the Senses, might be more efficacious with many, in constraining them to leave off Sugar, than those arguments which are only sentimental."[46] In the heart of the essay itself, Burn warns readers that they may experience the same unpleasant physiological reactions that afflicted his earlier listeners: "But if in doing this, I should offend their delicacy, by occasioning some very uneasy, and disagreeable sensations, they will be so kind as recollect, that it is only in this way I can expect to succeed in my main design."[47]

Burn believes that disgust works where logic and sentiment fail. Despite agreeing with other abolitionists that consumers have a direct connection to slavery, he has noticed that many consumers avoid such a recognition: "Abstain from Sugar, and Slavery falls. The consequence is as clear as the noon-day Sun; yet how difficult to persuade some, that when they eat Sugar, they figuratively eat the Blood of the Negro."[48] Figurative language can prove troublingly easy to ignore as a mere fiction; the proximity created by cannibalistic metaphors is only semantic, not physical.[49] In Burn's view, spurring his readers to action depends on convincing them of real physical contact: "[M]y business at present is, by plain matters of fact, of which I have frequently had ocular demonstration, to convince the inhabitants of Great Britain, who use Soft Sugar, either in Puddings, Pies, Tarts, Tea, or otherwise, that they literally, and most certainly in so doing, eat large quantities of that last mentioned Fluid, as it flows copiously from the Body of the laborious Slave."[50] Burn's language is that of abundance—his ample listing of the many tasty items benefiting from sugar ("Puddings, Pies, Tarts, Tea") is luxuriant both in content and in alliteration, and his word choice insists on the "large quantities" and "copiously" flowing sweat, which in turn recall the "torrents of Blood and Sweat" he described a few lines earlier.[51]

Excess characterizes the entire essay, and the overabundance Burn ascribes to disgusting bodily fluids is matched only by the racist exuberance with which he strains for sufficiently grotesque descriptions. He describes one enslaved man who while stamping sugar into hogsheads is "perspiring at every pore, with his head as wet as Gideon's first fleece."[52] Such "excessive Perspiration" not only emits "nauceous effluvia" but also transfers head lice from his "reeking locks" to the sugar below.[53] Another "very disgusting fluid," an "ingredient still more nauseous" than the lice and sweat that have come before, emanates from sores caused by yaws on the ankles and feet, profuse enough for Burn to envision an afflicted man with "*spring tide* at his ancles."[54] He closes his catalog of the contaminants that make their way into sugar with "that well-known, but offensive substance, usually lodged between the human toes, and under the nails."[55] The consumption of tainted sugar is disgusting, therefore, not because it is immoral, or because enslaved people have been radically commodified, or even because they suffer. It is disgusting because it represents the literal ingestion of bodies that he depicts as abundantly diseased and effusively contaminating.

Unlike descriptions of the physical suffering of enslaved people, which focus only on the Afro-Caribbean body, white abolitionist evocations of cannibalism bring the consuming body into focus alongside the body being consumed. Burn's imagery seeks to elicit not only disgust but also the suspicion that European bodies risk being dangerously altered by consuming tainted sugar. Burn expresses his certainty that imported sugar contains the sweat of enslaved people in striking terms: "But one thing I think, must be very evident to all my Readers, that every Hogshead of Sugar thus packed and imported into England from the West Indies, is more or less impregnated with this liquid from the human body."[56] Impregnation implies a foreign object implanted within a body (and the fact that this and similar tracts attracted a wide female readership gives this construction particular force), resulting in a significant transformation.[57] As an edible product, sugar entered the body and even, according to some contemporary medical professionals, altered it.[58] At the level of rhetoric, Burn's language tries to do something similar: His stories enter the body as read words, then physically transform the bodies as those words are digested. This transformation is both immediate (contorted faces and queasy stomachs) and, Burn hopes, lasting (aversion that triggers changed behavior).

Burn ends the essay by seeking to render rum as disgusting as other forms of sugar. He gives an account of a European wine merchant who purchases multiple barrels of Jamaican rum. When one barrel proves much tastier (and thus more popular with the merchant's clients), the merchant opens the barrel to investigate and discovers the burned remains of a Black man. Although Burn eventually reveals that this particular corpse was hidden in the rum cask by a fellow enslaved person who had murdered him, he nonetheless makes the startling assertion that secreting the roasted body of an animal or person into the barrel is a known way of improving the taste.[59] The tasters in this anecdote are as horrified as Burn hopes readers of this essay will be: "At the sight of which [the body], neither the Wine-merchant, nor his customers, wished to have any more of the best sort."[60] By itself, the corpse cannot render the sugar product disgusting—indeed, the body markedly improves the taste—but the sudden realization that the corpse is the real source of sweetness can. Even at his most gruesomely literal, Burn mirrors the message of more familiar abolitionist cannibalistic metaphors. Sugar consumers knew that sugar's delicious sweetness was the result of the excruciating labor of enslaved people, but that mere recognition was not enough to alter their behavior. In exposing sugar's skeleton in the closet (or rum cask, as it were), abolitionists attempted to make that connection more immediate by defetishizing the commodity and contending that the consumption of sugar also meant the consumption of its producers as well.

SOUTHEY'S ANTISLAVERY SONNETS AND THE LIMITS OF CONNECTION

Robert Southey, an associate of William Wordsworth and Coleridge who would later become England's poet laureate, wrote an antislavery sonnet sequence in 1794 and published it in 1797. Like so much abolitionist writing, the sonnet sequence attempts to establish a strong connection between consumers and producers. In addition to the familiar cannibalistic metaphor in the lines "Oh ye who at your ease / Sip the blood-sweeten'd beverage!," Southey emphasizes interrelation by putting the figures and events of the slave trade on a continuum that links bestial violence, slave traders, commerce, and everyday consumption.[61] Repeated phrases and images throughout the sequence create threads of connection and assert that these elements are not discrete tragedies in distant corners of the world, but causally related events that reverberate out from the greed at the heart of slavery. The sequence consists of six sonnets describing events across multiple continents—in Africa, the Caribbean, Europe, and even briefly during the Middle Passage—and touching on everything from personal grief and torture to widespread war and attempted rebellion. Despite the emphasis on interrelation, however, Southey's focus on physicality underlines the distance between British consumers and enslaved people.

The first sonnet condemns wars in Africa caused by European greed, while the second shows the devastating impact of slave trade kidnappings on the loved ones left behind. In the third sonnet, a description of a brutally punished enslaved man transitions into an excoriation of sugar consumers who ignore such suffering. The fourth sonnet returns to the enslaved man who, finally alone, can weep for his lost lover in Africa, who herself still weeps for him. In the fifth sonnet, he decides to seek vengeance against his enslaver. Rather than depict the attack, Southey opens the sixth sonnet with disturbing evidence of its failure—the gibbeted rebel is being eaten alive by birds—before ending with a warning about divine justice against supporters of the slave system.

From the start, Southey uses repetition to insist on causal connection. The speaker begins the first sonnet by addressing warring Africans and imploring "Hold your mad hands! for ever on your plain / Must the gorged vulture clog his beak with blood?" He then poses a pointed question about the cause of violence: "what dæmon prompts to rear / The arm of Slaughter?"[62] Despite arguments that the fact that Africans fought and enslaved other Africans justified European participation in the slave trade, Southey squarely blames the European demand for slavery for enflaming African wars. What daemon prompts the slaughter? The speaker answers his own question by pointing to a slave ship—a "bark of anguish"—at the end of the poem:

> For the pale fiend, cold-hearted Commerce there
> Breathes his gold-gender'd pestilence afar,
> And calls, to share the prey, his kindred Dæmon War.[63]

The "fiend" Commerce, linked to white traders through the word "pale," is the primary cause of death; War simply follows Commerce's call to "share the prey." Similar images of violence, insanity, and ravenous animals pervade the rest of the sonnet sequence. Sonnet 3 establishes the resemblance between plantation violence and African wars by beseeching the overseer in familiar terms: "hold—hold thy merciless hand, / Pale tyrant!"[64] The "mad hands" of the Africans in sonnet 1 anticipate the memories that drive the enslaved man's "soul to madness" in sonnet 5, inspiring him to stage a rebellion in order to "sweeten[] with revenge, the draught of death," a phrase which itself recalls the consumer in Europe "who at [her] ease / sip[s] the blood-sweeten'd beverage" in sonnet 3.[65] The gibbeted man in sonnet 6 has become "living food" for birds, just as his blood has already infused the beverage enjoyed by consumers, and he suffers from the violent attentions of a "gorging Vulture" that echoes the "gorged vulture" of sonnet 1.[66] The act of drinking sweetened tea becomes, in Southey's vision, a process that both causes and mirrors everything from wars in Africa to the vicious punishment of enslaved people and even rebellion in the West Indies.

In addition to recurring imagery that highlights interconnection between all aspects of slavery, Southey uses poetic form to collapse distance between seemingly separate terms. Each of the sonnets roughly follows the Petrarchan form, which consists of an octave and a sestet connected by a turn. In this sequence, Southey puts particular emphasis on the turn to stress the overlap of the sections, often creating surprising proximity between apparently different situations. Sonnet 3 provides an excellent example:

> Oh he is worn with toil! the big drops run
> Down his dark cheek; hold—hold thy merciless hand,
> Pale tyrant! for beneath thy hard command
> O'erwearied Nature sinks. The scorching Sun,
> As pityless as proud Prosperity,
> Darts on him his full beams; gasping he lies
> Arraigning with his looks the patient skies,
> While that inhuman trader lifts on high
> The mangling scourge. Oh ye who at your ease
> Sip the blood-sweeten'd beverage! thoughts like these
> Haply ye scorn: I thank thee Gracious God!
> That I do feel upon my cheek the glow
> Of indignation, when beneath the rod
> A sable brother writhes in silent woe.[67]

The first section runs to the middle of line 9 and depicts the brutality of everyday life on a sugar plantation, including hard labor, high temperatures, and physical violence. The second section leaves the Caribbean and instead focuses on distant consumers (presumably Britons)—the tea drinkers who resolutely ignore the cannibalistic valence of the beverage and the speaker whose empathy allows him to experience and acknowledge his connection to enslaved suffering. Like most poems in this sequence, the turn does not occur neatly between the eighth and ninth lines. Instead, the turn happens at the caesura of line 9, becoming a fulcrum around which an instrument of torture ("mangling scourge") and genteel comfort ("ease") are troublingly balanced. As much as the consumers may cling to their ignorance and comfortable distance, the realities of enslaved labor cannot be neatly contained, spilling over into their sitting rooms and teacups just as surely as the enjambment spills the eighth line into the ninth. What initially seems like disjuncture resolves into logical connection in the next line, as the cannibalistic contents of the cup resonate with the instrument of torture.

In sonnet 3, the line that initiates the turn also begins the poem's only rhyming couplet ("The mangling scourge. Oh ye who at your ease / Sip the blood-sweeten'd beverage! thoughts like these"). Five of the six sonnets in Southey's sequence feature a single rhyming couplet, but this is the only instance of a rhyming couplet occurring in the middle of the poem rather than in the final two lines. The cannibal scene breaks the rhyming pattern of the four-line stanzas on either side while also providing a pivot between the two sections. That break in form, along with the double punch of the immediately repeated rhyme, lends these lines particular prominence, effectively making cannibalistic consumption the focal point of the poem and, considering this is the only mid-poem couplet, a key moment of the entire sonnet sequence. The emphasis placed on cannibalism reflects its status as a preferred tool for bridging the gap between plantation torture and consumer comfort, but it also suggests cannibalism's knack for breaking away from its intended rhetorical role and drawing attention to the physical realm instead.

The intense focus on the body encouraged by the reference to cannibalism only highlights the physical imbalance between the sections of the poem on either side, dramatizing the difficulties in establishing a kinship not overshadowed by physical difference. While Southey's speaker scorns easeful drinkers and trumpets his ability to feel sentimental identification with the enslaved person, the language itself indicates that the imaginative rapprochement between enslaved person and distant consumer runs aground on the insurmountable difference between their physical situations. Despite mentioning the cheeks of both men, the speaker depicts the enslaved man's cheeks running with the bodily fluid spilled during his labor and abuse, while the speaker's cheeks are merely touched with "the glow / Of indignation." That glow further underscores the extent to which the speaker's discomfort recedes in comparison with that of the enslaved man, who experiences a heat much harsher than a mere glow as "The scorching Sun, / As pityless as proud Prosperity, / Darts on him his full beams." The sense of the sun as casting darts stresses that the enslaved body is liable to be pierced and mangled by outside forces while the speaker's body merely reacts physiologically to an inner emotion. Of course, the physical discrepancy is most obvious in the difference of positions—one man, safely in England, feels righteous indignation, while another "writhes beneath the rod."[68]

In the end, Southey's sonnet sequence moves in the direction of literalization. Sonnet 1 opens with a figurative "gorged vulture" representing African wars, but by sonnet 6 that metaphoric vulture has been literalized in the vulture (and other birds) that feed on the gibbeted man:

> High in the air expos'd the Slave is hung
> To all the birds of Heaven, their living food!
> He groans not, tho' awaked by that fierce Sun
> New torturers live to drink their parent blood!
> He groans not, tho' the gorging Vulture tear
> The quivering fibre![69]

The central image of the sequence—"the blood-sweeten'd beverage"—has become gruesomely literal, with the figuratively consumed enslaved person now actually being devoured and the blood imagined to be sipped in tea now actually gulped by birds. Although these grotesque literalizations serve to establish the material fact underlying the metaphors—the very conditions that make the metaphors so apt—they also, like Burn's pamphlet, accentuate the physical at the expense of a more transcendent sense of kinship. The almost prurient attention to physical suffering and the implements of torture—"quivering fibre," "twisted thong," "mangling scourge," "feast of gore," alongside the amply spilled bodily fluids—only highlight the vast distance between consumer and enslaved person, the distance these poems were meant to collapse.[70]

CANNIBALISTIC METAPHORS WITHOUT DEHUMANIZATION

Despite gestures toward kinship, the white abolitionist focus on physicality enforced difference and distance, emphasizing vast distinctions in position between British consumers and enslaved people and using disgust to inspire an anxious (and frequently racist) pushing away of people of African descent. As I have demonstrated, the urge to sever ties was a hallmark of consumption-as-connection, but it often instilled that urge through means that also propagated racism. While aversive physicality of blood-sugar metaphors spurred action, it also dehumanized enslaved people and overshadowed the critique of the inherently consumptive nature of chattel slavery. The Afro-Caribbean abolitionists Olaudah Equiano and Mary Prince recognized the power of consumption in condemning European violence and greed, but they notably eschewed blood-sugar metaphors. Instead, they worked to expose the cannibalistic undertones of slavery in ways that highlighted the fundamental humanity of enslaved people rather than sheer physicality or victimhood.

In his 1789 autobiography, Equiano tells of being kidnapped as a child in Africa and forced into slavery in the Caribbean. Equiano's famous fear that his captors planned to eat him echoes common West and Central African portrayals of European slave traders as cannibals.[71] When first observing conditions on the ship, he "no longer doubted of [his] fate" and, after fainting, manages to ask other Africans "if we were not to be eaten by those white men with horrible looks, red faces, and long hair."[72] What initially seems like the naïve fear of a child in fact demonstrates a canny grasp of the situation based on available information.[73] In the long tradition of labeling racial Others as savages, Equiano focuses on the unfamiliar appearances of the Europeans and concludes that they will behave in a fashion monstrously different from what he would expect from African slave traders. Although fellow prisoners explain that they are not to be eaten, but rather enslaved, Equiano returns repeatedly to the fear of being cannibalized, basing his terror on the observed behavior of his captors: "But still I feared I should be put to death, the white people looked and acted, as I thought, in so savage a manner; for I had never seen among any people such instances of brutal cruelty."[74] He continues by expressing his shock that the traders abuse certain white sailors as well, describing one who died after a flogging and whom "they tossed . . . over the side as they would have done a brute."[75] Equiano quickly learns the logic of forced labor: By claiming control over the body, the traders also assume the right to treat enslaved people (or low-ranking sailors) as animals fit to be abused and killed if necessary.

Upon arriving in Barbados, Equiano's fears of cannibalism are amplified by the behavior of prospective buyers—"They put us in separate parcels, and examined us attentively. They also made us jump, and pointed to the land, signifying we were to go there. We thought by this we should be eaten by these ugly men"—and the conditions in the slave pen, where the newly arrived Africans "were all pent up together like so many sheep in a fold, without regard to sex or age."[76] At auction, the zeal of the buyers strikes Equiano, not improbably, as appetite: "[T]he eagerness visible in the countenances of the buyers... serve[s] not a little to increase the apprehensions of the terrified Africans, who may well be supposed to consider them as the ministers of that destruction to which they think themselves devoted."[77] By imagining that enslavers wish to eat him, especially around moments of sale, Equiano intuits that he has entered a system bent on commodifying and consuming him. By describing the basis of his fear, he stresses his own ability to interpret a reality that, if not literal, nonetheless cuts to the heart of slavery's dehumanizing consumption.

Like Equiano, Prince skillfully uses eating imagery to denounce slavery's atrocities while asserting her own humanity. In her 1831 autobiography, she recounts the first time she was sold at auction: "I was soon surrounded by strange men, who examined and handled me in the same manner that a butcher would a calf or a lamb he was about to purchase, and who talked about my shape and size in like words—as if I could no more understand their meaning than the dumb beasts."[78] Prince mentions "cattle" and "sheep" earlier in this passage and elsewhere in the narrative, but here she switches to terms for young animals. Beyond emphasizing her youth (she notes "the people who stood by said that I had fetched a great sum for so young a slave"), the image of a butcher choosing a lamb or a calf suggests luxurious appetites, the willingness to pay a premium for meat at its most tender, thereby intimating that slavery was not a necessity, but rather a facilitator of extreme indulgence.[79] More importantly, Prince insists on her own ability to interpret and reject the premise of her sale. The prospective purchasers speak as if she cannot understand them precisely because they need to see her as saleable flesh, but her narrative attests to the fallacy of that belief by asserting her own humanity. Prince repeatedly compares mistreated enslaved people and livestock in order to drive home this point.[80] In the final paragraph of her narrative, she uses this comparison to protest the immorality of this treatment and the profound lie that justifies it: "They tie up slaves like hogs—moor them up like cattle, and they lick them, so as hogs, or cattle, or horses never were flogged;—and yet they come home and say, and make some good people believe, that slaves don't want to get out of slavery. But they put a cloak about the truth. It is not so. All slaves want to be free—to be free is very sweet."[81] Prince simultaneously stages slavery's horrific attempt to make human beings into meat and undermines it by starkly opposing her own indefatigable humanity. Significantly, she refuses the abject physicality of blood-sugar metaphors and instead locates sweetness in abstract freedom.

Equiano and Prince's strategic deployments underline the conceptual flexibility of cannibalism. Cannibalistic imagery did not require degrading physicality in order to critique slavery: By focusing on the consumptive logic of the slave trade, Equiano and Prince condemn slavery's depredations while still testifying to their own subjectivity. Cannibalism displayed similar flexibility as commentators with starkly different perspectives used it to define the meaning of the Haitian Revolution.[82] In the late eighteenth and early nineteenth centuries, many white writers expressed their terror of Black liberation through lurid images of blood-drinking and inhuman appetites among Haitian freedom fighters. At the same time, Black Haitian revolutionaries and Black activists in the broader Atlantic world used what Raphael Hoermann has called the "radical Haitian Gothic" to reverse such imagery back onto enslavers and colonizers.[83] Shortly after declaring Haitian independence in 1804, for example, Jean-Jacques Dessalines proclaimed, "I have given the French cannibals blood for blood . . . I have avenged America."[84] As Equiano, Prince, and Dessalines demonstrate, the rhetoric of cannibalism could be put to humanizing and even revolutionary antislavery ends.[85]

Unfortunately, the white British abolition movement's most iconic cannibalistic image—the blood-sugar metaphor—strove to incarnate suffering bodies, engendering a readerly disgust that risked targeting enslaved people as well as the slave system. In fixating on bodies, these metaphors participated in a broader tradition of obsessive physicality in white abolitionist writing, revealing how difficult many white British abolitionists found it to envision the humanity of enslaved people beyond the physical realm. The very quality that made cannibalistic metaphors so rhetorically effective—their ability to suggest an intimate connection that demanded consumer action—impeded the universal kinship many abolitionists purportedly sought. Through blood-sugar metaphors, white abolitionists successfully captured national attention, but they also exposed the profound difficulty of embracing antiracism without replicating the dehumanizing focus on physicality that was used to define racial difference in the first place.

TWO

AMBIVALENT CONNECTIONS IN FREE PRODUCE ABOLITIONISM

The problem with *Uncle Tom's Cabin* (1852), according to Black antislavery activist Frances Ellen Watkins (later Harper), is that it fails to portray slavery to the full extent of its consuming power. Harper writes in an 1854 letter, "Oh, if Mrs. Stowe has clothed American slavery in the graceful garb of fiction, Solomon Northrup [sic] comes up from the dark habitation of Southern cruelty where slavery fattens and feasts on human blood with such mournful revelations that one might almost wish for the sake of humanity that the tales of horror which he reveals were not so."[1] The consumptive terms in which Harper distinguishes fact from fiction return in her subsequent expression of gratitude that she can afford a "Free Labor" dress, made from cotton grown by free rather than enslaved people: "I can thank God that upon its warp and woof I see no stain of blood and tears; that to procure a little finer muslin for my limbs no crushed and broken heart went out in sighs."[2] Like sugar abstainers before her, Harper implies that the products of slavery may appear luxurious, but that their luxury masks the bodily fluids of the suffering laborers who produced them. To abstain from slave-grown produce, in this case by sourcing ethically grown cotton, is to recognize consumption-as-connection and avoid participating in a cannibalistic institution that "fattens and feasts on human blood." As in Coleridge's attack on sentimentalism without action, Harper positions consumption-as-connection as the concrete alternative to the distracting aesthetics of Stowe's fiction—the difference between the indelible traces of blood and tears and the more ineffable feelings engendered by novels. And yet, Harper didn't reject the sentimental mode generally or Stowe's fiction specifically—indeed, two of her antislavery poems are directly inspired by Stowe's characters—and even her construction here could be said to fuse the grotesquely concrete (the tears and blood staining the fabric) with intangible affect (the sighs present at the scene of production).[3] While sighs are unsettling, they are more likely to inspire concern or pity than aversion. Harper thus seeks to yoke the repellant contamination familiar from earlier formulations of consumption-as-connection to the sympathy inspired by evidence of suffering.

This chapter examines how antebellum U.S. abolitionists attempted to use consumption-as-connection to generate action without sacrificing sympathetic identification to outsized disgust. It is the second of two chapters investigating key moments in transatlantic antislavery consumer activism. While chapter 1 focused on the first major wave of abolitionist abstention in late eighteenth-century Britain, chapter 2 focuses on the second major wave: the free produce (or sometimes free labor) movement that emerged in the 1820s and continued through the 1850s on both sides of the Atlantic. Spearheaded by Quakers and predominantly practiced by Quaker and Black abolitionists, the free produce movement argued that, by restricting purchases to commodities produced by free laborers, consumers could reduce the profitability of slavery and entice enslavers to shift to free labor.

The free produce movement modified the earlier abstention movement in a few important ways. While the sugar boycott had sought to end the transatlantic slave trade, the free produce movement sought to end slavery altogether, in both the British West Indies (before emancipation in 1834) and the United States. The earlier movement essentially lasted just a couple of years, but the latter stretched over decades. This longer tenure allowed for more formalized organization, including numerous free produce societies, conventions, and even a U.S. newspaper, *The Non-Slaveholder*. The most significant innovation of the free produce movement was shifting emphasis from pure abstention to ethical consumption.[4] During the sugar boycott, avoiding slave-grown products had effectively meant going without, but free produce activists realized that access to sugar and cotton grown by free labor would enable consumers to strike a blow against slavery with less personal sacrifice.[5] They found a way to have one's (sugared) cake and eat it too.[6] During this period, free produce stores, some run by women and people of color, opened in cities including London and Bristol in England and Philadelphia, Baltimore, and New York in the United States.[7]

This second wave of antislavery consumer activism followed a period of relatively muted abolitionist activity in the wake of the British and U.S. abolition of the transatlantic slave trade in 1807 and 1808, respectively. By the 1820s, uprisings by enslaved people in Barbados and Demerara emphasized that ending the slave trade had failed to end slavery, as many abolitionists had hoped.[8] In response, the white British Quaker abolitionist Elizabeth Heyrick published the fiery pamphlet *Immediate, Not Gradual Emancipation* in 1824. Echoing previous antislavery consumer activists, her pamphlet insists on consumer complicity and advocates a boycott. Heyrick portrays the economics of slavery as abject consumption, as when she characterizes enslavers as simultaneously "receiv[ing], too long, the gains of oppression" and "fatten[ing] on the spoils of humanity."[9] Unlike earlier activists who targeted the transatlantic slave trade, she calls for abolishing West Indian slavery itself and abolishing it (as the pamphlet's title proclaims) without delay, helping inaugurate the era of abolitionist immediatism.[10] This pamphlet galvanized another mass sugar boycott in Britain that may well have attracted more supporters than the late eighteenth-century abstention movement.[11] The pamphlet was also printed in New York and Philadelphia and serialized in Benjamin Lundy's U.S. newspaper *Genius of Universal Emancipation*.[12]

Following Heyrick's lead, free produce formulations feature many hallmarks of consumption-as-connection. Articles and pamphlets declare enslavers to be merely the "agents" of consumers, who are themselves frequently described as the "abettors" and "immediate upholders" of slavery, or, as the prominent white U.S. abolitionist William Lloyd Garrison memorably writes, "the Alpha and Omega of the business."[13] An 1853 article in *The Non-Slaveholder* asserts that commodities create direct links despite physical distance: "Let us remember that while we are not separated from *traffic in the toil of slaves* however far removed we may be from the *scene of their sufferings in the physical world*, in the *moral* world we are standing beside them, receiving from their wearied hands the supplies which so abundantly minister to our demands."[14] As in earlier blood-sugar metaphors, free produce activists invoked proximity by envisioning radically defetishized commodities in which the enslaved laborer was not erased but remained physically and psychically present. The same article describes, for example, "merchandize fraught with the human sighs, tears, and life-blood."[15] Once again, these newly envisioned connections were designed to be quickly and instinctively broken, as when the white U.S. Quaker Elizabeth Margaret Chandler published a fictional letter urging women to "fling from them the luxuries that are purchased by such means, as if they were a deadly poison."[16]

And yet, free produce activists did not rely on physical disgust to the same extent as their sugar-avoiding predecessors. Bloodstained sugar still makes frequent appearances in free produce writing, but the lurid references to cannibalism in Fox and Coleridge have largely been replaced with more implicit injunctions to avoid the stain of guilt. While earlier abstainers focused almost exclusively on blood (and other noxious bodily fluids, in the case of Burn's *Second Address*), free produce writers typically balanced references to blood with simultaneous invocations of tears and sighs. This shift de-emphasizes physical contamination in favor of sentiment: people often recoil from blood but feel sympathy for the tears and sighs that serve as visible and audible indices of emotion.

Although free produce advocacy was transatlantic, this chapter focuses on the U.S. movement's widely read literature because it offers unique insight into the imaginative life of consumption-as-connection. Shortly after serializing Heyrick's pamphlet, for instance, Lundy's *Genius of Universal Emancipation* started publishing writing by Elizabeth Margaret Chandler, who became "the most widely read abolitionist author in the antebellum period" and produced multiple poems and essays advocating free produce.[17] Frances E. W. Harper's *Poems on Miscellaneous Subjects* (1854), later editions of which include her poem "Free Labor," was reprinted five times, with over 10,000 copies.[18] In addition to explicitly free produce writing by Harper and Chandler, this chapter analyzes canonical literary texts such as *Uncle Tom's Cabin*, *Walden* (1854), and *Moby-Dick* (1851), which have not traditionally been read as relating to the free produce movement. I nevertheless show that they illuminate key aspects of the ideology underlying abolitionist consumer activism and some of the unique concerns spurred by consumption-as-connection. My purpose is neither to reveal these works as secretly embracing free produce beliefs nor to adjudicate the ethics of their positions on slavery, but instead to explore how consumption emerges in nuanced ways in a range of antebellum U.S. literary production.

Unlike British sugar abstention campaigns, the mid-nineteenth-century free produce movement never attracted widespread support in the United

States.[19] Within the antislavery movement, many abolitionists dismissed it as unfeasible or a distraction from bigger priorities.[20] Despite having been a vocal early supporter of free produce, Garrison began deriding it in the 1840s, arguing that the products of slavery were "so mixed up with the commerce, manufactures and agriculture of the world ... [and] the credit and currency of the country" that any attempt to extricate oneself was necessarily quixotic.[21] The sense of inescapable entanglement that paralyzed rather than roused was directly related to the new ascendancy of cotton. By the mid-nineteenth century, what Sven Beckert has called the "empire of cotton" was firmly entrenched, driving national economies and industry on both sides of the Atlantic. It was much more difficult to avoid a material that made up most fabric and paper than it was a sweetener associated with indulgent taste, however much it had become an object of daily use. A favorite point of those wishing to illustrate the impracticality of free produce was the fact that even the paper advocates used for their pamphlets and newspapers would have almost always been made from cotton.[22] Moreover, slave-grown cotton's dominance made it difficult to effectively source or sell alternative goods. Despite global efforts to cultivate free labor crops, the supply chain struggled to provide adequate products at reasonable prices.[23]

In this chapter, I propose an additional factor in the failure of free produce to capture the popular imagination in the United States. Whereas disgust proved galvanizing to the earlier sugar abstention movement (even as it risked stigmatizing enslaved people), the free produce movement tempered its use of disgust with increased appeals to sympathy, thereby limiting the impact of its message. Julie L. Holcomb rightly identifies the "intense lurid focus" on ingesting the blood of enslaved people as a primary factor in the popularity of sugar abstention campaigns, but she argues that the wider range of products boycotted by the free produce movement offered less opportunity for horrifying imagery.[24] Examining U.S. free produce writing reveals that the reduced emphasis on revolting imagery resulted from more than just the larger variety of targeted products, however. Prepared to envision connections to slavery but reluctant to fully embrace revulsion, U.S. free produce writing exhibits an ambivalence that suggests an awareness of the disadvantages of disgust, even as it mitigates consumption-as-connection's ability to incite action. Free produce writers sought an antislavery rhetoric that could moderate aversion with sympathy and thus counteract the dehumanization of many consumption-as-connection formulations. Disgust, in other words, was deemed too powerful to forsake, but too dangerous to be left unchecked.

Scholars of the free produce movement have frequently noted the way its rhetoric seeks to fuse economics and morals, but it is also vital to recognize the way it combines disgust and sentiment.[25] In her important essay on what she terms "free produce literature," Jessica Conrad rightly notes the genre's hybrid form: "[F]ree-produce poetry depicted the sentimental stains of slavery on sensationalized objects of slave labor."[26] Conrad argues that this "blending" or "blurring" between sentimentalism and sensationalism ultimately serves sentimental identification, but I contend that horrific material proximity is not secondary to sympathy, but instead its conflicted and contradictory double.[27] Recognizing the relationship between revulsion and sentimental identification as one of ambivalent tension, in turn, allows us to grasp how antislavery advocates attempted to find a middle ground between a strategy with a proven track record of eliciting action and one that seemed to avoid the unsavory aspects of consumption-as-connection.

By reading free produce authors alongside contemporaneous authors who imagined comparable forms of long-distance implication without fully embracing consumption-as-connection, this chapter paints a fuller picture of the charged role of disgust in antislavery discourse. Writings by Harriet Beecher Stowe and Henry David Thoreau demonstrate how even antislavery advocates willing to envision connection through financial networks might eschew the disturbing physical contact via commodities implied by consumption-as-connection. Free produce writing by Frances E. W. Harper and Elizabeth Margaret Chandler explicitly portrays direct contact through slave-produced commodities, but it nevertheless oscillates between aversive physicality and more conventional appeals to intangible feelings designed to elicit sympathy. Finally, writing from Herman Melville presents a troubling alternative to abolitionist confidence that consumers who recognized how commodities implicated them in suffering would change their behavior. Melville vividly depicts commodities as containing appalling traces of anguish, but he suggests that the natural selfishness of consumers may override the disgust they ought to feel, even if they recognize the human costs of their commodities. The previous chapter showed that white abolitionist deployments of consumption-as-connection frequently dehumanized enslaved people through excessive physicality. This chapter suggests that such physicality may nevertheless be essential to triggering action, while also revealing (per Melville) that such action may not always move in the desired antislavery direction.

THOREAU AND STOWE'S FREE PRODUCE SENSIBILITIES

Thoreau and Stowe shared with free produce advocates a sense that everyday transactions could implicate people in geographically distant brutality. The texts I examine in this section depict nationwide systems of trade and (especially) finance as grievous entanglements with slavery, but they do not emphasize disturbingly defetishized commodities in their appeals to sever ties. They thus represent a kind of proto-consumption-as-connection, lamenting financial linkages to slavery but demurring on acknowledging the intimate contact suggested by everyday consumer objects. Their avoidance of portraying commodities as physical ties to suffering laborers in turn mirrors the ambivalent deployment of consumption-as-connection in explicitly free produce writing. Disgust may have been a powerful motivator, but its unsettling intrusion into everyday life proved at least partially incompatible with the kinds of long-distance implication these writers wanted to expose.

Thoreau famously took abstaining action to break immoral ties to slavery. The arrest that inspired "Resistance to Civil Government" (1849) sprang quite simply from Thoreau's belief that his tax dollars intimately connected him to the government-backed atrocities of slavery and the Mexican-American War. By refusing to pay, his logic went, he could avoid becoming grievously entangled in a national system of exploitation and violence. "I do not care to trace the course of my dollar, if I could," he declares, "till it buys a man, or a musket to shoot one with—the dollar is innocent,—but I am concerned to trace the effects of my allegiance."[28] Money becomes the medium through which crime is committed, and even if that crime occurs many transactions later, the money provides a source of continuity that connects the original holder with its ultimate consequences. As a result, Thoreau advocates action through avoidance: People need not undertake a blunt assault on social ills, but they should take care not to inadvertently sustain the institutions they abhor.[29]

Thoreau critiques immoral financial entanglements, but he does not place comparable emphasis on the ethical implications of slave-produced commodities. While "Resistance to Civil Government" advocates withdrawing financial support from slavery and war, and *Walden* advocates a much broader withdrawal from society, his concerns with consumption have little to do with the exploitation of laborers.[30] The commodities he isolates for specific critique (beef, coffee, butter) elicit no mention of having been produced by exploited labor, though he does note that poor laborers must work harder in order to afford them. Thoreau is disturbed not by the conditions under which these commodities are produced, but by the fact that they are superfluous luxuries whose purchase sets into motion monetary circulations that will eventually contribute to government-sanctioned violence. He asks readers to look below the surface of everyday goods and transactions, but what he finds there are impersonal ties to economic systems rather than interpersonal relationships with exploited laborers. Alda Balthrop-Lewis offers one potential exception in Thoreau's brief mention of New England factory operatives working in conditions that increasingly resemble those facing English operatives.[31] Tellingly, however, Thoreau follows this acknowledgment with a critique of the larger economic system ("[T]he principal object is, not that mankind may be well and honestly clad, but, unquestionably, that the corporations may be enriched").[32] His preceding paragraphs have emphasized not the way consumption materially links consumer and laborer, but the excessive consumption inspired by changing fashion. In fact, Balthrop-Lewis goes on to note that his journal entries describing textile mills suggest he is "slightly entranced" by the technological innovations on display—a response similar to his feelings about global trade, as I argue below.[33] By declining to defetishize commodities, Thoreau avoids the disturbingly physical connection they represent in favor of more abstract linkages.

Thoreau's willingness to ignore the conditions under which commodities were produced also permits him occasionally to indulge in a more pleasurable (and amoral) sense of connection. Despite his attention to the negative consequences of financial transactions, his often insistently fetishized depictions of commodities create surprising moments in which he seems to revel in the connections of trade. Thus, the railroad running past Walden Pond becomes an exuberant catalog of commodities: "I am refreshed and expanded when the freight train rattles past me, and I smell the stores which go dispensing their odors all the way from Long Wharf to Lake Champlain, reminding me of foreign parts, of coral reefs, and Indian oceans, and tropical climes, and the extent of the globe. I feel more like a citizen of the world at the sight of the palm-leaf which will cover so many flaxen New England heads the next summer, the Manilla hemp and cocoa-nut husks, the old junk, gunny bags, scrap iron, and rusty nails."[34] The cargo odors imaginatively transport an "expanded" Thoreau across continents, while the train inspires a vision of global commerce that allows him to continue enthusiastically tracing the circulation of commodities ranging from New England timber to Grand Banks cod to Spanish cowhides. Through the magic of worldwide networks, Thoreau experiences a brief but invigorating moment of transcendent connection.

Curiously absent from this moment is any reflection on the labor that produced those commodities. Thoreau's commodities instead appear as if their qualities were inherent rather than the product of human labor. Tears in ship sails become veritable authors: "Who can write so graphically the history of the storms they have weathered as these rents have done?"[35] Although Thoreau elsewhere expresses concern for the laborers who build the railroads, this passage casually erases the laborers who create and transport these goods (the sailors who could actually write the history of those storms, for instance). Likewise, for all his emphasis on slavery's dependence on national commerce, he muses here on the transport of products like cotton and molasses without the slightest mention of their very direct link to enslaved labor. When it came to the movement of money, Thoreau felt greatly concerned about the ultimate results of the transaction. When it came to the movement of goods, his concern tended to focus entirely on the consumer, not the laborer.[36] Thoreau's example demonstrates that visions of nationwide implication were not enough to conjure consumption-as-connection: Without the bracing confrontation with the commodity as the direct and horrifying emblem of personal involvement, networks could remain abstract, connections could remain attenuated, and even the products of slavery could occasionally be exhilarating.

Stowe echoes Thoreau's condemnation of immoral financial linkages, but she also proves more willing to consider the ethical dimensions of commodities. *Uncle Tom's Cabin* is a novel that strives to make connections, most famously by attempting to forge sympathetic ties between readers and distant sufferers. In this model of sympathy, the emotions engendered by the novel allow readers to feel intimately linked to enslaved people by imaginatively sharing the pain of slavery. By sending out the feelers of emotional recognition, the logic goes, readers realize the common humanity of enslaved people and are thereby recruited to the antislavery cause. Both antebellum and modern commentators have nevertheless been dubious about sentimental fiction's ability either to create real connection or to effect real change.[37] At a basic level, sympathy's dependence on identifying with a suffering body tends to reinscribe rather than reduce the distance between sympathy's subject and object—one being the emotionally distraught (but finally comfortable and safe) reader, the other being the person actually enduring the depredations of enslavement. Moreover, critics have frequently condemned sentimental fiction for facilitating private feelings instead of public action. Even those scholars who have argued for the fundamental power of sentimental novels tend to assume that sentiment-based morality remains firmly rooted in the domestic sphere. In this vision, sentimentalism shapes public life not through direct intervention, but by making the home "a dynamic center of activity, physical and spiritual, economic and moral, whose influence spreads out in ever-widening circles," as Jane Tompkins puts it.[38] In the portrait that emerges of the novel, Stowe emphasizes imagined kinship, not direct links; influence, not action.

Consumer objects play a significant role in mediating between the public and private spheres throughout *Uncle Tom's Cabin*. The novel portrays what Lori Merish has called "sentimental ownership," in which consumption offers the power to inculcate domestic spaces of feminine care through carefully curated objects.[39] According to Gillian Brown and Merish, Stowe uses these domestic spaces to critique the male-dominated market orientation of the broader world. While these scholars rightly identify Stowe's suspicion that market ideologies could corrupt domestic spaces, I maintain that Stowe also raises the possibility that those markets represent another channel through which antislavery influence might meaningfully flow. Considering *Uncle Tom's Cabin* through the lens of free produce thinking reveals how the power implied by sentimental ownership might be extended to enact even farther-reaching effects, using the very economic networks that seemingly threaten domestic values.[40] If sentimental novels portray women as powerful in the domestic sphere, then free produce ideas stress that the small everyday purchases that characterized household management could also directly shift vast economic systems. The resulting vision of simultaneously inward- and outward-facing consumer power captures how capitalism offers certain actors a feeling of control—the invigorating sense that they can shape both their personal lives and the society around them.

When the narrator of *Uncle Tom's Cabin* condemns Northern merchants who "trade in the souls and bodies of men as an equivalent to money," the denunciation might initially appear to be just another lament against the public sphere's nefarious commerce.[41] In fact, Stowe's careful and repeated attention to the sophisticated financial systems underpinning slavery also reveals the resonance between her novel and free produce ideology. *Uncle Tom's Cabin* shares with free produce advocates the belief that market forces represented direct connections to slavery and the desire to undermine Northern readers' sense of comfortable separation from it. Nevertheless, as I will show, Stowe does not follow these ideas to what might seem to be their logical conclusion—a direct call for consumer action. In laying the groundwork for free produce activism but ultimately retreating into the realm of feeling, *Uncle Tom's Cabin* replicates the ambivalence that characterized U.S. free produce writing.

Just as free produce advocates emphasized complicity in slavery despite geographical distance, Stowe's antislavery writing strives to collapse the apparent separation between North and South. In *The Key to "Uncle Tom's Cabin"* (1853), which provides documentary evidence to prove the plausibility of *Uncle Tom's Cabin*, Stowe asserts that, should any clergyman doubt the extent to which slavery has infiltrated the North, a quick investigation will show "that the roots of the poison-tree have run under the very hearthstone of New England families, and that in his very congregation are those in complicity with this sin."[42] Roots emblematize hidden connections waiting to be uncovered, at which point they suddenly disclose seemingly separate things (free states and slave states, for instance) to be part of the same system. Moreover, roots model connection as a living network of ongoing exchange. For Stowe, the real-life counterparts to these figurative roots were the commercial and financial networks that allowed even distant people to participate in and benefit from slavery. According to the narrator of *Uncle Tom's Cabin*, the ascendancy of the domestic slave trade risks collapsing "all the broad land between the Mississippi and the Pacific" into "one great market for bodies and souls."[43] As far as Stowe was concerned, financial transactions had already rendered slave trading a national system; *The Key to "Uncle Tom's Cabin"* chastises Northerners who "trad[e] in slaves . . . whether by partnership with Southern houses or by receiving immortal beings as security for debt."[44] As Walter Benn Michaels puts it, "Rejecting the claims of southern apologists that slavery provides a social and economic refuge from capitalism, Stowe imagines it instead as a mirror of the social and economic relations coming to the fore in the bourgeois North."[45]

In the antebellum period, the expansion of slavery directly fueled the development of increasingly sophisticated financial instruments, including chains of credit that linked slaveholders to investors in the North and abroad.[46] Stowe was deeply aware of these innovations. In the chapter entitled "The Slave Warehouse," the narrator elaborates the wide range of financial exchanges facilitated by slave market transactions: the warehouse is a place where "that soul immortal . . . can be sold, leased, mortgaged, exchanged for groceries or dry goods, to suit the phases of trade, or the fancy of the purchaser."[47] Beyond the various ways in which enslaved people could be converted to financial instruments or consumer goods in the market itself, Stowe notes that national systems of credit allowed similar conversions at much greater geographic distances. After a Louisiana enslaver loses the family fortune, his New York–based creditor, "a Christian man, and a resident in a free State," experiences "some uneasiness" at the prospect of selling enslaved people to cover debts, but ultimately decides it is "rather too much money to be lost for a principle."[48] The routes of business easily transcend the Mason-Dixon line, connecting New York to New Orleans with lines of credit and remittance just as surely as the novel's rivers connect various slave depots.

Stowe also echoes free produce ideology in her depiction of commodities as preserving the conditions under which they were produced, though she focuses more on psychic pain than abject physicality. Stowe's narrator opens the chapter in which Tom is transported down the Mississippi with an awed description of the river's power and the global trade it both resembles and facilitates: "What other river of the world bears on its bosom to the ocean the wealth and enterprise of such another country?—a country whose products embrace all between the tropics and the poles! Those turbid waters, hurrying, foaming, tearing along, an apt resemblance of that headlong tide of business which is poured along its wave."[49] Initially recalling Thoreau's rapturous account of the freight train, this bracing vision of commerce is soon interrupted by a disturbing reality. "Ah!" the narrator interjects, "would that they did not also bear along a more fearful freight,—the tears of the oppressed, the sighs of the helpless, the bitter prayers of poor, ignorant hearts to an unknown God."[50] Like the defetishized sugar and cotton imbued with the sighs and tears of enslaved people in free produce writing, Stowe's steamboat is laden with human suffering as much as market goods. On one level this is simply because the boat transports both slave products and enslaved people; on another level, Stowe's figuration reminds us that, in the antebellum South, the boat's "everywhere predominant cotton-bales" were inseparable from the enslaved labor that produced them, much as the mass commodification of enslaved people was inseparable from America's growing dominance in global markets.[51] As Martha Schoolman has written of this passage, it is "significant because it emphasizes slavery as the reality beneath the dream of economic development, calling attention to slavery not only as the producer but also literally the product—the 'fearful freight'—of capital expansion."[52]

In addition to conveying grave concerns about national and international commercial networks, *Uncle Tom's Cabin* includes moments that open the prospect of market interventions that serve the antislavery cause. The novel offers support for both of the free produce movement's major premises—that distant consumers were complicit in slavery and that abstaining from slave-grown commodities while purchasing free labor commodities would eventually end slavery. At the end of the mordantly titled chapter "Select Incident of Lawful Trade," in which, among other instances of familial separation, an enslaved woman has committed suicide after her child was sold, the narrator chides readers who would smugly judge the trader: "But who, sir, makes the trader? Who is most to blame? The enlightened, cultivated, intelligent man, who supports the system of which the trader is the inevitable result, or the poor trader himself?"[53] Stowe may not explicitly spell out the nature of this problematic support, but the following chapter implies that consumption is a vital component. In "The Quaker Settlement," consumption has become so thoroughly kind that even "the chicken and ham had a cheerful and joyous fizzle in the pan, as if they rather enjoyed being cooked than otherwise."[54] The home presided over by Rachel Halliday is, as many critics have noted, a domestic wonderland in which antislavery activism joins harmoniously with female-dominated sentimental morality, but its refreshing effect is heightened by immediately following such a horrendous account of the slave trade.[55] The Quakerism of the Hallidays may also evoke those Quakers who advocated free produce. A chair, for example, is described as having "a patch-work cushion in it, neatly contrived out of small pieces of different colored woollen goods."[56] In this ideal domestic economy, items are carefully repurposed rather than quickly replaced by market goods, and in this household, much of the fabric is apparently woolen—a term that suggests a kind of simple poverty, but that also significantly means made of wool, not cotton.[57]

To note the ways the Halliday household seems to avoid problematic market entanglements may appear to follow the critics who see this Quaker home as a matriarchal paradise blissfully, even radically, separate from the public sphere, but this isolation (and its supposed moral superiority) is overstated.[58] The Hallidays participate in multiple national and transnational networks. Most obviously, they are members of the Underground Railroad, helping fugitives like Eliza and George Harris on their escape to Canada. More subtly, their household isn't quite as insulated from the market as it first appears. Many of their breakfast items would have been market acquisitions, and certainly the cotton in Rachel's "muslin handkerchief" and the sugar in her neighbor Ruth's bowl have not been grown locally in Indiana.[59] If we are looking for consumer activist sentiments, cotton and sugar pose the difficulty of being typical slave-grown commodities. Nevertheless, there is the possibility that these market goods still fit a model of moral consumption. Among the real-life inspirations for the Hallidays seem to have been Levi and Catherine Coffin, Indiana Quakers who were prominent conductors on the Underground Railroad and who aided a fugitive named Eliza Harris.[60] Levi Coffin was also a passionate advocate for free produce and ran a free produce store in Cincinnati during Stowe's last three years there.[61] The Cincinnati store, which widely circulated flyers, supplied free labor cotton and groceries (including sugar, molasses, and coffee) to customers throughout the Midwest.[62] Given the novel's wariness about market connections, it is possible that, in the idealized paradise of the Halliday household, even the sugar and cotton represent purchases designed to use the market for social good.

Despite the ways free produce ideology would seem a natural corollary to Stowe's vision of slavery's nationwide networks, *Uncle Tom's Cabin* lays the foundation for a free produce argument without explicitly making it. It is conceivable that, continued discussion of free produce in antislavery periodicals and the presence of a large free produce store in Cincinnati notwithstanding, Stowe herself was not familiar with the concept until after *Uncle Tom's Cabin*. Stowe claimed that she and her husband "had not before attended to the subject" of free labor produce before their trip to England in 1853, though they both became staunch advocates after that, with Calvin Ellis Stowe donating $500 in support of a free produce factory in 1854.[63] More likely, the free produce emphasis on direct action contradicts the sentimental premise of Stowe's novel, in which the narrator famously instructs that the best thing readers can do is to *"feel right."*[64] While *Uncle Tom's Cabin* establishes the basis for a free produce vision, Stowe was finally unwilling or unable to follow that vision through to its ultimate conclusion in readerly implication in the suffering of enslaved people. Rather than connecting people with an imagined bond of shared humanity, a true embrace of free produce would require the recognition of the destructive chains of commerce and the subsequent willingness to fight slavery on a pragmatically commercial basis rather than a loftily moral one. Though Stowe strongly advocated that Northerners extricate themselves from the financial networks that linked them to slavery, she hesitated to trace those networks (and the commodities that travelled them) all the way onto the tables and into the armoires of Northern homes, focusing instead on associating those homes with the revolutionary possibilities of the positive links of sympathy.

Both Stowe and Thoreau offered clear-sighted indictments of the ways economic networks threatened to entangle distant people in slavery, and yet both ultimately avoided explicitly condemning personal consumption habits. Thoreau was undoubtedly opposed to war, slavery, and the exploitation of wage laborers, but he did not perceive consumer activism as a meaningful tool in the fight against them. Whereas Stowe recognized consumer goods in domestic spaces as morally significant, she ultimately declined to redefine those spaces as the scenes of abject consumption-as-connection. *Uncle Tom's Cabin* eschews blood-soaked sugar in favor of sentimental embrace. At some level, it is possible to argue that Stowe made the implicit case that cultivating "right feelings" would eventually lead to right action via consumer activism. Across the Atlantic, at least one abolitionist organization made this argument directly. In an 1850s pamphlet published by the Newcastle Antislavery Society, an English man shocks his family by announcing that they are enslavers because they purchase slave-produced goods. He explains that "it is the affecting exposure in Mrs. Stowe's book that has driven the subject home, and compelled me to look at it seriously."[65] By truly feeling the horror of slavery, the pamphlet implies, readers will be forced to recognize and modify their own connections to the institution. At another level, however, Stowe's reticence resembles the ambivalence I will investigate in the next two sections of this chapter. Free produce writing by Chandler and Harper indicates a similar tension between instilling the sentiment that might result in sympathetic identification and triggering the disgust that might result in real change.

PHYSICALITY, COMMODIFICATION, AND REVERSING THE MARKET'S "FEARFUL ALCHEMY"

In an 1857 speech at the Fourth Anniversary of the New York City Anti-Slavery Society, Frances E. W. Harper declared that everyone would be inspired to fight slavery if its atrocities were more readily perceptible rather than disguised by the currency form: "Such a sight should send a thrill of horror, through the nerves of civilization and impel the heart of humanity to lofty deeds. So it might, if men had not found a fearful alchemy by which this blood can be transformed into gold. Instead of listening to the cry of agony, they listen to the ring of dollars and stoop down to pick up the coin."[66] Through the "fearful alchemy" of financial exchange, the apparently benign materiality of coins replaces the horrific material realities of slavery—material realities that, in Harper's estimation, would spark immediate and widespread action if they were seen or heard in their true forms. Reversing this alchemy is similar to defetishizing the commodity—stripping away the deceptive gold to reconstitute the true (and appalling) form beneath. While Harper describes both the suffering and the gold in terms of seeing, hearing, and touching, she suggests that restoring the presence of underlying suffering would create sensorial immediacy ("a thrill of horror") that would in turn compel antislavery action. Without such galvanizing experiences, critiques of immoral financial networks can remain abstract and ineffectual, much as Stowe and Thoreau demonstrate squeamish reluctance to concretize distressing financial connections in the form of blood-soaked commodities.

Harper's sense that the currency form obscures the source of wealth would be true of any form of exploitation, not just slavery. The ability to envision the laboring body as inhering in commodities was a specific function of chattel slavery, however. Consumption became a means of imagined connection precisely because chattel slavery categorized enslaved people as commodified objects of exchange alongside the products of their labor. If the logic of the slave system eroded distinctions between human beings and commodities, consumption-as-connection crystallized that logic by suggesting that to consume slavery's products was to consume the enslaved people who had produced them. Antislavery advocates seized on this conceptual framework to create the kind of physical immediacy Harper encouraged. To appreciate the unique relevance of defetishized commodities to understandings of chattel slavery, it is worth considering a test case in which we might expect to see similar formulations—the exploitation of white wage workers engaged in the production of consumer products. Despite the discussions of "wage slavery" that became increasingly prevalent in the nineteenth century, wage laborers were not themselves commodified, removing the imaginative foundation for consumption-as-connection. While advocates were willing to compare exploited laborers to enslaved people, they did not imply that factory products contained bodily effusions from factory operatives, for example.

English poet Thomas Hood's wildly popular poem "The Song of the Shirt" (1843) illustrates that even a text devoted to awakening consumer conscience avoids collapsing laborer and commodity when the laborer is figuratively rather than literally enslaved.[67] In it, the tragic figure of a white British seamstress, destitute despite working constantly, dramatizes the plight of textile workers by singing a woeful song while she stitches. As with other invocations of "white slavery," the poem's comparison between the worker and enslaved people focuses not on the wrongs of slavery, but on the horrible degradation of a white woman reduced below her rightful social position:

It's O! to be a slave
Along with the barbarous Turk,
Where woman has never a soul to save,
If this is Christian work![68]

A Christian white woman is thereby ignominiously lowered to the position of enslaved non-Christian, just as the poem's opening lines lament that she is "A woman ... in unwomanly rags," where her poverty precludes the garments proper to one of her race and gender.[69]

Even as it asks readers to attend to the consequences of their textile consumption for a figuratively enslaved white woman, "The Song of the Shirt" does not weave her suffering into the shirt itself. The poem implores men to remember "It is not linen you're wearing out, / But human creatures' lives!"[70] The parallel between the destruction of shirts and the destruction of workers represents the poem's most emphatic linking of consumer product and human toll. Nonetheless, "lives" is decidedly less tangible than the tears and blood that so often characterized antislavery versions. Indeed, the poem quite pointedly insists that the woman's shirts contain only her labor, not any piece of her body:

> A little weeping would ease my heart,
> But in their briny bed
> My tears must stop, for every drop
> Hinders needle and thread!⁷¹

Preserving the seamstress's bodily integrity, the poem maintains that, however much she suffers due to consumer desires, she herself cannot be mistaken for an object of consumption. That distinction animates the premise of the poem itself. The "Song of the Shirt" is sung at the scene of production rather than consumption. Unlike free produce texts in which the sighs and moans of the enslaved emanate from cotton dresses, this poem keeps the laborer's voice attached to her person instead of the commodity (not to mention offering nine stanzas of complete sentences as opposed to the inchoate affect of pain).

Conversely, the human commodification that characterizes chattel slavery made it easier for free produce activists to portray the enslaved body as inhering in the commodity itself. The implication of bodily presence, in turn, counteracted the tendency toward abstraction with a vision of tangible contact. In her essay "Slave Luxuries," Chandler imagines a familiar and appalling table scene: "I have fancied that the death-sigh of some unfortunate victim of oppression might be yet trembling on the bosom of a jelly, and the rich flavour of a conserve conceal the briny tears that have mingled with the saccharine crystals that enter into its composition. A pound-cake seems like the sepulchre of the broken heart with which it may, perhaps, have been purchased, and the delicious ice to wear the red tinge of human blood."⁷² This sensorially dense scene uses sound, sight, and taste to create what Conrad calls "horrific materiality."⁷³ As in Harper's speech, Chandler asserts that few women would continue to use slave-grown sugar after direct exposure to slavery's depredations, if they "had beheld the horrors" or "could witness . . . all the agony."⁷⁴

For free produce advocates, imagining direct contact was only useful if it also triggered action. As in Chandler's "blood-polluted banquet" above, free produce texts emphasize a full range of sensory experience to provoke the recoil characteristic of consumption-as-connection.⁷⁵ The beginnings of the stanzas in Chandler's poem "Slave Produce" illustrate the mechanics of this process. The first three stanzas respectively start with commands to "Eat!" "List thee, lady!" and "Look!"[76] These imperatives explicitly appeal to the reader's senses before continuing with descriptions of sugar stained with blood and tears and cotton containing sighs, shrieks, and groans. After three stanzas directing the reader to tune into her own perceptions, the fourth and final stanza begins by specifying the appropriate response to such appalling bodily immediacy: "Yet fling them off from thy shrinking limb," echoing the second stanza's injunction to "turn aside, / With a loathing heart, from the feast of pride."[77] Facing the tangible links between one's own body and slavery's depredations spurs a precipitous casting off of the connecting commodities—a severing of immoral ties. In an 1855 article in *Frederick Douglass' Paper*, Harper follows invocations of sight, sound, and taste with a similar hope that people will "shake our hands from sharing in [slavery's] spoils, and participating in its crimes."[78] Harper's imagery suggests not only pulling back from depraved connection but also shaking off something distasteful or contaminating. To see blood stains on one's own hands, clothes, and food was the ultimate antidote to the "fearful alchemy" of market obfuscation.

FREE PRODUCE OSCILLATIONS BETWEEN SYMPATHY AND DISGUST

The free produce embrace of aversive physicality was ambivalent, however. Soon after her lurid description of the "blood-polluted banquet" in "Slave Luxuries," Chandler poses a question that captures the central quandary of the free produce movement: "Yet why should the sight of blood be needed, when they know it has been shed, to awaken their sleeping sensibilities?"[79] There is a sense of exasperation here—the deep frustration that people need, doubting Thomas-like, to see, hear, and even taste the evidence of suffering to act on what they already know. Chandler dutifully trots out the abstentionist set piece of the grotesque and tainted feast, but she concurrently registers her irritation that such disgusting imagery is necessary to incite action.

Free produce reticence toward the revolting materiality of commodities contrasts with earlier abstention rhetoric. Evocations of bloodstained sugar are still present, but they are now accompanied by tears and sighs. Tears represent an intermediary position: they are a physical substance, but one that emblematizes strong emotion; they are a body fluid, but do not conjure disgust like blood, sweat, or mucus. Among bodily secretions, tears are uniquely non-disgusting, according to William Ian Miller, due to "their source, their clarity, their liquidity, their non-adhering nature, their lack of odor, and their clean taste."[80] In addition to tangible bodily substances, free produce writing frequently adds intangible expressions of feeling: cries, groans, and sighs. Even when depicted as inhering directly in commodities, these sounds elicit horror at human suffering rather than revulsion at contact with a contaminating body. Torn between a redeeming vision of human kinship and the "sight of blood" that Chandler grudgingly acknowledges is often crucial, free produce advocates like Harper and Chandler oscillate between imagery meant to stimulate sympathy and that meant to provoke disgust. The attempt to use both approaches without entirely merging them, to graft sentiment onto disgust, might have been a pragmatic commitment to using all available tools. It also suggests a desire to marshal the more noble emotions of readers instead of depending solely on the fear of contamination. Harper and Chandler did not, like Stowe and Thoreau, avoid depicting the aversive physicality of commodities, but they nevertheless exhibited some of the same reluctance.

Free produce writing exhibits the ambivalence between sentiment and disgust by veering between ineffable emotion and concrete physicality. In her newspaper article "The Free Labor Movement," for example, Harper paints a scene that combines both elements: "We enter the wardrobe and the sighs and groans of the slave are lingering around the seams of our clothes, and floating amid the folds of our garments. But who will say, when Carolina's rice, with snowy whiteness, tempts the taste, perhaps the hands that gathered this were severed from some loved and lost embrace? Who will gaze upon the manufactured cotton, and see the stain, the stain of blood and tears upon its warp and woof?"[81] The ghostly emanations of the sounds of distress—haunting but intangible—give way to a careful examination of rice. In this context, attention to a tempting white foodstuff would have cued many readers to anticipate the cannibalistic imagery of blood, but Harper instead swerves away from the physical fact of the commodity and toward the scene of labor (hands gathering) and the familiar sentimental focus on familial separation ("were severed from some loved and lost embrace"). Nevertheless, she quickly tacks back to a commodity in its minute materiality, detecting the remnants of bodily substances in the very "warp and woof" of cotton cloth.

Both Chandler and Harper depict disturbing physical contact while also working to elevate sympathetic responses to a comparable level of influence. This impulse registers in moments that collapse the material and emotional realms. The speaker of Chandler's poem "Oh Press Me Not to Taste Again" attempts to merge the physical and non-physical when she refuses slave-grown sugar, declaring, "I cannot feed on human sighs."[82] This statement conveys repudiation, but it also captures the contradictory desire to wrest the actionably concrete from impalpable human emotion. No one can actually feed on human sighs, whatever their moral investments. In Harper's poem "Free Labor," the speaker proclaims her free labor dress

> Too light to bear a smother'd sigh,
> From some lorn woman's heart,
> Whose only wreath of household love
> Is rudely torn apart.[83]

In Harper's construction, the anguish of familial separation is transmogrified into a physical weight that cannot be borne by the "light" fabric. When Harper depicts tangible (non–free labor) fabric as transmitting intangible pain, she participates in what Kyla Schuller has identified as the nineteenth-century discourse of impressibility, in which sentimentalism was understood to use refining emotions to help regulate the body's physical sensations. According to Schuller, Harper's poem posits that impressibility "link[s] producers and consumers across space and time through the mediating role of inanimate objects that are nonetheless heavy with human experience."[84] Using objects redolent with human feeling to link producers and consumers across space and time also describes consumption-as-connection, of course. Because the physical realm in consumption-as-connection is defined by disgust, however, the desire to include stirring human experience alongside materiality in Harper's poem also indicates a desire to balance revulsion with sympathy.

Perhaps the clearest indication of free produce ambivalence toward inducing disgust comes in Harper's poem "Free Labor," which simultaneously raises the specter of consumption-as-connection and abjures any possibility that the speaker herself has been tainted. Through a series of negative declarations, the speaker consistently expresses relief that her dress will feature "no cry to God" and "No stain of tears and blood"; it is "Unladened" and "Unburden'd" by sighs.[85] The poem's tense enacts similar distance. Although it begins in the present ("I wear an easy garment"), subsequent stanzas imagine the dress in future terms with a litany of "shall" statements.[86] The last two stanzas combine the congratulatory future tense that characterizes most of the poem with an alarming evocation of past wrongdoing:

> Then lightly shall it press my form,
> Unburden'd by a sigh;
> And from its seams and folds shall rise,
> No voice to pierce the sky,
>
> And witness at the throne of God,
> In language deep and strong,
> That I have nerv'd Oppression's hand,
> For deeds of guilt and wrong.[87]

Without the negation of the preceding lines, the final stanza reads like a chilling confession of transgression. Harper ends the poem with a vision that would be particularly troubling to her presumed Christian readers, intensifying their desire to pursue the unburdened virtue of the poem's projected future. While the poem itself conveys horrifying physicality and human suffering alike, its construction propels readers into a future where that reality is already negated and in the past. Its rhetoric offers a beacon of appropriate consumer behavior and moral rectitude to its readers, but only by preempting any actual contact with the horrifying physicality that Harper concurrently evokes and disavows.

MELVILLE'S UNIVERSAL CAPITALISM OF THE SEAS

Free produce advocates were ambivalent about the rhetorical uses of cannibalism. They used it to mobilize disgust, but they also downplayed abhorrent physicality in favor of more sentimental connections. Herman Melville was a different story. Through representations of commodities that became more, not less, marketable because of the human suffering they had occasioned, Melville offered a deeply pessimistic view about the possibility of escaping the worldwide trade networks he considered manifestations of the nature-wide propensity for living beings to devour one another. Considering Melville's depiction of cannibalistic commodities allows us to recognize a strange optimism in even the most abject free produce formulations. Despite reservations about images like blood-soaked sugar, Harper and Chandler use them in the hope that their upsetting materiality will provoke reflexive antislavery action. Melville's writing betrays no such confidence that direct confrontation with horrifying commodities will change consumer behavior. His version of consumption-as-connection freely imagines how individual appetites link people to vast networks, but it does not presume any automatic impulse to break those ties, no matter how disturbing the consequences.

For all its admiration for the bravery of sailors and the undeniable exhilaration of the chase, *Moby-Dick* also captures the brutal, occasionally heartbreaking violence at the core of whaling and the fact that such violence serves consumer whims. Ishmael's sympathetic description of the blind whale with a missing fin (his stump mirroring the novel's many mangled sailors) insists on human terms for his death: "But pity there was none. For all his old age, and his one arm, and his blind eyes, he must die the death and be murdered, in order to light the gay bridals and other merrymakings of men, and also to illuminate the solemn churches that preach unconditional inoffensiveness by all to all."[88] Not only is this pitiable death deemed a murder, but it is also a murder in favor of the desire to better illuminate frivolous parties and hypocritical churches. Ishmael evinces a similar disgust while attempting to establish "The Honor and Glory of Whaling" in the chapter of that name, praising the fact that "the first whale attacked by our brotherhood was not killed with any sordid intent."[89] He goes on to specify that what makes modern whaling sordid is the consumer economy it supports: "Those were the knightly days of our profession, when we only bore arms to succor the distressed, and not to fill men's lamp-feeders."[90] Beyond the violence toward whales, the many fatalities among human whalers cast a pall on the illumination those whales so conveniently provide. After describing the frequent deaths of sailors, Ishmael admonishes readers, "For God's sake, be economical with your lamps and candles! not a gallon you burn, but at least one drop of man's blood was spilled for it."[91]

Melville's remarkable linking of whale oil and blood marks the commodity with the stain of cannibalism. As in the antislavery figure of blood-soaked sugar, Ishmael implies that, by consuming whale oil (and "filling lamp-feeders" evokes eating even though this oil isn't food), purchasers also consume the whalers who produced it. Melville's portrayal of cannibal commodities takes a significantly different view of consumer motivation than do the abolitionist versions, however. Whereas abolitionists saw the ability to imagine the suffering in the commodity as laying bare the horrifying truth of slavery and thus changing consumer habits, Melville often presents that suffering as stimulating rather than stifling consumption. In *Typee* (1846), the narrator, Tommo, conveys the market appeal of cannibalism. He observes that he has never believed Captain Cook was cannibalized and represents a Native Hawaiian who staunchly maintains otherwise as an opportunistic huckster. Because of the man's "morbid desire for notoriety," according to Tommo, he "gave himself out among the foreign residents of the place as the living tomb of Captain Cook's big toe!"[92] When fellow islanders bring the man to trial to silence such claims, his eventual victory "was the making of his fortune; ever afterwards he was in the habit of giving very profitable audiences to all curious travellers who were desirous of beholding the man who had eaten the great navigator's great toe."[93] Such a turn of events corresponds with what Daniel Cottom has identified as a tipping point in Western depictions of cannibalism: Starting in the eighteenth century, the explosion of narratives about cannibalism marked a shift to an era in which "cannibals were being merchandised as objects of consumption."[94] As with the whale oil that recalls drops of human blood, these travelers can imagine Cook's body as present, if transformed, and the result is not horror, but unseemly (and profitable) titillation.

Gruesome shop signs showing whalers being devoured by whales offer a similarly grotesque means of driving profits. Although Ishmael derides the sensationalism of these signs, the bloodthirsty whales nevertheless model the consumer demand actually responsible for the suffering of sailors. He scornfully dismisses such imagery: "As for the sign-painters' whales seen in the streets hanging over the shops of oil-dealers, what shall be said of them? They are generally Richard III. whales, with dromedary humps, and very savage; breakfasting on three or four sailor tarts, that is whaleboats full of mariners: their deformities floundering in seas of blood and blue paint."[95] Implicit in Ishmael's criticism of the sign's verisimilitude, however, is a disturbing tribute to its success as a marketing device. Scenes of dying sailors are common on shop signs because they attract customers. Far from shying away from the human cost of the commodity, oil dealers and oil buyers have made it the emblem of their economic exchange.

By Ishmael's estimation, everyone is constrained to cycles of consumption in which consumer appetites perpetually fuel destruction. Whereas antislavery consumer activists turned to cannibalism as the epitome of unnatural and horrifying consumption, Melville suggests that cannibalism in fact defines the world, in humans and animals alike. His depictions of cannibalism provide a preview of the second section of this book, which examines the metaphors of cannibalism and hungry animals that encapsulate slavery's consumptive logic. Melville combines these two metaphoric strains, explicitly invoking cannibalism while depicting animals that evoke both brutal appetites and bodily commodification. Ishmael proclaims cannibalism to be pervasive and endless: "Consider, once more, the universal cannibalism of the sea; all whose creatures prey upon each other, carrying on eternal war since the world began."[96] Cannibalism here does not denote humans eating humans or even species consuming the same species; instead, it represents violent devouring within any unifying category (in this case, an ocean habitat) as a kind of cannibalism. By counting any sea creature feeding on any other sea creature as cannibalistic violence, Ishmael suggests that such cannibalism may be "universal" precisely because it is part of the natural order. The few critics who have considered Melville's figurative cannibalism rather than his treatment of literal cannibalism and its cultural meaning have seen these images either metaphysically or as indicating an overt antislavery position.[97] In fact, the connections between slavery and cannibalism in *Moby-Dick* offer an antislavery message only insofar as slavery appears as yet another symptom of the brutal economic forces Melville condemns. By portraying the global transport of commodified bodies (whether African captives or the remnants of whales) in terms of cannibalism, he orients contemporary modes of exploitative consumption within a larger context of universal appetite. Melville concludes that, deplorable though they may be, these exploitative modes are as natural as they are inescapable.

The chapter "Stubb's Supper" uses the universality of cannibalistic destruction to present a version of consumption-as-connection in which the simple act of eating metaphorically links individuals to global networks of violence. As Stubb, the *Pequod's* second mate, dines on a steak cut from a freshly killed whale, he is mirrored by the sharks feeding on the whale below the water; the subsequent passage details other instances of shark banquets directly reflecting the human behavior above them (and merits quoting at length):

> Though amid all the smoking horror and diabolism of a sea-fight, sharks will be seen longingly gazing up to the ship's decks, like hungry dogs round a table where red meat is being carved, ready to bolt down every killed man that is tossed to them; and though, while the valiant butchers over the deck-table are thus cannibally carving each other's live meat with carving-knives all gilded and tasselled, the sharks, also, with their jewel-hilted mouths, are quarrelsomely carving away under the table at the dead meat; and though, were you to turn the whole affair upside down, it would still be pretty much the same thing, that is to say, a shocking sharkish business enough for all parties; and though sharks also are the invariable outriders of all slave ships crossing the Atlantic, systematically trotting alongside, to be handy in case a parcel is to be carried anywhere, or a dead slave to be decently buried . . .[98]

Cannibalism provides a conceptual handle for the larger horror of men turned into meat (be it "red meat," "live meat," or "dead meat"). War transforms combatants into "butchers" who are "cannibally carving each other's live meat"—the cannibalism adverb not the result of a desire to eat human flesh, but a function of taking what is the same (it is not just the enemy's live meat, but "each other") and radically stripping it of that sameness (in this case, humanity) in order to convert it to food. The conversion to food encapsulates precisely what is wrong in these situations—food offers little value beyond bodily sustenance and possibly pleasure, so making men into meat is tantamount to trading the soul of another for a fleeting nutritional boost. Of course, the boost here is not enjoyed by those who fight above, but those sharks who happily receive the "dead meat" below. Melville insists upon their mutual mirroring, however, replicating terms like "carving" and "meat" for men and sharks before declaring both to be "pretty much the same thing."

The cannibalistic violence of war is further tainted by money—Melville might as easily have called his overarching principle the universal capitalism of the sea. The "gilded and tasselled swords" are reflected in the "jewel-hilted mouths" of sharks, but the insidious role of greed is most explicit in slavery. Like the slave trade that sought to radically reduce human beings to saleable flesh by forcibly transporting them across the Atlantic, these sharks are "handy in case a parcel is to be carried anywhere"—the word "parcel" encompassing the dehumanizing transformation of people into portable commodities. Melville critiques the fungibility of enslaved bodies, but his critique also takes advantage of the way (as Saidiya Hartman has argued) that fungibility implies the availability of enslaved people for imaginative projection—in this case, to conveniently embody Melville's larger message about greed.[99] Again, the sharks merely reflect the conversion to meat that has already occurred above the water. The radical commodification that would reduce human bodies to parcels available to be tossed overboard and devoured is, significantly, the result of global networks of power and exploitation; the slave trade bound countries on both sides of the Atlantic, just as the earlier sea-fight example represents a clash between nations. Stubb's meal suggests this vast violence on a small scale. He greedily dines on the whale he killed three chapters earlier, reaping personal pleasure from commercial killing. Underscoring the resemblance between his eating and the whaling industry, the narrator judgmentally notes that the meal's illumination by whale oil lantern amounts to "feed[ing] upon the creature that feeds his lamp."[100] Underscoring the resemblance between Stubb and the sharks that evoke multiple registers of human consumption, the ship's cook Fleece pronounces Stubb "more of shark dan Massa Shark hisself."[101]

In Melville's vision, trade networks connect far-ranging whalers with lamp-lit parlors, implicating consumers in a worldwide system built to commodify and consume bodies. Like the abolitionists who campaigned against slave-grown products, Melville seeks to reveal the role everyday purchases play in distant suffering. Unlike those abolitionists, he implies that attempts to disrupt the consumer cycle will be subsumed by larger devouring forces that are endlessly self-perpetuating. Dismantling the commodity fetish means restoring the sense of relations between people instead of objects, and in Melville's disturbing vision, those relations are almost necessarily consumptive. Ishmael's formulation of the "insular Tahiti" among the cannibalistic seas in the soul of man comes with a final admonition: "God keep thee! Push not off from that isle, thou canst never return!"[102] The universal cannibalism of the sea is postlapsarian, suggesting that to be anything less than a true *isolatoe*, entirely cut off from relationships with other human beings, is to participate in an inescapable cycle of eating and being eaten. The dream of restoring less exploitative relations, however appealing, is simply the dream of an isolated paradise to which we can never return.

Melville's pessimistic view provides a fitting bridge to the next chapter. While the first two chapters have examined consumption-as-connection in an abolitionist context, the third chapter analyzes blackface minstrelsy to show that the ability to envision the enslaved laborer as inhering in commodities did not presuppose an antislavery outlook. Like the abolitionist formulations that present distressing links urging their own severing, the consumption-as-connection that appears in blackface minstrel songsters is aversive, resulting in recurring images that disavowed connections between white audiences and enslaved people. As in Melville's troubling theory that consumers are sometimes enticed rather than repulsed by human anguish, blackface minstrel songs gleefully depict commodities as interchangeable with enslaved laborers to spur the consumption of performances and minstrel songbooks. My first two chapters demonstrate that the efficacy of disgust in inspiring antislavery action also risked fueling anti-Black racism. Chapter 3 shows that racism could be the objective of such constructions as well as a harmful byproduct. The free produce ambivalence between galvanizing revulsion and engendering sympathy exposes the abolitionist reluctance to fully embrace consumption-as-connection. The following chapter establishes that this reluctance was well founded.

THREE

BLACKFACE MINSTRELSY AND THE DISAVOWAL OF CONSUMPTION'S CONNECTIONS

One of the most popular songs in early blackface minstrelsy, "Miss Lucy Long," includes two references to corn.[1] A catalog of the title character's beauty proclaims, "Oh! Miss Lucy's teeth is grinning, / Just like an ear ob corn."[2] Two verses later, the song's speaker (and Lucy's admirer) vows,

> If she makes a scolding wife,
> As sure as she was born,
> I'll tote her down to Georgia,
> And trade her off for corn.[3]

What begins as a humorously agricultural romantic tribute ends by testifying to the dehumanizing effects of the slave trade, where Lucy's body can be converted into corn. In the logic of the song, even the smallest corporeal details—straight teeth—become markers of her commodification. The threat of trading Lucy for corn does not come from an enslaver, however, but from her own lover, a Black man who furthermore tries to blame Lucy's fate on her failure to embrace wifely docility.[4] The song offers a surprisingly stark depiction of chattel slavery, a system that treats human beings as consumable objects, but it ascribes responsibility for that consumption to enslaved people themselves. This chapter explains why.

Blackface minstrel performances abounded in moments in which enslaved people were imagined as interchangeable with slave crops. Describing enslaved people with skin like tobacco or sweat like sugar, blackface minstrel songs and skits effectively defetishized commodities to envision the material links between enslaved laborers and consumers. Blackface minstrelsy thus adopted the logic of consumption-as-connection by suggesting that consuming tobacco and sugar also entailed the consumption of enslaved people. Such an insight would seem to pave the way for acknowledging consumer complicity in slavery, just as it had for so many eighteenth- and nineteenth-century abolitionists. Yet even in moments when slavery's products were defetishized, blackface minstrelsy refused to acknowledge that the consumers of those products would have included the mostly white, mostly working-class Northerners who dominated U.S. minstrel audiences. The song "Miss Lucy Long" also encapsulates the refusal to implicate Northerners. The song was composed and initially performed by the first blackface minstrel troupe, which, despite being founded in New York and led by a white Ohioan, was called the Virginia Minstrels. Just as "Miss Lucy Long" denies white complicity by depicting a Black man willing to commodify his enslaved lover, its original performers obscured Northern connections to slavery by assuming the mask of Southernness alongside that of Blackness.[5]

This chapter reveals that blackface minstrelsy harbored a sense of consumption-as-connection similar to that embraced by abolitionist consumer activists, but that blackface minstrelsy expressed it very differently. In abolitionist versions, consumption-as-connection appeared in overt and disturbing acknowledgments of consumer complicity. Abolitionists foregrounded aversion, using grotesque images of abject commodities to provoke recoil and spur people to sever ignominious ties to slavery. In blackface minstrelsy, conversely, consumption-as-connection was covert, discernible only through careful analysis of what was omitted as well as what was explicitly represented. The telling absence of any indication that white Northern consumers were connected to slavery, despite the frequent presence of figurations in which commodities and enslaved laborers are interchangeable, demonstrates the aversive nature of such connections. If the links implied by commodities did not trouble blackface minstrelsy's predominantly white, working-class audience, there would have been no need to disavow them. Aversion remained central to consumption-as-connection, but the aversion in blackface minstrel formulations produced not repulsive metaphors, but rather a recurring fantasy of separation that portrayed slavery as a self-perpetuating system in which enslaved people willingly facilitated their own commodification and white Northern consumers played no role.

This less blatant consumer aversion is consistent with the fundamental character of blackface minstrelsy. As Eric Lott has famously argued, blackface minstrelsy represented a complex combination of disdain and desire for Black culture.[6] Examining minstrelsy through the lens of consumption-as-connection reveals a similar combination of aversion and appetite. As I argued in the previous chapter, Melville's pessimistic depictions of consumption-as-connection portrayed revolting images as enticing rather than repelling spectators. Similarly, while blackface minstrel formulations indicate aversion by disavowing Northern connections to slavery, the insistent repetition of such formulations simultaneously betrays the audience's desire to imagine enslaved people in terms of slave-produced commodities.

As the final chapter in the first section of this book, chapter 3 shifts from abolitionist to non-abolitionist uses of consumption-as-connection. Examining blackface minstrelsy in the United States from the 1830s to the 1850s, it covers the same period and location as chapter 2 even as it investigates texts with radically different goals. The leap between chapters 2 and 3 is thus ideological instead of chronological or geographical. Because it analyzes the relationship between blackface minstrel performance and racial and class dynamics specific to the United States, this chapter focuses on U.S. blackface minstrelsy. It is nevertheless worth noting that, despite its origins and enormous popularity in the United States, blackface minstrelsy was also a transatlantic and eventually global phenomenon. American blackface minstrel performers began touring Britain in the 1830s, inspiring souvenirs, publications, and eventually numerous British blackface minstrel troupes.[7] As in other chapters of the book, it is important to remember that ideas about consumption and slavery were reverberating throughout the Atlantic world, even when my argument foregrounds the U.S. context.

The first three sections of this chapter consider pervasive blackface minstrel images that relate everyday consumption to chattel slavery while also deflecting any sense of white Northern involvement. Reassuring white audiences that they bore no disturbing ties to slavery or enslaved people, these images illuminate the complexities of consumption-as-connection as a conceptual framework. They show that blackface minstrel audiences, like antislavery consumer activists, were contemplating how economic networks linked people to slavery even at a geographic distance. Crucially, the ability to discern consumption-as-connection did not guarantee an antislavery outlook; it was equally available to popular cultural forms that, in the case of blackface minstrelsy, presented the enslaved status of Black Americans as a source of entertainment and fun. If the presumed basis of consternation in abolitionist consumption-as-connection tropes was the ethical horror of being implicated in a heinous system, in blackface minstrel versions it was the white supremacist horror of being linked to Black people. In effect, blackface minstrelsy's disavowal of connection lays bare the racist fears of contamination underlying many white abolitionist uses of consumption-as-connection, even as its catering to audience desires hints that white abolitionist repetitions of grotesque imagery could indicate titillation as much as indignation.

The final section of the chapter extends my analysis of consumption to the material culture of blackface minstrelsy to complicate critical understandings of minstrelsy's class identity. While the first three of the chapter's sections examine how blackface minstrelsy portrays the consumption of commodities like tobacco and cotton, the fourth section shifts to examining blackface minstrelsy as an object of consumption via widely popular printed sheet music and lyric books. Considering blackface minstrel lyrics about consumption alongside the consumer objects in which large numbers of people encountered them, I argue that scholarship on antebellum blackface minstrelsy has been too narrowly focused on theatrical performance. To get a full view of minstrelsy's cultural impact, scholars must look beyond theaters and into the homes, fields, and factories where minstrel songs were sung, and sung all the time, by amateurs. Moreover, the context of consumption-as-connection brings into sharp relief the significance of blackface minstrel print material. Depictions of slavery as a self-perpetuating system offered white audiences a fantasy of separation from consumption's grievous entanglements. By evaluating the form of sheet music and printed songsters in addition to their content, I demonstrate that at-home minstrel performance allowed white working-class aficionados to further assert their separation from enslaved people by assuming the mantle of middle-class respectability, even as they also reveled in crude lyrics and topics associated with raucous working-class entertainment. Beyond the common scholarly understanding of minstrelsy as a contradictory engagement with Black culture, the ambivalence that attends minstrelsy at home also reveals a contradictory combination of attraction and aversion to the white middle class.[8]

THE METONYMIC MINSTREL IMAGINATION: SEEING ENSLAVED PEOPLE IN COMMODITIES

No song better represents the minstrel trope of indistinguishability between enslaved person and product than "Jim Jawbone," which appears in a book of blackface minstrel lyrics published around 1850. From the beginning, the song portrays its enslaved namesake as interchangeable with the crop he produces. Suckled on and cradled in tobacco as a baby, Jim, like Topsy, doesn't grow up so much as just "grow," "blooming" like the tobacco buds all around him.[9] His later development continues the pattern:

> As Jim growed up, de more he show
> His vegetable breed, sa;
> His 'plexion from de sable crow,
> Turned like de yallar weed, sa;
> His limbs growed so jist like de plant,
> When cutting time come round, sa,
> He took 'em for tobacco stalks,
> An' cumself clar down, sa.[10]

In a remarkable metamorphosis, Jim's developing body transforms into a facsimile of a tobacco plant. He eventually becomes so indistinguishable from the crop he tends that he gets confused and accidentally harvests himself.

Hidden in this song's jocular tone and casual violence is an astute interpretation of chattel slavery, in which enslaved people both produced and represented valuable commodities. By 1860, enslaved people were effectively the nation's biggest agricultural asset, representing a monetary value "three times the value of the entire livestock population, twelve times the value of all American farm implements and machinery, [and] twelve times the value of the entire U.S. cotton crop."[11] The exhaustion of tobacco fields in the Upper South had long meant that more money could often be made selling enslaved people to the Deep South than in producing tobacco. As an 1853 *New York Tribune* editorial reprinted in *Frederick Douglass' Paper* mordantly puts it, "We congratulate the 'Gentlemen Farmers' of Virginia that they are still able to realize a handsome profit from a well selected stock of 'pretty plough boys and young girls,' and by this judicious rotation of crops, turn their exhausted soil to a good account."[12]

Like "Jim Jawbone," many blackface minstrel songs gleefully blur the boundary between person and commodity. Sometimes this means metonymic humor that plays up a perceived similarity in color between certain slave crops and dark skin, describing enslaved people who are "coffee colored" or "de color ob brown tobackur" or referring to tobacco as "de nigger plant, / Dark as our own skin boys."[13] One song compares a woman's eyes to "two egg shells in a pot of coffee," while another dispenses with logic altogether in its declaration that an enslaved woman has a head "like a tobacco plant."[14] Significantly, both crops only achieve this supposedly skin-like brown color after being cut and cured (tobacco) or roasted (coffee beans): It is at the point that they near readiness for consumption that these plants are deemed to resemble enslaved people. Even without a visual connection, some similes liken the physiology of Black bodies to slave crops, as when a woman in the popular minstrel play *Bone Squash* proclaims that her "perspiration flows jist as copiously as de 'lasses [molasses] from de hogshead."[15] In other moments, enslaved people appear either as vital components of crops, as in descriptions of the bodies fertilizing sugar or corn, or as crops themselves, as in the frequently repeated verse "In Souf Carolina de nigga's grow, / If de white man will only plant his toe, / Den dey water de ground wid bacca smoke, / And out ob de dirt dar heads will poke."[16] According to one song, the Black body is none other than the tobacco plant's original seed: "Natur planted a black baby, / To grow dis weed divine."[17]

Seeing slavery's products as inextricable from the laboring body laid the conceptual groundwork for understanding consumption as a form of intimate connection—a vision in which smoking tobacco or drinking coffee also meant taking enslaved bodies into one's own body. Such a conceptual move was, of course, the precondition for the abolitionist consumer activism I examined in the last two chapters: To convince consumers of their problematic link to slavery, abolitionists first had to convince them that it was impossible to separate enslaved labor from its products. It is noteworthy that even non-abolitionist commentators demonstrated the same understanding. Lott, one of the few critics to mention this tendency, attributes minstrelsy's anxious collapse of people into things as an attempt "to clinch the property relations these songs fear are too fluid."[18] As Lott rightly observes, such figurations indicate anxieties about "fragil[e] . . . racial boundaries," but these figurations also reveal that white audiences saw everyday consumption as a key means by which those fragile boundaries could be breached.[19]

In imaginatively merging enslaved people with products, minstrel songs reflect a broader cultural trend in which the naming and marketing of consumer goods echoed the logic of consumption-as-connection. Antebellum merchants sought to exploit the widely imagined metonymic link between people of African descent and slave crops by selling tobacco products named as if they were part of a Black body. "Negro head" tobacco was a specific (and popular) type of plug tobacco, for instance.[20] Such naming conventions defetishized the commodity without espousing antislavery sentiments, but they were not entirely free from some of consumption's more troubling implications. When the San Francisco *Daily Evening Bulletin* published the one-liner "CANNIBALISM—Chewing 'niggerhead'" in 1862, it literalized the product name and thereby attempted to render absurd the economic relations suggested by the metaphoric slur.[21] Writing about repeated references to "Negro head" tobacco in Charles Dickens's *Great Expectations,* Elaine Freedgood argues that such terminology represents "a fetishistic form of remembering" in which painful histories are simultaneously evoked and denied.[22] Beneath the surface of the *Daily Evening Bulletin* joke, for instance, lurks the recognition that consuming tobacco tangibly and grievously connected consumers to the enslaved laborers who cultivated it. Even though the racist humor is far from antislavery in impulse, it nevertheless registers the same kinds of discomfort on which many abolitionists sought to capitalize: both the fear that such a connection might have been profoundly immoral (rendering the consumer a cannibal) and the white racist aversion to close physical contact with Black bodies.

The ability to see commodities produced by slavery as inseparable from enslaved people dismayed abolitionists and non-abolitionists alike. While many abolitionists responded with concrete action via consumer activism, minstrel audiences were more interested in an imaginative dodge wherein the lines of connection circled back to the enslaved population (or at least into free Black communities). Thanks to this rerouting, slavery's grievous entanglements bypassed the Northern white communities where antebellum minstrel performances were most popular. A minstrel end men's gag published in 1863 offers a fittingly circular solution to the problem of consuming tobacco when it became indistinguishable from Black bodies: "PETER, didn't I see you goin' down Laurens street dis afternoon, wid a young lady in your mouth and a cigar on your arm? / No, Sam, 'twas de cigar I had in my mouth; de young Wenus was on my arm."[23] Beyond the telling erotics of mixing up one's objects of (oral) pleasure, this joke depends on the capacity of white audiences to imagine the interchangeability of a Black woman and a cigar. It also sidesteps any sense of cross-racial contact through consumption by making the consumer Black as well.

The rest of this chapter will examine how this imaginative sleight of hand worked to figuratively absolve white minstrel audiences of troubling connections to slavery, and why such a sleight of hand would have been necessary in the first place. Why would performers of blackface minstrelsy, a form rooted in anti-Blackness and strongly associated with the white Northern working class, feel compelled to disavow the links forged by white consumption? And how does that compulsion shift our understanding of minstrelsy's audience?

WILLING COMMODITIES: BLACKFACE MINSTRELSY BLAMES THE VICTIM

Free produce abolitionists and minstrel audiences may have shared a desire to dissolve or deny their consumption-based connections to slavery, but they had very different motivations. Abolitionists wanted to avoid the guilt of supporting chattel slavery. By and large, white working-class minstrel audiences had no qualms about chattel slavery, but they were terrified of being enslaved themselves.[24] The minstrel fantasy of separation allowed white Northern workers to ignore the fact that their tobacco, sugar, and cotton tangibly connected them to an exploitative system they already worried was too similar to their own working conditions. Moreover, blackface minstrelsy repeatedly envisioned enslaved people as willing participants in their own commodification, offering a tacit contrast to the white working-class unrest that strenuously protested so-called "white slavery" and "wage slavery." As

David R. Roediger notes, the more common "white slavery" frequently carried an implicit support or acceptance of "black slavery."[25]

The enslaved people portrayed in minstrel songs can be counted on to produce demand as well as the products to meet it. These portrayals replace the larger circulations within the U.S. economy with a self-destructive cycle in which enslaved people perpetuate their own enslavement. Along with the numerous instances in which enslaved people become the very crops they tend, these songs suggest that Black bodies are eminently suited and available to be entirely absorbed into the economy, and that the economy runs entirely on their self-inflicted and self-perpetuating labor.[26] This imagined economy, efficient though it may be, is not painless. It is characterized by enslaved people who whip, punch, and kill one another, and by other enslaved people who toil their entire lives only to have their corpses appropriated to grow more crops. Such a pattern of images essentially blames the victims of slavery for their enslavement. By portraying a self-perpetuating circularity in which enslaved people create and enforce their own condition, these minstrel images mask the potentially uncomfortable reality that Black people continued to be enslaved because Southern enslavers continued to profit from trading products to eager consumers in the North and abroad.

Jim Jawbone once again embodies the larger trend. Even after accidentally harvesting himself, Jim keeps working:

> So poor Jim Jawbone had to die,
> All by dis sad slipstake [mistake], sa,
> He hung him up wid stalks to dry,
> Upon de 'bacca brake, sa[.][27]

The "had to" suggests that Jim's demise is inevitable, and indeed it might have been the only way to untangle the thorny confusion that occurs when Jim becomes as much crop as man. Jim's death marks not so much the end of his life as the full realization of his commodity status. Far from rebelling against the circumstances of his death, Jim dutifully hangs himself to dry alongside the other harvested tobacco being readied for market.[28] He enacts his own conversion to commodity. The final verse ends, appropriately enough, with Jim's consumption, not by a distant purchaser of the tobacco, but by the speaker of the song, who (given the stereotypical dialect) seems to be a fellow enslaved person:

> Dis pipe I cut out ob de bone,
> Dat growed out ob his shin, sa,
> An' de more I smoke de 'bacca out,
> De more keeps coming in, sa[.]²⁹

The song's speaker takes a grisly souvenir—Jim's shinbone—and turns it into a pipe with which to smoke the rest of Jim. Jim's body, which was previously both crop and the means of cultivating that crop, has now become the crop and the means of consuming it.

Significantly, "Jim Jawbone" replaces the consumer whose money would have actually driven the production of tobacco—a Northern white man, say—with a Southern enslaved man. Although Southerners, both enslaved and free, certainly consumed tobacco, most tobacco products were shipped through the Northern market instead of being directly consumed, and this song neatly elides any sense of Northern involvement by offering an entirely self-contained fantasy of enslaved people as product, producer, and consumer.³⁰ Lyrics frequently depict enslaved people as voracious consumers of tobacco. As its imperative title suggests, the song "Gib Us Chaw Tobacco" identifies the crop as the central wish of its multiple enslaved speakers. The song promotes tobacco as a pain reliever, a digestive aid, and, most curiously, a tooth whitener, but its most frequently lauded benefit is its ability to "free de soul from grief."³¹ The song is frank about enslaved suffering, but it locates a cure not in freedom, but in consumption—a consumption that, moreover, drives demand for a crop that in turn reinforces slavery. The chorus of "Jim Jawbone" follows a similar trajectory:

> Success to de tobacco leaf,
> An' nigga's Jawbone Grinny,
> Sing may dey raise for our relief,
> De plant ob ole Virginny.³²

The enslaved cultivators of tobacco thus urge increased cultivation. By this song's logic, growing tobacco is a self-interested pursuit rather than violently enforced labor—the plant "raise[d] for [the] relief" of enslaved people rather than the source of enslaver wealth.

Even when they are not consumers, the enslaved people in these songs still drive consumption. Multiple songs mention tobacco signs. These antebellum advertisements used images of enslaved people to indicate tobacco stores, effectively deploying enslaved people to fuel consumer demand.[33] In their explanations of the phenomenon, songs once again reveal the extent of the metonymic minstrel imagination as they insistently conflate enslaved people with a slave crop. According to the song "The Tobacco Sign,"

> Along de streets whar e'er you go,
> You see a wooden nigger grinning at you oh
> His skin's de color ob de leaf so fine,
> An' it's jist the thing for a bacco sign.[34]

"Gib Us Chaw Tobacco" follows its declaration that "Natur planted a black baby, / To grow dis weed divine" with "Dat's de reason why de niggers, / Am made a 'baccy sign."[35] Occasionally songs push the limits of the metonym by suggesting that Black bodies and tobacco signs are identical. "A Hoo!" ends with an enslaved man who "died ob decline, / And dey dried him for a 'bacco sign."[36] "The Tobacco Sign" explains opposition to the annexation of Texas by joking that the conflict is "all 'bout de live tobacco sign."[37] Describing enslaved people as "live tobacco signs" reveals the extent to which the market for slavery's products was superimposed back onto enslaved producers, as if they were mere signifiers of commodities.

Unlike other minstrel tropes of commodification, tobacco sign tropes do not absolve audience members from consumption; demand in these cases still comes from tobacco store customers. Nevertheless, tobacco sign tropes do suggest that enslaved people directly stimulate such demand. One song instructs tobacco sellers looking to improve business that "If he wants to raise de trade up fine, / Let him raise a black tobacco sign."[38] The repeated "raise" points to agriculture in addition to the obvious meaning of "increase"—however far the tobacco shop might be from the tobacco field, "raise" underlines the correlation between increased demand and increased production. Furthermore, this same song repeatedly insists that enslaved people willingly participate in the process. For one man, modeling for a sign is lucrative enough to purchase his manumission: "He bought his freedom at forty-nine, / By standin' for a 'bacco sign." The final verse implies that, even without direct profits, tobacco signs provide enviable posthumous celebrity:

Oh, one ting cheers de nigger's head,
Dat he'll be livin' when he's dead;
For soon as grim death cuts his twine,
He turns into a 'bacco sign.³⁹

Ever happy to keep production churning, this enslaved man looks forward to his postmortem fame as an advertisement. Appropriation transforms into cheerful participation as blackface minstrelsy imagines enslaved people enthusiastically offering up their image to increase the sale of tobacco.

To note that minstrel songs portray enslaved people as natural commodities who willingly participate in their own commodification is not to suggest that they portray enslaved life as free from suffering. Yet even at moments of apparent sympathy for affliction, minstrel songs separate their white audience from the enslaved people they depict. As multiple critics have observed, minstrelsy frequently and candidly represented slavery's hardships, and the songs I have been analyzing are no exception. In "Jim Jawbone," the "poor" protagonist's tragic confusion between himself and tobacco is a "sad slipstake"; in "Gib Us Chaw Tobacco," tobacco's cataloged properties include "soov[ing] de heart an' lip" after violent punishment ("If Missy scold or Massa whip, / Or driver break our back"); in "The Tobacco Sign," the man who buys his own freedom "sweet liberty did crave," indicating his profound discontent with bondage.⁴⁰ Brian Roberts has argued that minstrel portrayals of enslaved anguish represent potential moments of solidarity between white working-class audiences and enslaved people, but these portrayals actually work to distinguish white from Black laborers.⁴¹ Just as commodity-driven descriptions in minstrel songs acknowledge that enslaved people are consumed alongside slave commodities but refuse to implicate distant white consumers in the process, minstrel depictions of slavery's depredations concede that many enslaved people need to be forced to labor under threat of violence but suggest that those enslaved people are willing to furnish that violence themselves.

In the song "Old Master's Death," enslaved people assume the role of white authority to strengthen the slave system, thereby effectively absolving white people of participation in the brutal spectacle it describes. The song begins by describing violent resistance—an enslaved man murders his enslaver—but ends on a thoroughly antirevolutionary note, as the other enslaved people hang the murderer: "So we left him a hanging, an example to all. / *Let him hang!*"[42] The need to discipline is thus removed from the expected duties of the plantocracy and its allies and is assumed instead by the enslaved people. They not only carry out the execution, but they also do it in precisely the kind of spectacular way adopted by white authorities to deter future transgression.[43] These displacements represent fantasies of cooperation instead of coercion. In tacit distinction to white workers who strenuously resisted perceived encroachments on their free labor, the enslaved people in the song are enthusiastic participants in their own exploitation, working actively to police and maintain their enslaved condition.[44]

No minstrel figure more obviously represents the willingness to police than the Black driver, an enslaved man put in a position of authority over other enslaved people. Many critics have noted that the pain caused by cruel enslavers appears in minstrel songs alongside the more familiar instances of plantation nostalgia and encomia of kindly enslavers dead and gone.[45] But critics have overlooked a crucial detail in minstrelsy's depictions of suffering within slavery: Cruelty often comes at the hands of a Black driver rather than a white enslaver.[46] In this respect, the minstrel fantasy mirrors a historical reality—many enslavers considered a Black driver an essential fixture in plantation management—that also served an enslaver fantasy of separation.[47] Like the minstrel tropes of intraracial violence that elide white implication in the slave economy, enslavers may have turned to Black drivers in part to displace responsibility for violence back onto a member of the community being harmed.[48] Peter Randolph, who had been enslaved, perceived drivers as a means of turning Black people into conduits for both enacting and disguising white violence: "In this manner, [drivers'] hearts and consciences are hardened, and they become educated to whipping, and lose all human feeling. This is the way the slave-holders take to hide their own wickedness. They ... use this as an argument against the poor colored man, to show how cruelly they would treat each other if they had the power."[49] A comparable desire to mask brutal anti-Black violence may have underpinned the phenomenon of Northern white mobs donning blackface while attacking Black people in race riots.[50] Together, these examples suggest that disavowal could appeal even to those white people engaged in direct enslavement and violence toward Black people. In frequent portrayals of Black drivers and fights between Black characters, blackface minstrelsy enacted a similar fantasy of white innocence for its more geographically distanced audiences.

WHEN COMMODITIES BECOME TRAPS, OR COTTON'S MYSTERIOUS ABSENCE

Minstrel depictions of self-commodification afforded white minstrel audiences the fantasy of separation—the sense that slavery was an efficient, self-driving system independent of their own behavior or input. That fantasy of separation also depended on a sense of freedom in consumption. While enslaved people were represented as helpless or even participatory in their own commodification and consumption, white audiences could imagine that they could choose what and how they consumed (while also remaining free from being commodified themselves). Cotton threatened to undermine that reassuring fantasy in two key ways: by being unavoidable as a commodity and by closely linking white labor to enslaved labor.

Cotton is notably absent from the minstrel tropes that imagine bodies as crops. Considering the repeated conflation of enslaved people with cash crops like tobacco and coffee and with subsistence crops like corn, it is surprising that minstrel shows did not spin similes with the biggest cash crop of them all—cotton. Although references to cotton abound in minstrel lyrics, they do not follow the pattern of product/producer merging we have seen with the other crops, typically appearing instead as more straightforward references to working in the cotton fields. I've found just one example of a minstrel simile between a Black body and cotton—"Her figure set dis heart a trottin' / Her shape is like a bale o' cotton"—though you might expect that slavery's most profitable and iconic commodity would be fertile ground for comparison.[51] Even in cases of more obvious visual logic such as the comparison between tobacco leaves and skin or corn kernels and teeth, cotton would offer a ready counterpart for certain aspects of physical appearance. Its color seems equally suited to supplying a simile of whiteness, for example, as eggshells and white corn are for eyes and teeth, respectively.[52]

Perhaps the most obvious way in which we might expect minstrel songs to metonymically associate Black bodies with cotton is in descriptions of hair. The supposed texture of Black hair was often glossed as "wool" (another typically white, fluffy agricultural product spun into cloth). Although we now associate wool only with sheep or other animal hair—an association that highlights the dehumanizing thrust of this epithet—"wool" was also used in the nineteenth century to mean cotton.[53] The dual meanings of "wool"

Figure 1. "'He Had No Wool on the Top of His Head . . .'" *Frank Leslie's Illustrated Newspaper,* December 28, 1861, p. 96. (Courtesy of the American Antiquarian Society)

would presumably make it even easier to link cotton and the hair of enslaved people, but minstrel song lyrics seem to use the epithet solely in the sense of sheep. The line "Her hair was like merino wool" explicitly mentions a breed of sheep, while the lines "For de wool dat he shave off his head, / Would make a bery good feather bed" in "Old Dan Tucker" describe the wool being shaved (as by shearing) rather than picked like cotton.[54] Minstrel songwriters thus avoided an imaginative connection between cotton and Black bodies that was already semantically available through "wool"—a connection that other sources were more than happy to make. An 1861 political cartoon about Britain's failure to effectively cultivate cotton in Africa makes a direct correlation between the crop and Black bodies through the imagined resemblance between cotton and hair (see fig. 1). The cartoon's caption even quotes "Uncle Ned," an immensely popular minstrel song by Stephen Foster: "He had no wool on the top of his head, / Where the wool ought to grow—ought to grow."[55] The cartoon, of course, leaves no doubt that the wool it means is of the cotton variety.

If we accept that equating Black bodies with slave crops represents a recognition that consuming slavery's products involves consuming enslaved people, it is surely significant that minstrel audiences could envision the consumption of enslaved people via tobacco or coffee in a way that they could not or would not with cotton. The absence of cotton in these minstrel tropes reveals important anxieties among the audience. In sidestepping cotton when it came to conflating enslaved people and crops, blackface minstrelsy established not only the limits of white working-class willingness to imagine one's relationship to the larger slave economy, but also the limit of humor's power to soothe racial and class anxieties.

One reason for working-class apprehensions about cotton was its inescapability. Tobacco, addictively necessary as it may have felt to its users, was an indulgence compared to the necessity of clothing oneself. Northern consumers could hardly forgo cotton produced by enslaved labor: In the decades before the Civil War, the U.S. South provided 80 percent of the cotton spun in Great Britain and 100 percent of domestically spun cotton.[56] Whether purchased cloth was imported from England or delivered from New England textile factories, if it was cotton, it had almost certainly originated with enslaved labor. The ubiquity of slave-grown cotton might have led to unpleasant feelings among working-class people with a wide range of opinions about slavery itself. Many opponents of the system resented the seemingly inescapable necessity of supporting it to clothe themselves, while others may simply have begrudged needing to buy products that further enriched planters and their Northern and British industrial partners.

In fact, close financial ties between Southern planters and the Northern textile magnates who depended on their cotton provoked multiple anxieties within the working class.[57] The discourse about "wage slavery" concentrated on white Northern factory workers and often inspired pro-labor rhetoric that demonstrated racist fears of being like Black people. In 1860 Clara Brown, a white striking shoe worker from Lynn, addressed fellow workers at a meeting and deployed a racial slur to urge them to demand higher pay, admonishing, "Don't let them make niggers of you."[58] In response to striking journeymen tailors' being convicted of conspiracy in New York City, an 1836 handbill laments that the supposedly slave-like status of exploited white workers makes them effectively consumable (though in a more broadly cannibalistic way than through a specific commodity): "The Freemen of the North are now on a level with the slaves of the South! with no other privileges than laboring that drones may fatten on your life-blood!"[59] That same year, striking white female operatives in the Lowell textile mills marched while singing,

> Oh! Isn't it a pity, such a pretty girl as I—
> Should be sent to the factory to pine away and die?
> Oh! I cannot be a slave,
> I will not be a slave,
> For I'm so fond of liberty,
> That I cannot be a slave.⁶⁰

Many strikes occurred, like that of Clara Brown and her fellow shoe workers, in non-textile industries, but the readiness to evoke the language of slavery among workers in textile factories and clothing trades like tailoring suggests a particular attunement to the fundamental connection between Northern cloth and Southern slavery. As Black abolitionist Sarah Parker Remond observed of British factory workers, "The free operatives of Britain are, in reality, brought into almost personal relations with slaves in their daily toil. They manufacture the material which the slaves have produced."⁶¹ Redmond saw this connection as grounds for identification and solidarity, but many white workers saw it as degrading.

The conditions under which cotton came to market made it especially challenging for the white working class to maintain a comfortable sense of separation from slavery. Raw cotton required extensive labor to transform it into usable products, and much of that labor came not from enslaved people but from white workers in the Northeast and England. Unlike tobacco, of which nine-tenths of the manufacture (excluding cigars) occurred in Southern factories powered by enslaved labor by 1860, cotton products represented white labor as well as Black.⁶² That fact would have been evident to the white working-class audiences of minstrelsy's epicenter, New York City. Beyond white labor in New England and English textile factories, the cotton trade depended on workers in New York. Most Southern cotton was shipped to New York before being reshipped to Europe. In addition to the laborers who would have been employed unloading, transporting, weighing, and packing cotton at New York docks, working-class connections to cotton extended to trading and manufacturing clothing: By 1860, New York received the vast majority of textile imports to the United States, and it had been a center of ready-made clothing manufacture for decades.⁶³

White minstrel audiences were more willing to consider enslaved people in terms of tobacco because tobacco represented Black labor and white leisure consumption. With tobacco, white workers could countenance the bodily merging between person and product because that merging did not implicate their own labor. Cotton, conversely, represented Black *and* white labor and the necessary consumption of clothing. To suggest bodily connections between enslaved people and cotton, however obvious, would have also raised the specter of "white slavery," a notion ultimately too uncomfortable for minstrel audiences to tolerate.

BLACKFACE MINSTRELSY AT HOME: DOMESTIC PERFORMANCE AND CLASS AMBIVALENCE

Fully understanding the motivations behind minstrel fantasies of self-contained slavery requires considering where those fantasies played out. Not necessarily on the minstrel stage, where I have found no record of the song "Jim Jawbone" having ever been performed, but in the places where amateur singers brought these printed lyrics to life.[64] The print forms in which minstrel songs were distributed illuminate an additional reason that minstrel audiences were so invested in imagining enslaved people as actively contributing to their own commodification and consumption. Performing these songs at home further emphasized the separation from Black people that white minstrel audiences sought by signaling certain forms of middle-class respectability. The print forms that brought songs like "Jim Jawbone" into American homes are pivotal to the cultural work of minstrelsy, and theater-focused research on antebellum blackface minstrelsy must be extended to include them.

In its preface, *Matt Peel's Banjo,* an 1858 collection of minstrel songs, offers an inconsistent vision of minstrelsy's purportedly working-class identity. Clearly concerned about the "many [who] have decried this style of amusement as being vulgar, or not exactly refined," the preface insists that people "in every walk of life" love the art form. Yet the examples that follow this claim are entirely (albeit internationally) working class: "We hear the farmer's boy whistling them as he turns up the rich soil with the plough, and the factory girl, amid the roar of machinery, lightens her toil by singing them; while the traveler, 'far from home,' hears them chanted by the shop-boy of London, the *ouvrier* of Paris, and the peasant of Italy."[65] As Paul Watt has noted, these prefaces are often more "potted" than accurate, but they nevertheless tell us a great deal about the image minstrelsy was trying to project.[66] These contradictory claims about the appeal of blackface minstrelsy are revelatory in two respects. First, they betray ambivalence about minstrelsy's class identity. Second, they emphasize widespread amateur performance. Despite its prominence in cities like New York, blackface minstrelsy extended beyond professional troupes in formal theatrical settings.

It is fitting that *Matt Peel's Banjo* focuses on minstrelsy outside the theater: As a songster, the collection was designed to facilitate portability. Songsters were small, cheap, mass-printed anthologies of songs that were organized around any number of themes, including political movements, temperance, and blackface minstrelsy. They typically included song lyrics but no musical notation. They were thus made for singing, rather than playing, and they depended on a singer's previous familiarity with the tune. They were small enough to be easily portable, and their diminutive size and even more diminutive print would have encouraged physical proximity. Songsters nestled easily in people's hands, encouraging them to gather close and lean in. They enabled users to perform the songs themselves and were well suited to private settings.

Although scholars have long depended on blackface minstrel songsters as a source of lyrics, they tend to read those lyrics back into a raucous theatrical setting instead of considering what songsters themselves have to say about blackface minstrelsy and American consumer culture. Most obviously, a booming publishing industry sold minstrel songs cheaply and widely to customers who may never have set foot in the Bowery Theater or Mechanics Hall but who sang minstrel songs at home and work. Moreover, in addition to popular standbys like "Miss Lucy Long" and "Old Dan Tucker," the songsters were full of songs that never made it to the minstrel stage, perhaps because they were filler, or perhaps because some of their themes were more relevant to the context of a songster than to the stage in the first place.

Christy's Nigga Songster (ca. 1850), the songster in which "Jim Jawbone" appears, is an unusual example of the form, but its quirks shed considerable light on the obsessive attention to consumption within its lyrics. As a consumer object, it is an intriguing mixture of cheap and classy. It was priced at twenty-five cents, putting it within the normal range of antebellum songster prices (and equivalent to the price of admission to many minstrel shows and thereby accessible to many working-class consumers).[67] There are many indications of the cheapness of its printing, from sloppily reproduced wood engraving illustrations, to typographical irregularities, to unexplained jumps in pagination. The songster often looks as if the printer simply grabbed leftover plates from other songsters and hastily anthologized them. Its very title, with its racist slur in dialect form, exemplifies the kind of language that disturbed more refined commentators about minstrelsy.[68]

And yet, despite the apparent carelessness of its printing, the songster also has features that seem to aspire beyond its position as cheap popular print. Most striking is its cover. While the majority of blackface minstrel songsters appeared in wrappers (paper covers), this one features a sturdy board cover, with an ornate panel-stamped design and even gilt on its spine.[69] This songster is built for display on a shelf: Not only is its most flamboyant and expensive decoration reserved for the spine (the part that would have been visible), but the spine also delicately excises the title's slur, reading simply *Christy's Minstrel*. In a world where books "rival[ed] parlors as symbols of refinement," such a book could send a powerful signal of gentility with its binding alone. Catharine Maria Sedgwick's novel *Home* (1835) demonstrates the importance placed on a book's appearance as well as contents. In it, the admirable Barclay family eschews superfluous decoration, but they allow themselves the "luxury, which long habit and well cultivated taste had rendered essential to happiness,—a book-case filled with well selected and well bound volumes."[70] This songster was not an etiquette manual, of course—its content could hardly be said to reflect "well cultivated taste"—but its relatively good binding suggests a craving for middle-class respectability not normally associated with blackface minstrelsy. In fact, the publisher T. W. Strong chose to print this songster with the same sort of panel-stamped design he tended to use for his many children's books, as if to emphasize the innocuous and even edifying possibilities of the content within.[71]

Considering the materiality of this minstrel songster as well as the songs within it reveals a key ambivalence: On one hand, the songs feature grotesque racism and bawdy humor at odds with self-contained middle-class politeness; on the other hand, it cloaked those songs in a surprisingly respectable form. The songs themselves may have evoked theatrical minstrel shows and the white, working-class men who frequented them, but singing those songs at home evoked the parlor song, a marker of bourgeois respectability in this era.[72] Although songsters did not necessarily mean singing at home—their pocket-sized portability meant they could be carried to work or to a tavern just as easily—they certainly brought minstrel performance out of the theater and into more personal spaces. Moreover, a songster introduced minstrel songs into its possessors' bodies, asking them to forge intimate musical performances out of the lyrics on the page and a tune they already knew. As what Robin Bernstein would call a "scriptive thing," the songster demanded much more active participation than attending a blackface minstrel show would have.[73] Because the participation it scripted was singing, it took on a specific charge as a potentially refining force. The musicologist Nicholas E. Tawa cites an 1854 encyclopedia entry on the ballad as evidence of the social function of music: "Americans, Moore writes, 'are eminently a working people.' For them, songs could serve as a much needed means for relaxation, while at the same time introducing 'refinement of taste' and a degree of 'moral feeling.' All people, he claims, are 'susceptible to the influence of music.'"[74] The content of blackface minstrel songs may have been distinctly unrefined, but the practice of singing them for personal enjoyment may have nevertheless signaled genteel self-improvement.

To suggest that blackface minstrelsy displays middle-class aspirations counters a strong critical consensus about minstrelsy's anti-bourgeois ethos. Even as recent scholars have worked to complicate minstrelsy's racial investments, sometimes going so far as to argue for its antiracist impulses, they have been less willing to reconsider its supposed antipathy to the middle class. In the commonly held view, blackface minstrelsy had uniquely working-class origins that helped to forge white working-class identity in the 1830s and 1840s. The corollary of these working-class origins was minstrelsy's supposedly fervent anti-bourgeois position, characterized by an embrace of "rascality" (in Douglas A. Jones's words) that repudiated staid middle-class values.[75] Invested in minstrelsy as a vehicle of interracial working-class resistance, W. T. Lhamon Jr. repeatedly evokes minstrelsy's "recalcitrance," which he defines as the form's "broad interracial refusal of middle-class channeling that working men and women of all hues mounted."[76] While William J. Mahar denies that minstrelsy satirizes any particular class, he maintains that it unflinchingly targeted "the pretentiousness that accompanied American elitism."[77] Even Brian Roberts, whose *Blackface Nation* is unusually attuned to the intersections of blackface minstrelsy and middle-class mores in antebellum popular culture, cannot quite relinquish the definition of minstrelsy as "the rejection of middle-class values of uplift and polite sociability."[78]

Many scholars see the recurrent minstrel figure of the "Black dandy" as embodying anti-middle-class sentiments. In fact, such figures represent yet another way in which minstrelsy could facilitate genteel performance, even if fleetingly or ambivalently.[79] According to Mahar, the blackface dandy stereotype "struck at the American distaste for pretentiousness and enhanced the pleasure derived from ridiculing those who claimed to be what they truly were not."[80] In equating dandies to confidence men, Mahar is indebted to Karen Halttunen's work on middle-class identity. If we push the connection further, however, we can recognize that the very act of condemning such pretenders could be considered its own performance of middle-class sincerity. As Halttunen argues, the greatest perceived threats to the antebellum middle class were the "confidence men and painted women" who undermined the equation between genteel exteriors and inner refinement.[81] Exposing pretenders thus reinforced middle-class mores rather than critiqued them.

Christy's Nigga Songster, for example, is filled with mocking portrayals of Black dandies as improper consumers, including both illustrations and lyrics in which racist caricatures of women sport outlandish finery:

De female dandies in a stew,
Am gettin bustles made bran new,
And puff 'em out like air balloons,
To take 'em straight up to de moon.[82]

These excitable female consumers aim so far above their proper station, they literally put on airs. Given the way the songster's enhanced binding and the bowdlerized title on its spine betray a grasping at refinement, its attempts to ridicule those without proper "taste" are revealing. The songster includes a parody of the opera aria "The Gipsy Girl's Dream, or I Dreamt I Dwelt in Marble Halls" titled "De Nigga Gal's Dream; or, I Loved Coon Still de Same," in which a Black woman dreams she lives in relative luxury, with every kind of creature comfort and delicacy at her disposal, and yet she discovers that raccoon remains her favorite dish.[83] There is a kind of racist wish fulfillment here—the idea that, no matter how upwardly mobile Black people may become, their inherent differences in taste will prevent them from truly breaking into the upper classes. By racializing class identity, the song bars the path to social advancement to all Black people, while leaving it open to the white working class.⁸⁴ In an era in which increased European immigration had destabilized whiteness itself, such depictions dramatize the means by which some Irish, Jewish, and other performers staked a claim to white identity by differentiating themselves from perceived blackness.⁸⁵

There is widespread scholarly agreement that, by the time *Christy's Nigga Songster* appeared around 1850, blackface minstrel shows had become popular with the middle class as well.⁸⁶ Nowhere is the increased compatibility between minstrelsy and middle-class taste more apparent than in *Uncle Tom's Cabin* and its cultural reverberations. Despite being a paragon of middle-class respectability, Stowe's novel incorporates blackface tropes and performance dynamics, while theatrical minstrel performances quickly incorporated characters and plotlines from Stowe's novel.⁸⁷ The middle class may have grown more comfortable with both blackface minstrelsy in the theater and the inherent theatricality of everyday life in this period, but the singing of blackface minstrel songs at home had already long been accepted as compatible with middle-class decorum.⁸⁸ While Tawa notes that the bound music collections of many well-to-do women included minstrel songs but replaced their suspect lyrics with more appropriate verses, he also acknowledges that other music collectors felt no such compunction and included the original songs.⁸⁹ Other evidence suggests that minstrel songs caused little anxiety for many middle- and even upper-class domestic practitioners. Before he grew up to compose minstrel standards like "My Old Kentucky Home," a nine-year-old Stephen Foster was allowed to mount backyard minstrel performances in the 1830s with his brother and other boys from their white middle-class Pennsylvania neighborhood.⁹⁰ In an 1845 letter, the affluent white mother Julia Ward Howe, who would later make her own decidedly respectable mark on music by penning "The Battle Hymn of the Republic," punctuates airy observations about her new clothes from Paris with descriptions of entertaining her two young children by singing the minstrel song "Jim Along Josie."⁹¹ The title page of *The Ethiopian Glee Book* (1848) proclaims itself to be "A Collection of Popular Negro Melodies, Arranged for Quartett Clubs"; the collection's racial epithets, stereotypical dialect, and unrefined subject matter notwithstanding, its musical notation indicates that it has been arranged for people with enough musical training and resources to harmonize four voices and accompany them on the piano.⁹²

With its shoddy print, lack of musical notation, and economical price point, the *Christy's* songster was not aimed at people with extensive resources. Nevertheless, to understand that blackface minstrelsy in the home was hardly anathema to middle-class gentility is also to grant the possibility that, counterintuitive as it may seem, the singing of blackface minstrel songs outside the theater could be an enactment of white respectability just as much as a ribald embrace of impolite fun. By recognizing how *Christy's Nigga Songster* enables certain kinds of middle-class performance even as it revels in lower-class material, we gain a new understanding of minstrelsy's cultural work. As a form invested in Black captivity, as Jones has argued, blackface minstrelsy is also a vehicle for imagining white mobility.[93] If the primary audience for this particular songster was white working-class people who were attracted to the songs but also to the style of the object; who enjoyed singing at home but also believed that such singing indicated a certain refinement, then we can see why these minstrel forms would have been committed to reinforcing the separation between their audience and an imagined Blackness that represented the opposite of bourgeois life. Songs like "Jim Jawbone" propose just such a fantasy of separation—one in which white Northerners have no connection with enslaved people—not through economic networks, and certainly not through any similarity in laboring conditions. While this songster shares with abolitionists a sense of consumption-as-connection, it defuses that recognition by offering its audience a different vision: a world in which enslaved people consume themselves, and the white working class is free to consume objects that promised a better, more refined life.

PART TWO

METAPHORIC CONSUMPTION IN THE DISCOURSE ON SLAVERY

FOUR

FEEDING THE BODY POLITIC

Slavery, Cannibalism, and Identity in the United States

Consumption-as-connection resulted from novel economic meanings of "consume" in the eighteenth century, but it also tapped existing cultural understandings of consumption. The first three chapters of *Grievous Entanglement* explored how consumption-as-connection represented specific commodities like sugar, cotton, and tobacco as material links between enslaved producers and distant purchasers. The final two chapters shift from actual products to the metaphors of consumption that explained the economics of chattel slavery through established ideas about human difference and exploitation: specifically, the centuries-old discourse on cannibalism and prevalent imagery of ravenous animals poised to devour human beings. Untethered from the stuff of actual commodities, metaphors of cannibalism or hungry animals could accentuate or downplay particular aspects of consumption-as-connection depending on the goals of the commentator. Considering such metaphors clarifies the imaginative landscape that gave consumption-as-connection purchase. These images of brutal devouring evocatively captured the inhuman viciousness of making humans consumable under the economic logic chattel slavery. In tracing these wider-ranging metaphors, the final two chapters of the book also range more widely in chronology and geography than the first three chapters, moving from the sixteenth to the nineteenth century and including texts from Europe and the United States.

By the time consumption-as-connection emerged, cannibalism had already been used for centuries to demarcate Otherness and justify imperial domination, as well as to critique those very practices by emphasizing the human costs of excessive greed. This chapter starts by reading European and American texts that establish why the long-standing discourse on cannibalism proved so pertinent to chattel slavery. The paradigmatic use of cannibalism to deny humanity, for instance, illuminates why the antislavery advocates discussed in chapters 1 and 2 found it so rhetorically effective. This chapter then turns to the antebellum United States, where enduring European ideas about cannibalism evolved to encompass the specific conditions of U.S. slavery.

Understanding the relevance of cannibalism to U.S. slavery requires recognizing crucial distinctions between the United States and Britain. Most significantly, slavery was practiced within the United States as opposed to being largely relegated to the British colonial periphery. The founding of the United States had been dominated by conflict over the place of slavery, and eventual constitutional compromises made slavery essential to the new nation's economy and politics "[i]n the interest of both profit and unity," in Edward E. Baptist's words.[1] From the beginning, U.S. commentators had to confront the fact that slavery was geographically proximate and politically central. The United States also had a significantly larger Black population than Britain. Black Americans, both free and enslaved, led the fight against slavery, and their activism forced white Americans to grapple with the morality of slavery, even as their presence triggered white supremacist anxieties about the appropriate racial makeup of a nation.[2]

These conditions made cannibalism uniquely relevant to slavery in the antebellum United States. Debates over the place of Black Americans and slavery within the nation resonated with the characteristic ambivalence of cannibalism, which oscillated between admitting sameness and enforcing difference. As a result, commentators frequently portrayed the U.S. body politic as cannibalistic while agonizing over the nation's ability to truly incorporate people they considered fundamentally different, whether because of race or their status as enslavers. In addition to these distinctively American applications, U.S. commentators also used cannibalism tropes to denounce the economics of chattel slavery, a usage that would have been germane throughout the Atlantic world. After analyzing these two strands of antebellum U.S. cannibalism metaphors, this chapter transitions to Nathaniel Hawthorne's *The House of the Seven Gables* (1851), which exemplifies the many intersecting currents of the discourse on cannibalism in this era. On one hand, Hawthorne deploys cannibalistic imagery as antislavery advocates did, to condemn destructive appetites. On the other hand, he racializes those appetites in ways reminiscent of earlier imperial arguments for the domination of colonial Others. Once again, the multivalent implications of consumption did not dictate a specific political outlook.

My argument builds on vital contributions by Kyla Wazana Tompkins and Vincent Woodard, who have established that imagining Black bodies as edible was central to the white psyche in nineteenth-century America. Tompkins's *Racial Indigestion* convincingly demonstrates that depictions of eating, food, and the mouth inform conceptions of race and especially white national identity. Tompkins traces the manifestations of "white America's twinned emotions—desire and fear," and Woodard's *The Delectable Negro* extends that point by insisting on the erotics inherent in even the most heinous racial violence.[3] Both scholars briefly gesture to the relationship between eating imagery and the underlying economics of slavery: Woodard acknowledges that he frequently uses the word "consumption" precisely because it evokes the "economies that make possible the consumption of the slave along with other traded commodities"; Tompkins observes that "the representation of African Americans as food themselves . . . circulates as a common trope for the objectification and commodification of slave bodies."[4] My work develops these suggestive remarks by revealing the specific relevance of consumption as a concept in this era and by showing how images of eating directly engaged the economics of chattel slavery. Beyond evoking the commodification of enslaved people, cannibalism metaphors fused centuries-old ideas and new economic meanings of consumption to present enslavement as interpersonal violence fueled by excessive greed.[5] Invocations of slavery as cannibalism did more than signify barbarity; they encapsulated a system that makes humans consumable by other humans.

OTHERNESS AND EXPLOITATION IN CANNIBALISM DISCOURSE

Before examining how cannibalism shaped the discourse on slavery in the antebellum United States, it is useful to establish why cannibalism provided such a powerful conceptual vehicle for enslavement and exploitation in European and American culture. Although cannibalism appears in numerous classical texts—Greek myths abound in man-eating gods and monsters as well as parents devouring their children, and Herodotus describes anthropophagi living near Scythia in the fourth book of his *Histories*—the word "cannibalism" entered modern European languages only after Europeans arrived in the Americas.[6] On November 23, 1492, Columbus's journal describes his Arawak interpreters warning him about a distant land where "Canibals" elicited "great fear . . . because those people ate them."[7] Standard definitions of "cannibal" identify the word as an alternate form of "Carib," the Indigenous people who also lent their name to the Caribbean and who, the *Oxford English Dictionary* intones, "are recorded to have been *anthropophagi*."[8] Scholars have challenged this neat etymology, however, arguing that Columbus may have seized upon the term because of the ways it reinforced his own preconceptions.[9] The term "cannibalism" thus entered European languages through misunderstandings and potentially even willful misrepresentations. It is possible that Columbus's Arawak informants were defaming long-standing enemies to gain strategic advantage, presaging the way Columbus's own defamations of Indigenous people would pave the way to more violent Spanish domination. In fact, accusations of cannibalism directly contributed to Spanish practices of enslavement in the New World. Although Queen Isabella initially condemned Columbus for enslaving Indigenous people, she issued a royal decree in 1503 allowing any of the Americans who were cannibals to be enslaved.[10]

From the beginning, the term "cannibalism" carried significant stakes, serving to justify colonial incursion and to delimit humanity. Less than a century after Columbus first recorded the term in his journal, cannibalism also helped to critique the very Europeans who had made it a mark of inhuman otherness deserving subjugation.[11] In a famous articulation of the "noble savage" trope, Michel de Montaigne's essay "On Cannibals" (1580) contrasts the principled impulses (honor and vengeance) behind the cannibalism of Indigenous Brazilians with the depraved brutality of Europeans:

> I am not so anxious that we should note the horrible savagery of these acts as concerned that, whilst judging their faults so correctly, we should be so blind to our own. I consider it more barbarous to eat a man alive than to eat him dead; to tear by rack and torture a body still full of feeling, to roast it by degrees, and then give it to be trampled and eaten by dogs and swine—a

practice which we have not only read about but seen within recent memory, not between ancient enemies, but between neighbours and fellow-citizens and, what is worse, under the cloak of piety and religion—than to roast and eat a man after he is dead.[12]

Montaigne's position on cannibals is typically understood as relativistic comparison—cannibalism may be bad, but it is hardly the end-limit of human depravity. Beyond its condemnation of European state-sanctioned violence, the essay is attuned to the consumptive implications of the colonial project. After reflecting on the momentousness of "that other world which has been discovered in our time," Montaigne observes the great gap between human curiosity and human understanding, a condition he refers to as "our eyes [being] bigger than our stomachs."[13] In Montaigne's figuration, the acquisitive greed of colonial expansion is best captured by appetite, one that (by the logic of his comparison) may be even worse than cannibalism. With a mere evocation of eyes and bellies, he "defines the limitations of an incorporative epistemology of imperialism," as Kelly L. Watson puts it.[14]

A century and a half later, Jonathan Swift's trenchant satire "A Modest Proposal" (1729) would exemplify the cannibalism implied by colonialism with a parodic glee rendered more devastating by its underlying despair. In this, the most iconic text of cannibalism as a metaphor for human exploitation, Swift demonstrates several of the ways in which cannibalism would be brought so forcefully to bear on questions of slavery in the following century. Perhaps most notably, Swift deploys cannibalism as a metaphor to achieve a precise rhetorical purpose. In this way, his landlords-as-cannibals metaphor represents what Wayne C. Booth has referred to as a "weapon metaphor," wielded in an adversarial situation in the hopes of achieving a context-specific goal. By way of example, Booth describes a trial lawyer who referred to his client, a small utility, as a catfish on the verge of being gutted by a larger utility's fishing knife.[15] What makes this example a weapon metaphor—and an essential aspect of the way metaphors of cannibalism shaped the discourse on slavery—is that it allows the literal and figurative meanings to remain in productive relation to one another: "But after the auditor has reconstructed such acceptable meanings, they are not, with this kind of metaphor, separated from the *stated* meanings and then in some sense repudiated. . . . The original meaning, what might be called the uninterpreted picture, remains as part of the final picture in a way that is not true of stable ironies. The big utility is forever a knife-wielding threat."[16] The contrast between a weapon metaphor and what Booth refers to as stable irony is particularly salient for "A Modest Proposal." Although Swift uses irony that is readily and consistently discernible, his evocation of cannibalism also suggests that the proposal is not so far from reality as we would like to believe. Swift condemns the exploitation of Ireland with an image of landlords blithely dining on babies that does not quite dissolve with the recognition of the satire.

Unlike the early colonial texts in which purported cannibalism becomes an excuse for enslavement, "A Modest Proposal" yokes the horrors of ingesting human flesh to those of radically commodifying it. The most pervasive echo of slavery in the essay is the narrator's meticulous accounting of the profits yielded by human bodies as he carefully computes the cost of maintaining a child and compares it to prospective market prices. This cost analysis initially seems poised to recommend enslaving Irish children to save on their upkeep, but the narrator concludes that their sale will not earn enough money.[17] This fact does not dissuade the narrator from commodification but rather redirects his attention to the commodification of more profitable babies. The pervasive livestock imagery throughout the essay emphasizes dehumanizing exploitation and evokes chattel slavery by imagining humans as valuable, tradable breeding stock ("Men would become as *fond* of their Wives, during the Time of their Pregnancy, as they are now of their *Mares* in Foal, their *Cows* in Calf, or *Sows* when they are ready to farrow").[18] Cannibalism and profit collide as Swift's narrator declares, "I believe, no Gentleman would repine to give Ten Shillings for the *Carcase of a good fat Child*; which, as I have said, will make four Dishes of excellent nutritive Meat, when he hath only some particular Friend, or his own Family, to dine with him."[19] Unlike the Brazilians who, according to Montaigne's approving account, eat human flesh not for "nourishment," but for symbolic vengeance that actually venerates the enemy, Swift's narrator degrades the human form into nutrition devoid of any nonmaterial humanity—a "carcase," some "meat." Swift's narrator echoes the model of cannibalism Montaigne condemns, with a constant focus on economic gain that recalls the Europeans always hungry for more land.

In using the weapon metaphor of cannibalizing Irish babies, Swift presents a figurative extreme that indelibly marks its literal message, leaving readers with the sense that landlords, in reaping obscene pleasure and profit from the dehumanized bodies of their tenants, really do feed on them. Moreover, by the end of the essay, Swift reverses the presumed direction of the satire. While it may seem that "A Modest Proposal" functions by evoking a reprehensible extreme to make readers understand just how immoral the treatment of the Irish was, Swift ends the essay by suggesting that the treatment of the Irish, not the proposed cannibalism, represents the extreme term. Irony gives way to a more direct condemnation of the situation when Swift's narrator defies his would-be detractors: "I desire those Politicians, who dislike my Overture, . . . that they will first ask the Parents of these Mortals, Whether they would not, at this Day, think it a great Happiness to have been sold for Food at a Year old, in the Manner I prescribe; and thereby have avoided such a perpetual Scene of Misfortunes, as they have since gone through; by the *Oppression of Landlords*."[20] Being sold for food—Swift insists on the market pressures underlying this cannibalism—may be appalling, but it is less appalling than the actual enormities being perpetrated. Swift arrives at an implicit justification, however fleeting, for the infanticide that has been the source of revulsion and satire throughout the essay, because that infanticidal cannibalism is not as heinous as the prolonged systemic cannibalism that is its devastating alternative.

If Swift represents the more metaphoric vein of cannibalism discourse, it is important to note that the literal vein, in which people were suspected of actually eating other people, continued to have sweeping social and political consequences. Following in the tradition of Spanish colonialists using alleged cannibalism to justify enslaving Indigenous people, accounts of African cannibalism (along with human sacrifice and sexual voracity) bolstered proslavery claims about innate African depravity in the era of the transatlantic slave trade, despite those who questioned the credibility of such accounts.[21] In his *Philosophy of History*, Hegel uses accusations of cannibalism to assert the inferiority of Africans: "[T]he devouring of human flesh is altogether consonant with the general principles of the African race; to the sensual Negro, human flesh is but an object of sense—mere flesh."[22] Later, U.S. slavery proponents repeatedly evoked the supposedly rampant cannibalism in Africa to argue that enslaved people were better off in the United States. James C. Wilson, a proslavery clergyman writing in 1859, lists the purported benefits of being enslaved in the U.S. South (being well fed, well clad, and educated in Christianity) before contrasting them to the imagined difference from an enslaved person's African grandfather, "who knew nothing of God or Savior; who one day, at the caprice of his native prince, made war upon a neighboring chieftain, and made captives who were eaten or held in slavery, as the chance befell them; the next day, himself a captive, awaiting with trembling anxiety, the decision of his conquerer, whether or not he should be barbecued for breakfast."[23]

In the eighteenth and nineteenth centuries, travel narratives from the Pacific and Africa supplied new ideas about cannibalism that became fodder for discussions about slavery. Because many of the victims in cannibal narratives are described as enslaved captives, cannibalism suggests barbaric tyranny—a horrific state of unbridled authority that covers not only life and death but also the fate of the corpse after death, even to the point of ingesting it. An 1839 article in *The Liberator* cites the disturbing fact that, according to Joel Samuel Polack's travel narrative from New Zealand, people enslaved there could be killed and eaten at the "slightest caprice" of their enslaver.[24] The article continues by asserting that comparable violence underlies U.S. slavery: "Probably, however, the New Zealand 'patriarchs' have no market for their surplus human stock, like Maryland and Virginia, and so contrive to 'keep open a drain for the excess beyond the occasions of profitable employment,' by *eating the overplus!* What would be poor economy in Virginia, may be very good in New Zealand."[25] Satirically citing the American Colonization Society's claim that sending free Black people abroad would "keep open a drain for the excess of increase beyond the occasions of profitable employment," the author lambastes the internal slave trade by putting it on par with cannibalism—just another way to ensure the profitability of excess "stock."[26]

Cannibalism had helped to construct difference from the earliest colonial encounters, but the rise of scientific racism in the mid-nineteenth century gave such uses new force by depicting cannibalism as an innate biological trait.[27] An 1860 editorial in the *New York Herald* declares, "The men of that [negro] race are confessedly inferior to the white race. . . . The negro is the same now as he was four thousand years ago. He has no literature, no arts, no sciences; he is essentially a savage and a cannibal."[28] Insisting on the "essential" nature of the cannibalism within the "negro race in Africa," the author implies that people of African descent can never be entirely free from such heritable impulses. Predictably, the editorial continues by using these supposed facts to justify enslaving people of African descent. In his proslavery book *Slavery, As It Relates to the Negro, or African Race* (1843), Josiah Priest combines loosely interpreted scripture, ancient texts, and contemporary travel accounts to depict all people of African descent as irredeemably primitive and vicious—traits he links to their supposed physical makeup.

After alleging that Black people have more robust digestive tracts than white people, for instance, he proclaims, "The horrid and heart-appalling practice of *cannibalism* has, in *all* ages, attached more to the African race than to any other people of the Earth."[29] This racist fantasy proved persistent. Frantz Fanon identified the presumed cannibalistic heritage of Black people as a recurring focus of white racism far into the twentieth century.[30]

METAPHOR, AMBIVALENCE, AND THE BODY POLITIC

When Ralph Waldo Emerson likened slavery to boiling and eating babies, he joined numerous commentators in adapting the long-standing discourse on cannibalism to fit specific conditions in the antebellum United States. For Emerson, cannibalism still evoked otherness and profound exploitation, but it also expressed his acute anxiety about the legal and moral place of slavery in the nation. In a scathing journal entry from 1851, Emerson imagines that the 1793 precursor to the recently enacted 1850 Fugitive Slave Law was in fact a legal allowance for infanticidal cannibalism:

> It was a law affirming the existence of two states of civilization or an intimate union between two countries, one civilized & Christian & the other barbarous, where cannibalism was still permitted. It was a little gross, the taste for boiling babies, but as long as this kind of cookery was confined within their own limits, we could agree for other purposes, & wear one flag. The law affirmed a right to hunt their human prey within our territory; and this law availed just thus much to affirm their own platform,—to fix the fact, that, though confessedly savage, they were yet at liberty to consort with men[.][31]

To some extent, Emerson condemns the law in terms reminiscent of Swift, turning to cooked infants to express the extreme depravity of his opponents. They are, in Emerson's portrayal, every bit the barbarian that their cannibalism would imply—uncivilized, "barbarous," "confessedly savage," and with an apparently insatiable "taste for boiling babies." As in many depictions of savages, Emerson's opponents are more animal than human; he imagines enslavers as wolflike monsters masquerading as men: "[T]hough they had tails, & their incisors were a little long, yet it is settled that they shall by courtesy be called men; we will all make believe they are Christians; & we promise not to look at their tails or incisors when they come into company."[32]

For Emerson, the most horrifying consequence of this imagined cannibalism is the way it taints his own regional identity. In the metaphoric logic of this journal entry, Emerson could grudgingly accept Southern cannibalism only by carefully differentiating the two regions (described as "two countries," with "two states of civilization"). The new power given to the Fugitive Slave Law of 1793 by the Compromise of 1850, however, "bring[s] down the free & Christian state of Massachusetts to the cannibal level."[33] The figurative cannibalism of enslavers offers a variation on consumption-as-connection. Once again, consumption forges personal links to slavery despite apparent geographic distance. Like the consumer goods that revealed complicity, cannibalism here expresses the newfound sense that New Englanders now inhabited slaveholding territory. We can even detect some of the characteristic aversion of consumption-as-connection in Emerson's evocation of boiling babies—a practice so horrifying that non-slaveholding regions should be spurred into restoring the moral distance they previously enjoyed. Emerson's model uses cannibalism to imply serious consequences for national identity. Just as one taste of human flesh forever defines a person as a cannibal, the true incorporation of the South's cannibalistic ways into the nation transforms the nature of the entire country.[34]

By the mid-nineteenth century, the carefully maintained distinctions between slaveholding and free states had been eroded by legislation like the Fugitive Slave Law of 1850 and the Kansas-Nebraska Act of 1854. The United States represented an uneasy coalition between two regions that sought union while simultaneously fearing that real unity would require the destruction of their regional identity—the terrifying prospect of being absorbed into a hostile other. Cannibalism was a particularly apt metaphoric vehicle for these conditions because, according to Maggie Kilgour, it joins all acts of eating in breaking down categories of self and other. Eating, she asserts, "assumes an absolute distinction between inside and outside, eater and eaten, which, however, breaks down, as the law 'you are what you eat' obscures identity and makes it impossible to say for certain who's who."[35] Even more than other forms of eating, cannibalism embodies the tension between the recognition of sameness (hence what makes eating other people different from eating animals) and the enforcement of difference (putting other people into the category of food rather than person). Inherently granting likeness while also holding identification at bay, cannibalism resonated with people fretting over the future of their nation and wondering what it would mean to truly incorporate another group—be it Black people or enslavers or both—into the country as a whole. Unlike the Caribbean, in which enslavement in the colonies existed far from the metropole, the United States grappled with a slave system that existed within its national borders, resulting in a particularly fraught body politic.

A primary reason cannibalism lends itself so well to metaphors is the fact that its uneasy mixture of sameness and difference mirrors the way metaphors work. Paul Ricœur's theory of the "semantic impertinence" provides a means of understanding the *same/not same* tension that governs cannibalism. According to Ricœur, the figurative turn that renders the predicate fundamentally different from the subject nonetheless sparks awareness of a larger similarity: "In order that a metaphor obtains, one must continue to identify the previous incompatibility *through* the new compatibility. . . . 'Remoteness' is preserved within 'proximity.' To see *the like* is to see the same in spite of, and through, the different. This tension between sameness and difference characterizes the logical structure of likeness."[36] Cannibalism is similarly animated by a tension between shared humanity and radical reduction to nonhuman materiality in which neither alternative fully obscures the other.

Perhaps more than any of ways in which cannibalism is already evocative—of savagery, appetite, greed, or lust—it is its capacity to preserve remoteness within proximity that so powerfully suited cannibalism for making sense of U.S. slavery. A necessary precondition of chattel slavery was the nation's ability to absorb millions of Black people while staunchly affirming their fundamental difference. As a result, commentators repeatedly turned to cannibal metaphors when imagining a white body politic faced with the incorporation of Black people. These images don't suggest "eating the other" in bell hooks's sense, in which white people desire contact with racial Others to enrich and positively transform themselves. Instead, they encode a franker anti-Black racism that portrays such incorporation as pollution. According to the anthropologist Mary Douglas, "[S]ome pollutions are used as analogies for expressing a general view of the social order. . . . So also can the processes of ingestion portray political absorption. Sometimes bodily orifices seem to represent points of entry or exit to social units, or bodily perfection can symbolize an ideal theocracy."[37] In the images that follow, the sickly, reticent, or violated white people faced with ingesting Black people embody the racist disgust that always threatened even antislavery expressions of consumption-as-connection. As we have seen, consumption-as-connection formulations frequently leveraged white aversion to imagined contact with Black bodies to encourage breaking ties with the slave system. Many depictions of a white cannibalistic body politic used a similar mechanism to fantasize about breaking ties with Black Americans.

Although it dates from just after the Civil War, the cartoon "Too Black a Dose" illustrates the view that absorbing immigrants into the nation resembles consuming them and that people of African descent were too foreign to stomach (see fig. 2). Caricatures of Radical Republicans Thaddeus Stevens and Charles Sumner urge Uncle Sam to swallow the Black child they assure him (in the original caption) will "reconstruct [his] health." Though Stevens compares the child to food ("a good-sized oyster"), the prevailing metaphor is that of medicine. The child (and by extension, all Black Americans) becomes a "dose," thoroughly unpleasant but potentially helpful in restoring the health of the nation. Stevens and Sumner believe that the incorporation of Black people as full citizens will heal the nation, but sickly Uncle Sam protests in the caption that "I have swallowed an Irishman and a Dutchman, and don't feel much the worse, but that nigger would be the death of me."[38] The child himself balks more visibly, struggling to escape Sumner's grasp in horror at the prospect of being ingested. This 1867 cartoon visually captures what Matthew Frye Jacobson has called the "notion of variegated whiteness" that characterized U.S. racial classification between 1840 and 1924. In this period, American nativists sought to exclude various European immigrants from full political belonging. While various white races were placed in a presumed hierarchy with Anglo-Saxons at the top, white supremacists nevertheless downplayed such differences when questions of slavery or people of African descent arose.[39] *Davy Crockett's Almanack* (1837) portrays a fictionalized hero with a stronger stomach than the Uncle Sam in the cartoon: "I can walk like an ox: run like a fox, swim like an eel, yell like an Indian, fight like a devil, and spout like an earthquake, make love like a mad bull, and swallow a nigger whole without choking if you butter his head and pin his ears back."[40] The mythic frontiersman's statement makes the cannibalizing of a Black man a sign of masculine prowess. That this act culminates a hyperbolic catalog of superhuman violence, virility, and racial appropriation suggests that

Figure 2. "Too Black a Dose." *Frank Leslie's Illustrated Newspaper,* November 23, 1867, p. 160. (Courtesy of the American Antiquarian Society)

such feats of incorporation would be near impossible for less exceptional white Americans.[41]

Decades earlier, Thomas Jefferson articulated a similar sense of incompatibility between Black bodies and a nation he imagined to be white. In query 14 of *Notes on the State of Virginia* (1785), he discusses a proposal to gradually emancipate enslaved people and colonize them elsewhere, famously declaring that the white and Black races can never coexist peacefully: "It will probably be asked, Why not retain and incorporate the blacks into the state . . . ? Deep rooted prejudices entertained by the whites; ten thousand recollections, by the blacks, of the injuries they have sustained; new provocations; the real distinctions which nature has made; and many other circumstances, will divide us into parties, and produce convulsions which will probably never end but in the extermination of the one or the other race."[42] Jefferson's emphasis on the distinctions between the groups anticipates Emerson's journal entry about boiling babies. Imagining Southern enslavers to be monstrous cannibals, Emerson insists that regions defined by such wildly different moral codes can never be truly united, and any attempt to do so would necessarily destroy the character of one of the regions.[43] Although Emerson's journal entry focuses on a behavior (boiling babies/enslaving), he racializes that behavior by suggesting that Southerners are an entirely different species ("they had tails, & their incisors were a little long"). Jefferson emphasizes insurmountable racial difference ("the real distinctions which nature has made") to reach a similar conclusion about doomed union: trying to "incorporate" Black people within the nation will result in the annihilation of one group.[44]

Whatever their opinions about slavery, many white observers seemed, like Emerson and Jefferson, to derive comfort from the idea of insurmountable differences between North and South, Black and white, slaveholding and free. As long as the differences were recognized and policed, violent confrontation could be avoided and regional, racial, and political identities comfortably maintained. In his lecture "American Slavery" (January 25, 1855), Emerson once again carefully distinguishes between antislavery morality and a host of behaviors coded as primitive and barbarous: "Slavery is an evil, as cholera or typhus is, that will be purged out by the health of the system. Being unnatural and violent, I know that it will yield at last, and go with cannibalism, tattooing, inquisition, duelling, and burking; and as we cannot refuse to ride in the same planet with the New Zealander, so we must be content to go with the southern planter, and say, you are you, and I am I, and God send you an early conversion."[45] In this formulation, slavery resembles a disease, temporarily a part of the national body, but unmistakably foreign and dangerous. As in his earlier journal entry, Emerson uses cannibalism as a marker of enslaver depravity, though here that comparison serves the more hopeful sense that the abolition of slavery does not require vanquishing seemingly insurmountable evil but simply taking the next step in inevitable human progress.[46] In this public speech as opposed to the private journal, Emerson evinces a renewed sense that the two sides can grudgingly coexist within the same country (as Americans and New Zealanders can coexist on the same planet), providing that enslavers do not undermine his careful distinction between North and South ("you are you, and I am I").

But slavery advocates were constantly trying to undermine precisely that distinction by expanding slavery into new territories. The Fugitive Slave Law of 1850 and the Kansas-Nebraska Act of 1854 represented frank departures from the careful distinction between slaveholding and free states that had previously represented a kind of institutionalized ambivalence toward slavery. Laws that required Northerners to return fugitives or allowed the possibility of slavery above the parallel 36° 30′ eroded the regional differentiation that opponents of slavery had once found so reassuring. Cannibalism was a key feature in anxious musings over the altered character of the nation: It expressed the sense that certain kinds of incorporation could irrevocably transform identity, just as the absorption of certain people or practices seemingly threatened to profoundly alter the body politic. Like the antebellum United States, where two regions wanted union but also worried that union jeopardized their own identities, cannibalism combined similarity and difference. Moreover, cannibalism implied real danger, the sense that human lives were at stake as well as regional identity. Hence Emerson's list of transgressions comparable to slavery—"cannibalism, tattooing, inquisition, dueling, and burking"—all center around disfiguring or dismembering the body and, in the case of the first and last, treating men as meat and potential sources of profit ("burking" refers to murdering people using the method of William Burke, who smothered victims and then sold their bodies to medical science).[47]

Antislavery advocates asserted that allowing popular votes to expand slavery was akin to allowing one territory or state to legalize cannibalism and thereby destroy the entire nation. An 1855 article in the *North American Review* likens slavery to "polygamy, or castes, or sutteeism, or cannibalism"—all practices associated with people who would be racial or religious others to white Protestant Americans—before declaring that legalizing such depraved behavior could "blight, or cripple, or dishonor our glorious republic."[48] In an 1860 speech, Senator Benjamin F. Wade, a Republican from Ohio, takes the same logic through a test case. He imagines what would happen if the United States were to annex the Fiji Islands, where some people (according to Wade) were enslaved and occasionally cannibalized. In his hypothetical scenario, the Fijian senator would protest that "it is the law of my country. We have a right to roast and eat this property, and if you don't protect us in it, we will pull down the pillars of this Republic and involve all in one common ruin."[49] On the eve of the Civil War, Wade uses cannibalism to convey national danger ("we will pull down the pillars of this Republic") as well as

Figure 3. *A Dish of "Black Turtle,"* Nathaniel Currier and John L. Magee, 1852. Lithograph on wove paper, 28.1 x 41.8 cm. (Library of Congress, American Cartoon Print Filing Series, LC-DIG-ds-17452)

place U.S. slavery on a continuum with a system that would eat its chattel. In both Wade's speech and the *North American Review* article, further incorporating slavery into the nation would let a savage practice spill over its carefully bounded existence and taint the entire country with barbarism.

While the examples above explicitly turn to cannibalism to condemn the brutality of slavery, contemporary political cartoons lay bare the more implicit echoes of the cannibalism trope as it relates to incorporation and the body politic. These cartoons begin with implied incorporation, usually through a figure of speech, and then imagine it as literal consumption. The 1852 print *A Dish of "Black Turtle"* starts by referring to a publicized letter in which General Winfield Scott expressed his desire for a "hasty plate of soup," but ends by imagining that soup as containing the body of a Black man (see fig. 3).[50] Cannibalism once again evokes ambivalence—Scott, the Whig presidential candidate, was excoriated by antislavery activists for his support of the Compromise of 1850 (and with it, the Fugitive Slave Law), and here he is torn between accepting and rejecting the enslaved man on his spoon: "Here's a predicament! First I shall have to swallow this nigger to please the north & then take a compromise emetic and deliver him up to please the south. Faugh! what a dose of Ginger, but I am anxious to serve the country at $25,000 pr Annum so down he goes." Scott's resolution to swallow the man to please the North suggests rejecting the Fugitive Slave Law by refusing to return fugitives who have escaped to free soil; however, that rejection is not coded as welcoming formerly enslaved people to the North, but rather gobbling them up. The conception of slavery as cannibalism animates the enslaver in the upper right corner, who is familiar with the soup's taste: "I should think from the flavor of the Generals [sic] last plate of Soup that my darkey had tumbled into it." By the logic of this cartoon, fully incorporating either formerly enslaved people or slavery into the North is akin to a cannibalistic transgression.

An 1856 political print imagines the bloody conflicts in the wake of the Kansas-Nebraska Act as a violent feat of forced cannibalism (see fig. 4). The cartoon starts from "forcing something down someone's throat" as an idiom for compulsory acceptance, but its visual vocabulary heightens the sense of savage violence already established by the cannibalistic centerpiece. In the background, a house burns and a man has been lynched; meanwhile the enormous Free Soiler in the foreground has been bound with rope that evokes both

Figure 4. *Forcing Slavery Down the Throat of a Freesoiler,* John L. Magee, 1856. Lithograph on wove paper, 24.8 x 37 cm. (Library of Congress, American Cartoon Prints Collection, LC-USZ62-92043)

the hanged man (violent death) and the bondsman (violent enslavement). Notably, the prominent Democrats who torture the white man and his Black victim, including James Buchanan, Stephen Douglas, and Franklin Pierce, are themselves neither Southern nor enslavers. In the Emersonian logic of the cartoon, their willingness to compromise with proslavery interests has rendered them willing participants in cannibal acts. More importantly, their compromise forcibly requires cannibalism from opponents as well.

This cartoon graphically depicts Jefferson's anxiety over incorporating Black Americans into the nation. Although Free Soilers opposed slavery, many of them did so to exclude Black people from their state or territory and prevent competition with white labor. In the words of Democratic congressman David Wilmot, whose Wilmot Proviso proposed banning slavery in any new territories and sparked the formation of the Free Soil Party after it failed to pass, "I plead the cause of the rights of white freemen. I would preserve for free white labor a fair country, a rich inheritance, where the sons of toil, of my own race and own color, can live without the disgrace which association with negro slavery brings upon free labor."[51] The cartoon thus pursues two (not mutually exclusive) directions in establishing the horror of the Kansas-Nebraska conflict: one, that the figurative cannibalism of slavery acts like a contagion, infecting even those citizens with opposing beliefs; and two, that the figurative cannibalism of popular sovereignty threatens to force enslaved people into a territory where white supremacists do not want them, just as Black people have been only fitfully incorporated into the national body as a whole.

FIGURATIVE CANNIBALISM AND THE ECONOMICS OF SLAVERY

Beyond expressing ambivalence toward both slavery and people of African descent, cannibalism metaphors allowed antebellum U.S. commentators to capture slavery's economic exploitation. Eating provided a vivid figure for greed and personal gain. In an 1854 speech on the Fugitive Slave Law, for instance, Emerson uses what Dwight A. McBride calls "clearly economic language"[52] to lament that "whilst we reckoned ourselves a highly cultivated nation, our bellies had run away with our brains."[53] Henry David Thoreau's essay "Slavery in Massachusetts" (1854) echoes Emerson's imagery with a more explicitly cannibalistic twist. Positing that "we do not even yet realize what slavery is," Thoreau imagines proposing that Congress "make mankind into sausages."[54] He fiercely rejects their hypothetical resistance: "But if any of them will tell me that to make a man into a sausage would be much worse,—would be any worse, than to make him into a slave,—than it was to enact the Fugitive Slave Law, I will accuse him of foolishness, of intellectual incapacity, of making a distinction without a difference. The one is just as sensible a proposition as the other."[55] Although the economic connotations of cannibalistic sausage-making remain implicit, Thoreau likens slavery to human destruction in service of personal appetite. In a conceit reminiscent of Swift, Thoreau takes a laughable extreme—converting human beings to sausage—and then insists that it is no more extreme than what he critiques. The familiar logic of consumption-as-connection would have given force to Thoreau's sausage-making analogy. Antislavery audiences would have been attuned to insinuations that enslaved bodies lingered in everyday commodities and aware of arguments that refusing to break such connections implicated people in horrifying interpersonal violence.

Many commentators explicitly connected the economics of chattel slavery and cannibalism. In the process, they exposed the conceptual foundation of consumption-as-connection. The consumption of everyday commodities like sugar and cotton both mirrored and supported the market for the enslaved people that had produced them. The fact that the commodification of enslaved people rendered them economically consumable also enabled the perception that they were consumed along with those commodities. When the mediating commodity was removed and it became a question of personally profiting from the sale of enslaved people, however, it became even easier to imagine enslavers as directly feeding on the people they enslaved. Even agronomist and enslaver Edmund Ruffin (the man reputed to have fired the first shot of the Civil War) conceded the cannibalistic undertones of the internal slave trade: "The slave first almost starves his master, and at last, is eaten by him—at least he is exchanged for his value in food."[56] An 1819 article in a Philadelphia newspaper recounts a visit to the slave market in cannibalistic terms: "I have seen those soul-trafficers [sic] engaged in their unhallowed work. I have beheld them in their shambles, bartering the blood of their brother men. A cannibal ferocity scowled on their shameless visages. The fire of Hell glanced from their eyes. . . . It even seemed to burn back on itself with insatient greediness!"[57] This description goes well beyond using cannibalism as a placeholder for depravity: It compares slave trading and cannibalism in terms that stress their fundamental resemblance. The slave market has become a "shambles" where meat is butchered and sold. "Insatient greediness" makes the butchery even more heinous.

Olaudah Equiano's fear that European slave traders planned to eat him resurfaces in the disturbing hallucinations of an enslaved man encountered in Baltimore by Alexis de Tocqueville. His nightmarish vision disturbingly conveys the consumptive logic of the slave trade—the cannibal metaphor experienced as literal. As Tocqueville reports, "Today, 4th November, we saw in an Alms-house a Negro whose madness is extraordinary: there is at Baltimore a slave-trader who, it seems, is much feared by the black population. The Negro of whom I speak imagines that this man sticks close to him day and night and snatches away bits of his flesh."[58] The incident clearly struck Tocqueville's traveling companion Gustave de Beaumont as well. In his novel *Marie, or Slavery in the United States* (1835), Beaumont offers an expanded version. The narrator attributes the condition of the "furiously demented" enslaved man to "a professional slave dealer named Wolfolk"—a name changed only slightly from the actual slave trader Austin Woolfolk—who "made a big business of this and was, perhaps, the foremost dealer in human flesh in the United States."[59] Beaumont describes the results of Wolfolk's treatment of the man while transporting him for sale: "[O]n the way [he] was subjected to such brutalities that his reason had snapped. Since then, one fixed idea had possessed him, never giving him an instant's rest: he believed his mortal enemy was constantly at his side, awaiting the moment when he could cut out from his body strips of flesh for which he hungered."[60] Beaumont expands Tocqueville's brief note to assert that the brutalities of the slave trade directly caused the man's breakdown. Moreover, the hallucination has been elaborated into an explicit fantasy of cannibalistic torture, as the trader waits not only to carve living flesh, but to use it to sate his hunger.

Frederick Douglass extended conventional portrayals of slavery as a bloodthirsty monster to directly indict its underlying economics.[61] In his first autobiography, *Narrative of the Life of Frederick Douglass* (1845), Douglass focuses on bodily destruction in his description of slavery as "feasting itself greedily upon our own flesh," recalling William Lloyd Garrison's portrayal of slavery as "the Vampire which is feeding upon our life-blood."[62] In his more extensive second autobiography, *My Bondage and My Freedom* (1855), Douglass revises the description to clarify the relationship between economic exploitation and bodily destruction: Now slavery is "greedily devouring our hard earnings and feeding himself upon our flesh."[63] Variations of the phrase "the jaws of slavery" appear repeatedly in Douglass's writings: in speeches, in personal letters, and in each of his three autobiographies. Frequently it captures the horror of returning a fugitive to slavery, as in an 1846 letter to Garrison in which he laments that fugitives were "liable to be hunted at any moment, like a felon, and to be hurled into the terrible jaws of slavery."[64] The phrase echoes centuries-old constructions like "the jaws of death" or "the jaws of time," but the preceding sentence in this case reveals that Douglass means something more than just all-encompassing destruction. For Douglass, slavery denotes being "thought of and spoken of as property; in the language of the LAW, *'held, taken, reputed, and adjudged to be a chattel in the hands of my owners and possessors.'*"[65] Being hurled back into "the jaws of slavery" thus represents a very specific kind of destruction: to be once again reduced to chattel and thereby declared a consumable good.

For antislavery advocates, cannibalism encapsulated the suffering occasioned by the selling of human beings to feed another human's greed. When Douglass characterizes slavery as devouring enslaved bodies *and* wages or Equiano recalls his childhood fears about the slave traders who might eat him, they emphasize the resonance between slavery's economics and barbaric appetites. In the closing arguments of the 1856 trial of Margaret Garner, the woman who killed her child rather than return her to slavery (and who inspired Toni Morrison's *Beloved*), the Cincinnati attorney John Jolliffe proclaimed, "Slavery, Sir, is cannibalism, not the cannibalism which eats men, but that which puts the image of God upon the auction block."[66] The mere act of commodifying a human being—the moment at which a person's body becomes economically consumable by other human beings—becomes morally indistinguishable from cannibalistic violence.

There is no better indication that slavery as cannibalism had become a familiar trope than the fact that at least one proslavery advocate referred to the comparison as a commonplace before proceeding to rebut it. In an 1860 speech in New York in support of the Constitutional Unionist Party, the white Southerner Washington Barrow attempts a weapon metaphor in reverse—defusing the link between cannibalism and slavery by creating as much distance between them as possible. His speech lampoons common Northern depictions of enslavers, and the *New York Herald* account dutifully notes the audience's rollicking response: "I know that Sumner and Helper have said that we are barbarians, and have taught the people of New York and other States to believe that a slaveholder is a cannibal. Do I look like a barbarian? (Laughter.) Do I look like a cannibal—a man who could take the head and arms of a negro for breakfast, and the balance of his body for dinner? (Renewed laughter.) No, fellow citizens, I am no barbarian."[67] Barrow, a former congressman and diplomat, delights the crowd merely by calling attention to the presumably enormous gap between himself and a cannibal. The enthusiastic laughter accentuates what struck the audience as terribly obvious: The well-heeled white gentleman before them bore no resemblance whatsoever to their mental image of a cannibal, scantily clad and, to be sure, dark-skinned.

The proslavery advocate George Fitzhugh took a different approach. Rather than play up the purported absurdity of white cannibalism, he frankly acknowledged the conceptual resemblance between cannibalism and human exploitation but claimed that the true cannibals were the Northern "vampire capitalist class."[68] Anticipating Marx's contention that "[c]apital is dead labour which, vampire-like, lives only by sucking living labour, and lives the more, the more labour it sucks," Fitzhugh's proslavery treatise *Cannibals All! or Slaves Without Masters* (1857) argues that Northern capitalists take no interest in their employees beyond their ability to work.[69] Unlike enslaved people who are supposedly sustained by beneficent enslavers even when they can no longer work, Northern laborers depend on being able to earn wages to survive. "You are a Cannibal!" Fitzhugh declares to Northern capitalists, "and if a successful one, pride yourself on the number of your victims quite as much as any Fiji chieftain, who breakfasts, dines, and sups on human flesh."[70] Cannibalism as a figure for economic exploitation was conventional—so much so that an 1848 newspaper could jokingly style someone who "lives on other people" as "A Modern Cannibal"—but Fitzhugh is a notable outlier in trying to put that exploitative implication to proslavery purposes.[71] For the vast majority of those who used figurative cannibalism to make sense of the antebellum United States, the ways in which cannibalism seemed to capture both economic forces and obscene violence, all while foregrounding tensions between identification and difference, made it compellingly, almost unavoidably, resonant with chattel slavery.

THE STAIN OF THE CANNIBAL: HAWTHORNE'S *HOUSE OF THE SEVEN GABLES*

Commentators used cannibalism to different ends in the discourse on slavery: Its supposed literal practice became the mark of racialized savagery and a justification for enslavement, while its figurative dimensions made it a powerful tool for condemning commodification and exploitation. In the specific context of the United States, cannibalism tropes also expressed racist anxieties that incorporating Black people into the body politic risked sullying white identity. Nathaniel Hawthorne's *The House of the Seven Gables* provides a remarkable cross-section of this multivocal discourse. Hawthorne critiques the destructive greed of Pyncheon patriarchs by using cannibalism to suggest that they have been cursed not by witchcraft, but by their own appetites and willingness to profit from the pain of other people. At the same time, he portrays these cannibalistic qualities as racially marked, coding their barbaric behavior in terms of animalistic Blackness. Given Hawthorne's personal politics, it is not surprising that he did not leverage figurative cannibalism into a denunciation of U.S. slavery.[72] The novel nevertheless embodies the rhetorical flexibility of cannibalism, where cannibalistic metaphors express both the inhuman greed that leads to enslavement and white fears of racial degradation. As I have shown throughout this book, the recognition of consumption's broader ethical implications was compatible with a range of ideological positions. Just as consumption-as-connection facilitated anti-slavery activism as well as anti-Black racism, cannibalism offered a powerful conceptual vocabulary for both slavery's depredations and the alleged barbarity of non-white peoples.

When Hepzibah Pyncheon decides, with much agony, to reopen the cent-shop on the ground floor of the House of the Seven Gables, her first customer is a cannibal. Or rather, he is a white schoolboy whose first two selections are pieces of gingerbread in the shape of the iconic minstrel figure Jim Crow. Hawthorne mines this preference for humor: "No sooner had he reached the sidewalk (little cannibal that he was!) than Jim Crow's head was in his mouth."[73] The boy immediately returns to eat another Jim Crow, followed by a gingerbread elephant and camel. Despite the ultimate range of the boy's ample appetite (his final gingerbread tally includes two Jim Crows, a locomotive, camel, whale, and elephant), he has been marked by his initial choice. He's the "the little cannibal of Jim Crow" and "the little devourer of Jim Crow and the elephant" long before we learn his name, which even then is quickly followed by the cannibal epithet: "Ned Higgins, the devourer of Jim Crow and the elephant."[74] It doesn't matter what Ned eats—if a human being is in the mix, his identity becomes "cannibal." True to literary traditions in describing cannibals, Ned has an "all-devouring appetite" and a predilection for the human form.[75] The fact that he immediately wolfs down his victim recalls lurid missionary accounts of cannibals too eager to wait for human flesh to be cooked, while his decision to start with the head evokes popular accounts of South Seas headhunters (even if headhunters were typically described as preserving rather than eating the heads of their victims). Most saliently, given the prevalence of cannibalism in the discourse on slavery, the body consumed is, figuratively speaking, that of an enslaved Black man.

Coded as cannibalism, the collision between Hepzibah's financial need and Ned Higgins's excessive appetite racially marks both characters. When Ned returns for the second Jim Crow, "[t]he crumbs and discoloration of the cannibal-feast, as yet hardly consummated, were exceedingly visible about his mouth."[76] As Kyla Wazana Tompkins has shown, these stains indicate a kind of "racial indigestion" as the devoured image of a Black body also "infects" the white devourer "with its own 'primitive' likeness."[77] Not only is Ned transformed into a cannibal, but his stained face resembles what Tompkins calls a "photonegative of blackface makeup," with his mouth in exaggerated outline.[78] When Hepzibah grudgingly accepts payment for the cookie, "[t]he sordid stain of that copper-coin could never be washed away from her palm. The little schoolboy, aided by the impish figure of the negro dancer, had wrought an irreparable ruin."[79] According to David Anthony, these stains (along with many other racial signifiers in the novel) represent Hawthorne's attempt to use racial markings to mediate between upper and lower classes while also grappling with mass culture. Hence the Jim Crow cookie represents racial staining at the point where Hepzibah must enter into contact with the lower classes, as well as the unsettling proliferation of minstrel images and their dual signification of Blackness and working-class white people.[80]

Cannibalistic consumption is not just a racial marker, as Tompkins and Anthony persuasively argue, but also a metaphor of immoral commerce, especially in relation to slavery. The stains of the copper coin and gingerbread embody what Gillian Brown has called the "intensification of corporeality" in this commercial interaction, but they also intimate that such commercially induced corporeality is bloodstained and guilt ridden.[81] The reddish tinge of both copper and gingerbread evokes blood—the substance most likely to stain partakers of a cannibal feast and which is biblically associated with bloodstained hands.[82] Hepzibah's first commercial transaction is, figuratively, the sale of a Black man that leaves blood on her hands and on the mouth of his consumer.[83] The characteristic death of Pyncheon men—be it from apoplexy or Matthew Maule's curse—always seems to leave bloodstains on white beards and collars, and Hawthorne stresses the link between these stains and avarice.[84] When Colonel Pyncheon falsely accuses Matthew Maule of witchcraft in order to seize the land on which the House of the Seven Gables is eventually built, Maule's curse from the gallows is overtly cannibalistic: "God will give him blood to drink!"[85] Although Maule does not specify whose blood, popular tradition tellingly decides the blood is no other than Maule's own: "If one of the family did but gurgle in his throat, a bystander would be likely enough to whisper, between jest and earnest—'He has Maule's blood to drink!'"[86] Colonel Pyncheon's eventual death literalizes the cannibalistic exploitation implied by his willingness to see Maule put to death for personal gain, and Hawthorne emphasizes the comparably murderous greed of descendants such as Gervayse Pyncheon and Judge Jaffrey Pyncheon.

Evoking the centuries-old tradition of depicting cannibals as scarcely human, Hawthorne insists on the animalistic qualities of Judge Pyncheon to further distance him from social norms and, I will suggest, from whiteness. The narrator reports that people said, "in reference to his ogre-like appetite, that his Creator made him a great animal, but that the dinner-hour made him a great beast."[87] The *OED* defines an ogre as a "man-eating monster," and the image of the judge ravenously consuming a large spread combines cannibalism and animalistic excess to convey inhuman appetite, not unlike Emerson's portrayal of Southern enslavers as wolflike cannibals.[88] Consistent with the scientific racism that would make cannibalism a function of physiology, the judge's beastly nature emerges in his physical characteristics. He has a "dark, square countenance, with its almost shaggy depth of eyebrows" and "somewhat massive accumulation of animal substance about the lower region of his face."[89] Moreover, the judge's "animal substance" recalls his ancestor's "great animal development."[90] Judge Pyncheon is figured as a man-eating, animal-like devourer, and Hawthorne underlines the fact that these qualities, like race, come through the family line.

Hawthorne repeatedly indicates that Judge Pyncheon's greed racially marks him. The organ-grinder's monkey illustrates this process. Dancing and joylessly grabbing for coins, the monkey provides the ultimate "image of the Mammon of copper-coin, symbolizing the grossest form of the love of money."[91] Michael T. Gilmore has noted the resemblance between the monkey's performance and the way the judge manipulates his public image to increase his wealth, while Anthony identifies the monkey as a "thinly veiled caricature of a performative black masculinity."[92] In fact, these elements mutually reinforce Hawthorne's portrayal of the judge as someone whose avarice aligns him with animality and Blackness. Judge Pyncheon's famously overwrought smile represents a similar nexus of racialized performance and appetite. The narrator notes that a keen observer "would probably suspect, that the smile on the gentleman's face was a good deal akin to the shine on his boots, and that each must have cost him and his boot-black, respectively, a good deal of hard labor to bring out and preserve them."[93] The exaggerated smile conjoined with black boot polish powerfully evokes blackface. The judge's smile thus assumes a racially performative tinge. In the same way that minstrel shows and popular print imagery imagined Black characters with enormous mouths and shining white teeth, Judge Pyncheon becomes a sort of wolf in grandmother's clothing—parading as a respectable white citizen but being revealed (by those big teeth he has) to be in actuality something inhuman, savage, and Black.

In Hawthorne's depiction, Pyncheon patriarchs like the colonel and the judge have brought the ignominious mark of racialized barbarity upon their would-be white aristocratic family, just as surely as "Maule's blood" has stained their white shirts and white beards. Similar images of darkening whiteness characterize the house, framed with white oak that now appears "black," and even the faces of the judge and the colonel.[94] The judge's face reveals a "dark, full-fed physiognomy" and "a frown as black as the ancestral one," indicating that "darkness" is a family trait linked to appetite.[95] Early on, the narrator explains that a painting of Colonel Pyncheon better expresses his real character the more it darkens over time.[96] Near the end, in the fading light of the room in which Judge Pyncheon has died, the narrator uses a striking (and oft-noted) oxymoron to describe the face that will not quite fade into the darkness: "And there is still the swarthy whiteness—we shall venture to marry these ill-agreeing words—the swarthy whiteness of Judge Pyncheon's face."[97] Those ill-agreeing words brilliantly capture the way Hawthorne draws on multiple strands of cannibalism discourse. On the one hand, he adopts the same kind of cannibalism metaphor used by antislavery commentators to contrast the judge's outward social respectability with his underlying violence and greed. On the other hand, Hawthorne suggests that the unethical qualities of certain Pyncheons align them with Blackness, much in the way proponents of slavery and colonialism wielded cannibalism accusations to justify domination of racialized Others.

For Hawthorne as for abolitionist consumer activists, consumption offered powerful metaphors of exploitation and violence, but it also readily tapped well-established veins of white supremacist disgust. Antislavery advocates harnessed the ability of cannibalism to convey the inhuman violence of rendering people economically consumable, but they always risked simultaneously conjuring the racist tropes that had accompanied the figure of the cannibal for centuries. The next chapter will examine another set of consumption metaphors that presented similar opportunities as well as risks. Both Black and white abolitionists used hungry animal metaphors to encapsulate the economic consumption at the heart of chattel slavery. While white abolitionists used them in ways that risked naturalizing the consumption of Black bodies, Black abolitionists emphasized enslaved resistance to devouring forces.

FIVE

CONSUMING MONSTERS

Hungry Animals in the Discourse on Slavery

In *My Bondage and My Freedom* (1855), Frederick Douglass characterizes the men hoping to profit from his failed escape attempt as hungry animals: "Once shut up, a new set of tormentors came upon us. A swarm of imps, in human shape—the slave-traders, deputy slave-traders, and agents of slave-traders—that gather in every country town of the state, watching for chances to buy human flesh, (as buzzards to eat carrion,) flocked in upon us, to ascertain if our masters had placed us in jail to be sold."[1] Douglass reverses the dehumanizing gaze of slavery back onto the traders. If the logic of the system defines him as a kind of meat, then slave traders are no better than scavenging animals; instead of feeding directly off his flesh, they seek to feed off the profits of his sale. By linking eating with purchasing, Douglass figures the economic interests that fueled chattel slavery as monstrous consumption.

Starting in the late eighteenth century, Black and white abolitionists on both sides of the Atlantic used hungry animals—sharks, snakes, birds, and especially dogs—to signify the greed of enslavers and the consumptive logic of slavery. These hungry animal portrayals both resembled and revised consumption-as-connection. They represented yet another metaphoric vehicle in which eating encapsulated how chattel slavery rendered human beings economically consumable as well as vulnerable to physical and psychological violence. Even though these depictions featured neither slave-grown commodities nor their distant purchasers, they still implicated those who benefited from slavery. Like the slavery-as-cannibalism tropes in the previous chapter, hungry animal tropes effectively removed the mediating commodity. Unlike cannibalism, portrayals of hungry animals configured consumptive violence as interspecies rather than interpersonal, thereby attacking the greed of enslavers and their allies as inhuman depravity. In moving away from the abject horrors of blood-soaked commodities and the cannibal feast, hungry animal tropes also moved away from the disgust central to consumption-as-connection. As with disgust, however, hungry animal tropes provided a powerful affective spur to antislavery action but risked exacerbating anti-Black racism.

Hungry animals offered a fitting emblem for a system predicated on making people consumable, but their emphasis on the connection between animals and people of African descent posed problems. In addition to the possibility of playing into racist narratives about Blackness and animality, figuring slavery's violence as animal predation could imply that enslaved people were "natural" prey. This implication was accentuated by frequent white abolitionist portrayals of the Black people in these scenarios as passive victims. Moreover, antislavery formulations that focused solely on slavery's economic logic risked reinscribing that logic even as they critiqued it. But, as in efforts by Afro-Caribbean abolitionists like Olaudah Equiano and Mary Prince to challenge the dehumanizing propensity of abolitionist cannibalism imagery, Black American abolitionists modified hungry animal tropes to denature their deleterious tendencies. First, they eschewed the suggestion of naturalness or passivity by emphasizing resistance, depicting encounters in which enslaved people face, fight, or even kill aggressive animals. Second, while they used animals to condemn the financial interests that drove slavery, as Douglass does above, they went beyond an economic critique to provide a more nuanced portrait of the psyche of enslavers and the workings of slavocratic power. By using animals to embody enslavers' contradictory fusion of self-interest and irrational instincts, Black abolitionists seized narrative control and underscored Black subjectivity. Their hungry animal tropes recognized the centrality of consumption to slavery, but they evinced a more expansive understanding of that consumption while starkly rejecting the purported availability of enslaved people to be consumed.

Recent scholarship has illuminated the importance of animals in the discourse on slavery. Scholars including Brigitte Fielder, Jamie Bolker, and

Colleen Glenney Boggs acknowledge that while many comparisons of enslaved people and animals were dehumanizing, some presented opportunities to envision resistance or even radical sympathy.[2] Thomas G. Andrews asserts that animals help define the experience of enslavement in "interspecies slave narrative[s]" like Charles Ball's *Slavery in the United States* (1836).[3] I build on this work by focusing on the crucial but understudied intersection between animality and consumption in the discourse on slavery. Despite the fact that slavery's most iconic animal tropes figured enslaved people threatened by the monstrous jaws of a vicious animal, most existing scholarship overlooks the importance of eating in its focus on the inherent dehumanization of treating human beings as prey for animals.[4] The precise form of this dehumanization is significant, however: it was not just the animality, but the *consumability* that so deeply resonated with larger logics of slavery and white supremacy. As Bénédicte Boisseron has argued about the dogs that attacked fugitives from slavery, "Mutilation—performed by either a human or canine—was thought to remind the slave that she or he was, unlike the dog, a farm animal. But more importantly, like a farm animal, the slave is defined not only by his or her chattel status but also by his or her edibility."[5] Echoing Kyla Wazana Tompkins and Vincent Woodard on the pervasive portrayal of "the black body as food," Boisseron recognizes that this enforced edibility is related to commodification and even cannibalism.[6] I develop these insights by showing how abolitionists used animal appetites to give the abstract economic logic of slavery a devastatingly concrete form, all while demonstrating that slavery's supporters fused human incentives with inhuman instincts.[7]

This chapter begins by examining the images of hungry animals (especially sharks) that accompanied the rise of abolitionism in late eighteenth-century Britain and the United States, before briefly turning to the way similar images in blackface minstrelsy occasionally offered surprisingly similar economic critiques. The overlap between early, predominantly white abolitionist and blackface minstrel hungry animal tropes reveals that an economic critique alone was insufficient to counteract the tendency of such images to naturalize Black consumability. The chapter ends by considering how Black abolitionists worked to reappropriate such tropes. Although Black abolitionists frequently acknowledged the connection between hungry animals and slavery's economics, they shifted the focus to active resistance and emphasized that monstrous consumption took myriad forms. Because the enabling conditions of hungry animal tropes were not specific to a particular national context, this chapter includes material from Britain, the Caribbean, and the United States, ranging from the 1790s to the 1850s.

CONSUMING MONSTERS AND WHITE ABOLITIONIST ECONOMIC CRITIQUE

Whether in the middle of the Atlantic or the mouths of African rivers, sharks haunt descriptions of the Middle Passage. In his poem "The West Indies," the white British poet James Montgomery laments "Myriads of slaves, that perish'd on the way, / From age to age the shark's appointed prey," while the white British poet Robert Southey describes "the trooping sharks / [that] Track by the scent of death the accursed ship / Freighted with human anguish."[8] Southey characterizes the transatlantic slave trade in terms of the persistent ministrations of sharks, whose skill as hunters allowed them to home in on (and thereby emphasize) the suffering many Europeans willfully ignored. In his account of captives who resisted enslavement by committing suicide onboard ships waiting to cross the Atlantic, the prominent white British abolitionist Thomas Clarkson stresses conditions so brutal that even a shark's mouth could seem a sanctuary: "[M]any have accomplished their ends, and have found an asylum either in the mouths of sharks, or in the beds of their native rivers."[9] Many observers noted that these attentive sharks were not restricted to the coast of Africa, but actually followed slave ships across the entire Middle Passage, another gruesome point of connection in the Atlantic world.[10]

Sharks encapsulated the terrors of the Middle Passage, but they also became metaphoric vehicles through which predominantly white commentators condemned how the desire for consumer goods and financial gain facilitated the consumption of enslaved people. If the captives had been figuratively consumed in the sense that they had become saleable commodities, these sharks reflected that consumption in the threat of actual devouring. As I discussed in chapter 2, Herman Melville highlights the connection between eating and economics in *Moby-Dick* (1851): "[S]harks also are the invariable outriders of all slave ships crossing the Atlantic, systematically trotting alongside, to be handy in case a parcel is to be carried anywhere, or a dead slave to be decently buried."[11] His sharks vividly reproduce the violent conversion to consumability enacted by the slave trade.

The sense that hungry sharks embody the fundamentally consumptive nature of the slave trade and its supporters drives an unusual anonymous British broadside entitled "The Petition of the Sharks of Africa" (1792).[12] Written from the viewpoint of the sharks who swarm the slave ships on the coast of Africa, the broadside satirically urges Parliament to reject the bill to abolish the slave trade lest the sharks lose the source of their "rich repasts" and "many a delicious meal" of "their most favourite food—human flesh." These sharks represent pure appetite. They gleefully describe the feasts provided by occasional shipwrecks, "where the gnawing of human flesh, and the crashing of bones, afford to your petitioners the highest gratification which their natures are capable of enjoying." They conclude their appeal in the last line of the broadside by arguing that, should the trade be preserved, "your petitioners, and their wide-mouthed posterity, as by nature urged, will ever, ever PREY, &c." Both examples emphasize the fundamental differences between sharks and humans. Sharks are built to devour, with their wide mouths and bone-crunching jaws, and their nature significantly circumscribes their opportunities for pleasure, where eating human beings is "the highest gratification which their natures are capable of enjoying," and their inability to embrace religious doctrine punningly registers in their desire to "PREY" rather than pray.

Sharks, the broadside suggests, may be natural consumers of enslaved people, but certain humans harbor comparable (and inhuman) appetites: "Should the lower branch of the legislature be so far infatuated by this new-fangled humanity as seriously to meditate the destruction of this highly beneficial commerce, your petitioners have the firmest reliance on the wisdom and fellow-feeling of the Lords Spiritual and Temporal of Great Britain." The reference to "highly beneficial commerce" equates the financial gains of slave traders and plantation owners to the nutritional gains of sharks, recasting economic transactions as violent eating. The irony of "new-fangled humanity" stresses that the House of Lords (as opposed to the "lower branch" of the House of Commons) shares its "fellow-feeling" not with other humans, but with those who would viciously consume humans. This broadside exposes the underlying message in antislavery hungry animal tropes: The people who profit from the slave trade are no better than sharks—ferocious, remorseless, and focused solely on their own pleasure, even at the expense of human lives. The sharks have become, if not exactly agents, then totems—monstrous incarnations of the figurative capacity of some human beings to devour others.

The threat of being eaten by animals did not end with the sharks of the Middle Passage, and instances in which animals were used to torture enslaved people inspired further critiques of the link between consumer appetites and bodily destruction. Like the consuming sharks, punishments involving animals were a material reality in America and the Caribbean. In a description of Jamaica, Equiano includes the following in his list of the horrific abuses endured by enslaved people: "There were also, as I heard, two different masters noted for cruelty on the island, who had staked up two negroes naked, and in two hours the vermin stung them to death."[13] Similar punishments appear in the diaries of the English enslavers Thomas Thistlewood and Matthew Lewis. In what may be the most famous literary example, the fictional persona James in the white American immigrant J. Hector St. John de Crèvecœur's *Letters from an American Farmer* (1782) encounters an enslaved man who has been caged and fed upon by birds. The incident so disturbs James that he devotes an entire letter to melancholy ruminations on slavery and the human condition. James opens Letter 9 by describing Charleston as a bastion of wealth and pleasure, and he depicts that wealth with particular focus on luxurious food and drink, mentioning the "expences of those citizens' tables" three times in the first paragraph.[14] In excoriating wealthy white Charlestonians who "eat, drink, and live happy" while willfully ignoring the suffering of enslaved people, James tacitly links table luxuries to the excruciating labor that produced them—"those showers of sweat and of tears which from the bodies of Africans daily drop, and moisten the ground they till."[15] By joining spilled bodily fluids with epicurean indulgence, Crèvecœur anticipates the blood-sugar metaphors that would soon galvanize early British abolitionism, though he denounces ill-gotten luxury in general as opposed to a specific commodity.

Animals allow Crèvecœur to make inescapable the connections between enslaved labor and corrupt consumption. James's reflections soon turn to the fundamental willingness of human beings to destroy one another, something he imagines in terms of animals: "Man, an animal of prey, seems to have rapine and the love of bloodshed implanted in his heart."[16] James ends the letter by apologizing for its dismal content and describing the enslaved man he encountered: "From the edges of the hollow sockets, and from the lacerations with which he was disfigured, the blood slowly dropped, and tinged the ground beneath. No sooner were the birds flown, than swarms of insects covered the whole body of this unfortunate wretch, eager to feed on his mangled flesh and to drink his blood."[17] Teresa A. Goddu has argued that this "gothic scene" reveals that "America's mythic image masks a corruption hidden at its core," and I would add that the corruption becomes visible through animal predation.[18] The incident disturbingly reverses animal and human positions: A man is in a cage rather than birds, and birds feed on him instead of the opposite. "The blood slowly dropped, and tinged the ground beneath": The language here parallels the earlier description of Charleston's wealth (produced by "showers of sweat and of tears which from the bodies of Africans daily drop, and moisten the ground they till"), insisting through spilled bodily fluids that, under slavery, labor and torture are indistinguishable. Moreover, the devouring birds and insects, though literal, nonetheless recall the earlier figure of "man an animal of prey," asserting once again that to benefit from slavery is to be "eager to feed on [the] mangled flesh and to drink [the] blood" of enslaved people, either directly through torture or indirectly through sumptuous food and drink.

By replacing cannibalistic humans with voracious animals, such tropes contrasted the "natural" appetites of animals with the "unnatural" appearance of those same appetites in people. They thus depended on creating a strong moral distinction between the human and nonhuman. As the white British abolitionist Mary Birkett puts it in her "Poem on the African Slave Trade" (1792), enslavers are "More rav'nous than the foulest beasts of prey, / They but from Nature's powerful cravings slay."[19] Birkett suggests that wild animals may be excused for their instinctual appetites, but humans merit harsh condemnation because they have a choice in the matter. Such tropes participated in a long tradition of hierarchical thinking that imagined humans with a divinely ordained right to master the natural world. Far from post-Darwinian perspectives that would see sex and violence as natural drives in humans as in animals, this worldview contended that animal-like appetites were a moral aberration, a betrayal of Christian values and human character.[20] Furthermore, as scholars such as Joshua Bennett and Zakiyyah Iman Jackson have pointed out, the hierarchical thinking that divides humans from animals also drives racial hierarchies.

Like the excessive focus on Black physicality discussed in chapter 1, these white abolitionist tropes sought to humanize enslaved people but ultimately reinforced racial difference. Significantly, the "unnatural" aspect in hungry animal tropes was not the humans being consumed, but the humans exhibiting animal-like appetites. Saidiya Hartman has argued that antislavery portrayals of spectacular Black suffering "risk . . . fixing and naturalizing this condition of pained embodiment," and these hungry animal tropes take that naturalization even further by displacing the suffering from the world of human interactions to the natural world.[21] The proximity of animals and people of African descent in these depictions moreover renders the apparent gesture of inclusion an example of what Jackson has called "bestializing humanization," where, "[i]nstead of denying humanity, black people are humanized, but this humanity is burdened with the specter of abject animality."[22] Despite their condemnation of the human drivers of slavery, such tropes nevertheless represented people of African descent as animalized humans, fundamentally available for consumption.

Beyond naturalizing consumption, these depictions also tended to imagine enslaved people as passive victims. Even when resistance is acknowledged—the enslaved man described by Crèvecœur is being punished for killing an overseer; Clarkson describes captives jumping overboard to avoid enslavement—the consumption itself is endured rather than actively resisted. The dynamics of viewing or reading these scenes further emphasizes passivity. These tropes generated hierarchical empathy, which Martha J. Cutter has characterized in abolitionist visual texts as dependent on pity and "the idea that the pained body and psyche of the enslaved is a low, unfinished, disabled, childlike, or in some way inferior entity that needs the help and mediation of the white viewer."[23] In granting readers the power to refuse humanity to enslavers while simultaneously awarding it to enslaved people, early white abolitionist animal tropes offered their audience a sense of empowerment while also reducing enslaved people to inert recipients of white magnanimity. By portraying enslaved people as the passive victims of spectacular, naturalized violence, these tropes also participated in a process by which, as Hartman puts it, "the fungibility of the commodity makes the captive body an abstract and empty vessel vulnerable to the projection of others' feelings, ideas, desires, and values."[24] Early hungry animal tropes, in other words, reinscribed the very economic logic they attempted to critique by presuming the availability of enslaved people for their metaphoric constructions.

As with the appearance of consumption-as-connection in both pro- and antislavery texts, recognizing the conceptual foundations of chattel slavery did not foreordain any particular political orientation. Underscoring the fact that the economic critique in these early white abolitionist hungry animal tropes was insufficient to counteract their commodifying tendencies is the presence of similar tropes in white supremacist popular culture. From the antebellum era until well into the twentieth century, depictions of Black people at risk of being devoured by monstrous animals, often alligators, were a standby of racist kitsch. Critical attention to these viciously racist depictions has focused almost exclusively on their late-nineteenth- and twentieth-century incarnations, but they also dominated antebellum U.S. blackface minstrel print culture and performance.[25] The frank racism of these purportedly humorous representations exposes many of the implicit messages of white abolitionist hungry animal tropes. The sheet music cover for the minstrel song series *Songs of the Congo Melodists* (1844), for example, includes a vignette in the bottom left corner in which a bones-playing Black musician is entirely unfazed by an alligator approaching with jaws agape. The musician is mirrored in the bottom right corner by an anthropomorphized fiddling frog, and though the frog continues to play, he warily eyes an approaching open-mouthed snake. The visual logic of these vignettes implies that while both musicians, the Black man and the frog, are natural prey for aggressive reptiles, only the frog is wise enough to recognize it. Like white abolitionist hungry animal tropes, this illustration emphasizes Black passivity, naturalizes the consumption of Black bodies, and parallels the logic of the slave economy. Whereas the antislavery tropes reinscribe that economic logic by portraying enslaved bodies as mere vehicles for white imaginative projection, the minstrel sheet music illustration is franker about its commodification. The fact that the actual songs make no mention of alligators reveals the violent cover image to be pure advertising ploy—designed to grab attention and entice would-be buyers. Long after emancipation, similar images would be used to sell consumer products, postcards, and novelty stereographs.

White supremacist uses of hungry animal tropes can thus be read as an index of desire in which hungry animals replicate white consumer appetite not for the products of slavery, but for images of enslaved bodies under threat. Minstrel performances occasionally acknowledged this fact directly. In a comical prose interlude in one minstrel songster, the speaker describes taking a woman to an animal exhibition: "De show man said dat snake was twenty-five feet long from his head to his tail, and thirty feet from his tail to his head. He eats a whole ox at a mouth full, and some times eats niggers; and when Dinah hear dat she wouldn't stay any longer."[26] In Dinah's mind, the exotic creatures, part of a moneymaking Barnum-style entertainment, pose a direct threat—if she is not careful, the enormous snake could choose to devour her as she is told it has other Black people before her. The underlying implication—that Black people fueled popular (and Northern-inflected) entertainment—is particularly significant within the context of a minstrel show. Embodied in Eric Lott's construction of "love and theft," minstrel show performances represented a complex combination of desire and appropriation. Blackface minstrel images of hungry animals reflect a similar fusion of desire for and violence toward Black people. Another songster features a comic interlude in which the character Aunty Chloey tells the audience, "You needn't grin at me, you he-crocodiles!"—insinuating that the smiles of her predominantly white male audience carry a predatory quality.[27] And indeed, they did—just as this fictional enslaved woman, herself depicted by a white man in blackface drag, might be playing into a minstrel tradition of enslaved people at risk of being devoured, the very idea of an Aunty Chloey (and of what it meant to be Black) was being consumed by the audience. That these most obvious moments of audience implication came not in minstrel songs but in comic interludes is no accident—these were the moments when performers could be most virtuosic in improvising responses to a given audience's reactions and desires, and therefore the part of the show most flexible in its ability to lay those desires bare.[28]

In blackface minstrel songs, hungry animal tropes occasionally offer nascent economic critiques along similar lines as abolitionist versions. In the antebellum minstrel song "Git Along Home, My Yaller Gals," the hungry alligator replicates the enslaver's own consumption habits:

De alligator in de brake
Plays fast asleep when he wide awake;
He wants to suck some darkey in,
As massa do a glass ob gin.[29]

Like Crèvecœur's proposed equivalence between Charleston's consumer luxuries and the animalistic consumption of people, this image traces a direct line from the enslaver's consumption habits to the consumption of enslaved bodies. The minstrel song "Mississippi Sandy Shore" makes the link between the slave economy and hungry animals even more explicit:

On Mississippi's sandy shore,
Many an hour I've passed in glee,
Singing songs we sang before,
When we were down in Tennessee;
Transfixed with wonder I have been,
To see dat alligator's mouth,
He wants to suck dis nigger in,
An carry him away down south.[30]

Being "carried away down south" evokes the terrifying prospect of being sold away from family and friends to harsher plantations; indeed, this speaker already seems to have been transported from Tennessee to Mississippi. In this case, the alligator assumes the place of enslaver, reaping the benefits (albeit nutritional rather than financial) as the enslaved man is taken quite literally down the river. Using depictions of alimentary consumption to reveal forms of economic consumption was thus not an automatically antislavery gesture. While antislavery activists used these tropes to connect slavery's economic logic with its catastrophic human consequences in an attempt to effect Black liberation, blackface minstrel performers used the same connection to attract laughs and customers in a cultural form fundamentally committed to "black captivity."[31] The economic critique may have been an important aspect of antislavery hungry animal tropes, but it alone was insufficient to prevent replicating the commodification it rebuked.

RESISTING HUNGRY ANIMALS IN SLAVE NARRATIVES AND ANTISLAVERY SPECTACLES

When Frederick Douglass compared slave traders to buzzards, he likened the financial interests of those traders to animal appetites. Though the logic of the simile made him carrion, Douglass insisted on his own humanity by seizing control of slavery's dehumanizing logic and turning it back onto its practitioners.[32] As I will argue in this section, antebellum Black abolitionists adopted and adapted the hungry animal tropes that had emerged in late eighteenth-century white abolitionism. Black abolitionist hungry animal tropes frequently represented enslaved people not as passive victims but as active resisters; even when they did not, the form of those tropes contested the objectifying tendency of hungry animal tropes by foregrounding the subjectivity of enslaved people. When Douglass, Hannah Crafts, and Harriet Jacobs used hungry animals to critique the monstrous appetites driving slavery, they chose forms that testified to their own narrative control. When William Wells Brown turned to hungry animals to attract attention for his antislavery panorama and magic lantern slide lectures, he directed that attention to a subversive public performance. In the hands of formerly enslaved writers, hungry animal tropes did more than show the suffering of enslaved people and the monstrousness of those who profited from slavery; they offered a nuanced portrait of the impulses and motivations of enslavers as they intersected with literal and figurative animals. In the process, they capitalized on the tropes' ability to expose slavery's consumptive logic while both portraying and enacting resistance to that logic.

As critics have examined at length, Hannah Crafts reworked tropes of prominent British and American novels, staging her own literary freedom in both her generic choices and her "radical appropriation of white forms."[33] Whether or not she ever encountered Crèvecœur, her novel *The Bondwoman's Narrative* (ca. 1850s) boldly reimagines James's encounter with the caged man in order to spotlight the connection between consumption and torture that the Charlestonians supposedly tried to ignore. She describes a tree on which Sir Clifford, the progenitor of one of the novel's enslaving families, tortured enslaved people: "Many a time had its roots been manured with human blood. Slaves had been tied to its trunk to be whipped or sometimes gibbeted on its branches. . . . On such occasions, Sir Clifford sitting at the windows of his drawing room, within the full sight and hearing of their agonies would drink wine, or coolly discuss the politics of the day with some acquaintance, pausing perhaps in the midst of a sentence to give directions to the executioner, or order some mitigation of the torture only to prolong it."[34] Far from Crèvecœur's Charlestonians, who "neither see, hear, nor feel for, the woes of their poor slaves," Crafts depicts enslavers as embodying what Kelly Ross has called the "cruel surveillance associated with the slave system."[35] These enslavers socialize and luxuriate as they take in the spectacle of Black suffering "within the full sight and hearing of their agonies," as Crafts pointedly specifies. Torture seems to whet—or at least not diminish—Clifford's appetite for the finer things, whether his wine (which mirrors the blood watering the tree's roots) or his drawing room (the windows of which appear designed to frame the scene of anguish). The link between the suffering of enslaved people and the pleasure of enslavers is not a studiously ignored secret, but the very basis of enslaver conviviality.

Like Douglass, Crafts uses animals to critique the economic motives of enslavers and slave traders. The novel's villain, Mr. Trappe, has become wealthy by discovering the African heritage of his victims and then blackmailing them or selling them into slavery. Hannah, the protagonist and first-person narrator, overhears someone remark upon Trappe's death, "He had neither feeling, nor sympathy in common with other people. Love of gold had blunted all the finer sensibilities of his heart, and he would not have hesitated a moment to sell his own mother into slavery could the case have been made clear that she had African blood in her veins. No blood-hound was ever keener in scenting out the African taint than that old man."[36] Trappe's greed has made him less than human, without "feeling, nor sympathy in common with other people" and with an animal-like tenacity when it came to identifying and pursuing his victims (Hannah has earlier described his pursuit as "dogging our footsteps").[37] Even when describing literal bloodhounds, Crafts suggests that, under slavery, certain animal and human appetites are not neatly distinguishable. Hannah describes the dogs deployed by a neighboring enslaver to track fugitives as "long, gaunt, and lean, inexpressibly fierce with a cannibal look that made me tremble."[38] "Cannibal" is multivalent. First and foremost, it invokes a taboo practice to insist that, unlike depictions that naturalize animals eating humans, this consumption is fundamentally immoral and unnatural. Second, it uses cannibalism not only to imply a fearsome hunger for human flesh, but also to imply that the hungerer is a fellow human. In Crafts's usage, the ferocious appetite of these bloodhounds is shared by the slave hunters. The dogs hunger for the fugitives while the slave hunters work to prevent an enslaved couple's escape and to reinforce their status as commodities. Both actively work to consume them.

Hungry animals in Black abolitionist texts were more than metaphors for enslaver greed, however. For one thing, hungry animals were a material reality of slavery's landscapes, and formerly enslaved authors attested to the way enslavers conscripted natural forces to enforce slavocratic authority. Crafts portrays a white man who suggests that nature will take over if enslavers fail. He warns Hannah not to run away, because "you would almost certainly be caught, and if not, you would be certain to perish miserably, perhaps hunted and torn to pieces by dogs, or perhaps eaten alive by the vultures when reduced by famine and privation to a dying state."[39] These dangers influenced would-be fugitives. When planning an escape attempt, Douglass and his co-conspirators are overwhelmed by the number of things that could go wrong:

> Upon either side, we saw grim death assuming a variety of horrid shapes. Now, it was starvation, causing us, in a strange and friendless land, to eat our own flesh. Now, we were contending with the waves, (for our journey was in part by water,) and were drowned. Now, we were hunted by dogs, and overtaken and torn to pieces by their merciless fangs. We were stung by scorpions—chased by wild beasts—bitten by snakes; and, worst of all, after having succeeded in swimming rivers—encountering wild beasts—sleeping in the woods—suffering hunger, cold, heat and nakedness—we supposed ourselves to be overtaken by hired kidnappers, who, in the name of the law, and for their thrice accursed reward, would, perchance, fire upon us—kill some, wound others, and capture all.[40]

To his apprehensive mind, the escape route is fraught with ways he can be eaten or otherwise injured by animals. Douglass repeats "wild beasts." Although the list of likely calamities culminates not in a devouring animal, but "hired kidnappers," those kidnappers replicate the animal terms Douglass has so anxiously laid out. The fugitives have been chased by the slave hunters as much as by wild beasts. Both dogs and slave hunters are described as "overtaking" the fugitives, and both risk killing or wounding the fugitives, whether with guns or "merciless fangs."

Crafts includes a scene in which Hannah and a fellow fugitive further collapse the distinction between wilderness and the power of enslavers, fearfully projecting the latter onto the former: "Trees in the dusky gloom took the forms of men, and stumps and hillocks were strangely transferred into blood-hounds crouching to spring on their prey."[41] These writers demonstrate how enslavers strove to make animals—both wild and domesticated—extensions of themselves, revealing the literal foundation of hungry animal metaphors. According to Solomon Northup in *Twelve Years a Slave* (1853), "[I]t was difficult to determine which I had most reason to fear—dogs, alligators or men!"[42] But even as these narratives acknowledge fear, they testify to the willingness to overcome it. Despite the terror of the natural forces used by slavocratic power to discourage escape, these writers escaped anyway.

As Harriet Jacobs, who was herself bitten by a snake during her escape, declares in *Incidents in the Life of a Slave Girl* (1861), "But even those large, venomous snakes were less dreadful to my imagination than the white men in that community called civilized."[43]

The most iconic animal encountered by fugitives was, of course, the bloodhound, and formerly enslaved writers used dogs to portray the slave system as a fusion of instinctive impulses and careful strategy. Bloodhounds were a fitting emblem for thwarted freedom: Their skill in tracking fugitives suggested slavery's reach, their ability to inflict gruesome injuries mirrored slavery's uneven power dynamics, and their occasionally out-of-control appetites paralleled the libidinal investments of enslavers. Even as bloodhounds mirrored some of the elements of wild animal descriptions, they featured a crucial difference. The buzzards, snakes, and other "wild beasts" in hungry animal portrayals represented pure instinct. When Jacobs writes that "[h]ot weather brings out snakes and slaveholders, and I like one class of the venomous creatures as little as I do the other," she underlines predatory behavior that is instinctual—not the product of human reason, but an impulse as unconsidered as a reptile responding to higher temperatures.[44] Bloodhounds, conversely, represented a more troubling combination of instinct and training. These "weaponized dogs" were terrifying both because they were powerful animals and because their natural hunting abilities had been carefully honed by trainers committed to upholding slavery.[45] In Joshua Bennett's view, the dogs were "more or less inextricable from hegemonic whiteness as a set of sociopolitical protocols and practices."[46]

Bloodhounds epitomize how terrifying animals were used to uphold the slave system. In her study of dogs trained to hunt and kill Indigenous and Black people in the circum-Caribbean, Sara E. Johnson has provocatively argued that "[i]nasmuch as one can suppose that the human species' most primal fear is being eaten alive by wild animals, the deliberate use of semidomesticated dogs as weapons made it clear that the state was a fearsome predator ready to cannibalize human flesh by proxy."[47] Jacobs, Douglass, Crafts, and Northup (along with many others) all describe the possibility of being "torn to pieces" by bloodhounds at some point, and narratives report instances of fugitives being killed before the dogs can be pulled away. Notably, while the aggressive tendencies of the bloodhounds may have been an effective means of deterring some would-be fugitives, those same tendencies also worked against the presumed interests of enslavers. Fugitives were tenaciously pursued because they represented immensely valuable property, and a dog that might maim or even kill a fugitive would have posed a significant financial liability.

White abolitionist hungry animal tropes tended to portray consumption as motivated by greed—an inhuman profit motive. Black abolitionist writers revised these depictions to assert that consumption under slavery frequently defied economic rationality.[48] Bloodhounds in particular revealed not only the fundamental violence of the slave system, but destructive appetites that could not be reliably controlled, even when they seemingly worked against the financial interests of enslavers. Many proslavery advocates claimed that abolitionist reports of abuse must have been exaggerated, since such cruelty would harm valuable "property." In response, writers like Jacobs and Douglass maintained that slavery unleashed inhuman appetites that quickly exceeded the bounds of reason or morality. Certainly, Jacobs's narrative is in part a portrait of a man gripped by his own obsessive need for sexual power. She insistently links her enslaver's actions to appetite, describing him as a man "whose restless, craving, vicious nature roved about day and night, seeking whom to devour."[49] The connection to hungry animals is even more explicit in the Bible verse to which Jacobs refers, which compares the devil to a "roaring lion . . . seeking whom he may devour" (1 Pet. 5:8). Douglass starkly rejects the idea that enslavers are restrained by motives of interest. He declares "profit or loss" to be "but a very slender and inefficient restraint" on an enslaver in the grip of "pride, hatred, envy, jealousy, and the thirst for revenge."[50] Whether in bloodhounds or in enslavers, it is difficult to reliably control baser instincts when an excess of power is combined with an excess of passion or appetite (note that one of the spurs for this particular enslaver is, in Douglass's words, a "thirst for revenge").

Black abolitionists used hungry animal tropes to suggest that consumption lay at the root of enslavement, encompassing economic interests, physical threats, and instinctual desires. In depicting violent resistance to those animals, these writers also depicted an emphatic rejection of the fundamental basis of slavery. Sometimes that resistance appeared through metaphors that animalized human antagonists. When Northup fights his enslaver John Tibeats, he describes feeling "as if I had a serpent by the neck, watching the slightest relaxation of my gripe, to coil itself round my body, crushing and stinging it to death" and admits he is tempted to "kill the human blood-hound on the spot."[51] At other times, the resistance targets actual rather than metaphorical animals to challenge the larger slave system. The historian Walter Johnson has noted the similarities between accounts of killing slave-hunting dogs by former fugitives like Charles Ball and J. D. Green and accounts of violently resisting enslavers and their allies.[52] The physical resistance to enslavers described in slave narratives tends to be wrestling matches in which enslaved men beat white men instead of killing them, however. Scenes in which enslaved men physically resist pursuing dogs, conversely, involve knives, sticks, and swords and frequently result in unapologetic death. Given that hungry animal tropes conflated predator and enslaver, such scenes provided a stand-in for the kind of violent uprising that otherwise would have unnerved many white readers. Cutter astutely observes the way Henry Bibb's battle with wolves (which I will discuss below) intervenes in abolitionist debates in favor of violent resistance, though her focus on the wolves as representing slave catchers and Bibb's actions as "violent resistance to reenslavement" risks missing the way these tropes engaged not just with fugitivity, but with the slave system as a whole.[53] Solomon Northup describes whipping the enslaver's dogs at every opportunity to prevent having to fight them off during escape: "In this manner I succeeded at length in subduing them completely. They feared me, obeying my voice at once when others had no control over them whatever."[54] Such scenes turn earlier white hungry animal tropes on their heads, portraying enslaved people as active, whole, and, insofar as subdued animals represent white power, in revolutionary control.

Vicious animals also presented opportunities to display resistance in the abolitionist visual culture of this era. Although the widespread failure of most abolitionist iconography to meaningfully depict either Black resistance or Black perspectives has become a critical commonplace, I follow recent scholarship on Black interventions into visual culture to show how hungry animal imagery in the antislavery panoramas of the formerly enslaved U.S. abolitionists William Wells Brown and Henry "Box" Brown foregrounded consumption while shifting focus toward resistance.[55] Both men exploited the mid-nineteenth-century craze for panoramas that swept both sides of the Atlantic. Henry "Box" Brown (initially alongside James C. A. Smith, a free-born Black American) premiered the panorama entitled *Henry Box Brown's Mirror of Slavery* in Boston in 1850 and subsequently toured with it in New England before leaving for England in the fall. He would continue to show the panorama around England for the next decade.[56] William Wells Brown exhibited his panorama, *William Wells Brown's Original Panoramic Views of the Scenes in the Life of an American Slave*, throughout England and Scotland from 1850 until his 1854 return to the United States. Although neither panorama survives, we can glean information on the choices both exhibitors made in designing and presenting their spectacles by reading the written catalog (in William Wells Brown's case) and newspaper advertisements, which include descriptions and occasionally reproductions of the images.

These Black abolitionist panoramas reappropriated many of the commodifying tendencies of white hungry animal tropes. As in the white supremacist popular culture that used hungry animal tropes to attract attention (and money), William Wells Brown saw lurid images of dogs in pursuit of fugitives as promising promotional tools. For a later British lecture featuring magic lantern slides (in which he used a number of scenes from his panorama), he chose "Hunting the Slave with the Negro Dogs" as one of two illustrations for his advertising broadside.[57] Michael A. Chaney has called the image of a fugitive fleeing dogs a "popular set piece of antislavery iconography," and the fact that such an image could be used to drum up ticket sales underscores its currency—a readily reproduced image that commodified Black bodies in danger or pain.[58] This commodification was nevertheless strategically deployed to attract an audience for a subversive performance of resistance and agency. Daphne A. Brooks has persuasively argued that Henry "Box" Brown's panorama represented a kind of "escape artistry" wherein Brown used the panorama form's movement and geographic sweep to escape the constraints of the slave narrative and take control of his own story.[59] Commodification could thereby serve revolutionary ends: "Brown's *Mirror* creates and commodifies a self-consciously disruptive space, a chaotic zone that foregrounds the creative agency of the African American activist-turned-artist."[60] Within the revolutionary context of the panorama, showcasing encounters with dangerous animals allowed the exhibitors to capitalize on a familiar means of generating viewer interest while thwarting viewer expectations of passive victimhood.

Four out of the twenty-four views in William Wells Brown's *Original Panoramic Views* featured threatening dogs (or, in one case, wolves), including the first scene drawn from Brown's own life. Evidence suggests dogs and wolves also appeared in at least two scenes in Henry "Box" Brown's panorama.[61] In many ways, William Wells Brown's panorama followed the white abolitionist trend of portraying enslaved people as victims of vicious animals. The catalog describes that first scene from his life in terms of his decision to "climb a tree to save himself from being torn to pieces" and continues by offering several excerpts from American newspapers about the hunting of enslaved people with dogs, including incidents in which the dogs managed to drown or "considerably maim" the fugitive.[62] And yet, Brown balances these accounts of victimization at the hands of animals with a tale of heroic and violent resistance against them. His pamphlet quotes directly from Henry Bibb's narrative in which Bibb describes fighting off wolves with a bowie knife as he and his family try to escape. Both William Wells Brown and Henry "Box" Brown chose to depict Bibb's escape in their panoramas, suggesting the power they saw in it.[63] The image of Bibb and the wolves combines the sheer narrative drama of man versus beast with the familiar antislavery tradition of hungry animal tropes, but his actions do more than provide a bracing vision of frontier manliness, as some critics have argued.[64] Bibb's actions register resistance to both slavery and the iconographic tradition that would render him passively consumable. Bibb in this moment stands as an emblem of righteous, manly violence, courageously defending his family against long odds.

The resistance to hungry animals—especially bloodhounds—depicted by Black antislavery activists appeared in some white-produced illustrations as well. Jeffrey Ruggles has identified Charles C. Green's 1845 antislavery poem

Figure 5. Title page of *The Nubian Slave,* Charles C. Green, 1845. (Rare Book & Manuscript Library, Columbia University)

The Nubian Slave as a source for Henry "Box" Brown's panorama.⁶⁵ At least part of the appeal of this source for Brown may have been its iconographic attention to consumption and resistance. Once again, animalistic consumption serves as an introduction to the text and an enticement to read further: The title page for *The Nubian Slave* (see fig. 5) features not only a snarling dog but also a leering eagle (whips in talon), snakes coiling around the outer margin, and a strange animal-claw border around the title, as if predatory animals are the very frame or context within which slavery is to be understood. The text of Green's poem deploys a familiar portrayal of bloodhounds who pursue, attack, and then disappear without further mention. The accompanying illustration (a version of which also appeared in *Mirror of Slavery*) breaks free from its source material to depict violent resistance to the dogs (see fig. 6). In the poem, the titular character expresses his "stern defiance" by declaring to the pursuing slave catchers that they will not take him alive.⁶⁶ In the illustration, this verbal rebellion against white men has been transformed into physical violence against their dogs, one of whom apparently lies dead before him.

Figure 6. "Man Hunting," plate 7 of *The Nubian Slave,* Charles C. Green, 1845. (Rare Book & Manuscript Library, Columbia University)

Figure 7. *The Hunted Slaves,* Richard Ansdell, 1862. Oil on canvas, 36 x 60 in. (Artist's copy of 1861 original; National Museum of African American History & Culture)

The shift toward resistance registered in academic painting as well. The white Liverpool-born artist Richard Ansdell's painting *Hunted Slaves* (see fig. 7), for example, was exhibited at the Royal Academy in 1861.[67] It was well received, and even included in the British division of the International Exhibition in London in 1862, as well as reproduced as a print.[68] In the painting, the raised hatchet visually echoes the raised stick in the "Nubian Slave" illustration, while the corpses of dogs in both images testify to the fugitives' willingness to lethally wield their brandished weapons. In the same period, Thomas Moran, a white English-born but American-raised artist, painted *The Slave Hunt* (see fig. 8) on a trip to England. Moran's painting recalls J. M. W. Turner's famous *Slavers Throwing Overboard the Dead and Dying, Typhoon Coming On* (1840), in which a theatrically vivid sunset risks overshadowing the drowning enslaved people menaced by hungry fish in the foreground. The human action in *The Slave Hunt* similarly seems almost incidental to the dreamy drama of the natural world. Moran's canvas offers a crucial distinction, however. While both Turner and Moran portray animals threatening enslaved people, Moran depicts an enslaved person who fights back: One of the fugitives in *The Slave Hunt* carries a bloody knife and stick as he moves away from the corpse of a dog (see detail, fig. 9). In all these images, the dead dog lying at the fugitive's feet has become just as much of a

Figure 8. *Slave Hunt, Dismal Swamp, Virginia,* Thomas Moran, 1861–62. Oil on canvas, 34 x 44 in. (Philbrook Museum of Art, Tulsa, Oklahoma; gift of Laura A. Clubb)

Figure 9. Detail, *Slave Hunt, Dismal Swamp, Virginia,* Thomas Moran, 1861–62. Oil on canvas, 34 x 44 in. (Philbrook Museum of Art, Tulsa, Oklahoma; gift of Laura A. Clubb)

set piece as dogs in pursuit. Taking their cues from Black abolitionist writing and performance, these white artists used modified hungry animal tropes to draw the eye to raised and bloody weapons, insisting that these fugitives have resisted and will continue to resist.

In many ways, the critique of consumption struck at the heart of chattel slavery, underscoring how mundane purchases facilitated the physical and psychic suffering of commodified human beings. In the first wave of hungry animal tropes, predominantly white abolitionists generated the metaphor of the consuming monster out of the material conditions of slavery on the Middle Passage and in the Americas: The sharks, birds, and insects that threatened to devour enslaved people mirrored the inhuman appetites that drove the entire system. More than just another entry in slavery's catalog of depredations, depictions of hungry animals leveled an economic critique by making the consumption enabled by commodification excruciatingly literal. The focus on such scenes risked dehumanizing enslaved people, however. Beyond ignominiously associating enslaved people with animals and emphasizing their spectacular suffering, early white hungry animal tropes tended to portray enslaved people as flattened, unresisting victims. In the attempt to evocatively decry the commodifying logic of slavery, these tropes required enslaved people to be readily available as vehicles for that economic critique, effectively enacting the fungibility they were meant to condemn.

While Black abolitionists also saw in hungry animals a powerful trope through which to denounce slavery's multifaceted consumption, they reworked those tropes to highlight resistance rather than replicate commodification. The act of foregrounding their own subjectivity in the face of slavery's dehumanization allowed formerly enslaved writers to "tell a free story," in William L. Andrews's phrase, particularly when drawing on personal experiences to elaborate the meaning of metaphoric animal appetites and actual animal threats.[69] Beyond their emphasis on the perspectives of enslaved people, Black abolitionist hungry animal tropes frequently depicted overt resistance, sometimes through the willingness to violently attack pursuing animals, sometimes through the willingness to escape despite the hazardous animals upon which enslavers depended. Because hungry animals acted as figurative proxies for enslavers and also literally helped prevent escape, resisting hungry animals encapsulated both resistance to individual enslavers and an attack on the larger systems that perpetuated enslavement. Finally, whether a romance, gothic novel, or panorama, Black abolitionists staged resistance by reimagining the formats in which their hungry animal tropes appeared. As many scholars have demonstrated, Jacobs, Crafts, Douglass, and Henry "Box" Brown all took the problematic constraints of familiar generic and formal conventions and transformed them, with liberatory results.[70] The reappropriation of hungry animal tropes represented one such transformation—capitalizing on the opportunity to condemn the consumption at the heart of slavery without replicating that consumption at the heart of their work.

CONCLUSION

Henry Highland Garnet came relatively late to free produce advocacy. Despite nearly fifteen years of antislavery activism, Garnet, who had been formerly enslaved, only publicly embraced the importance of refusing slavery's products in 1849, shortly after the announcement of his planned speaking tour in Great Britain.[1] His promotion of free produce was nonetheless passionate and effective; his lectures inspired around twenty-six new British free produce societies.[2] Like many free produce advocates, Garnet expressed confidence that revealing the truth of consumption-as-connection would spark antislavery action, writing to the white Philadelphia Quaker abolitionist Samuel Rhoads that "[n]othing but light and information on the subject is needed to arouse the whole country to sally forth and to labor in the Anti-Slavery fields."[3] His speeches aimed to provoke the disgust so integral to consumption-as-connection, describing commodities as "actually spread with the sweat of the slaves, sprinkled with their tears, and fanned by their sighs" and urging audiences to "refus[e] to touch or taste . . . the products of the blood-stained fields."[4] For Garnet, disgust was crucial to inspiring audiences to reestablish ethical relations with other people, even at great distance. By offering a disturbing image of bodily contamination—eating sugar and wearing cotton imbued with sweat and blood—Garnet sought both to convince his audiences that their everyday consumption inextricably tied them to the cruelties of slavery and to channel their revulsion into antislavery consumer activism.

Aversion is the defining feature of consumption-as-connection. Unlike the imagined connections fostered by sentimentalism, in which people come to feel sympathetically bonded to distant others, consumption-as-connection uses disgust and guilt to elicit recoil, an instinctual urge to escape the taint of contact. As in Garnet's usage, these negative feelings are not an end, but rather the means of persuading people to restore ethical relations by severing the reprehensible ties that have just been exposed. Whereas critics have fiercely debated whether sympathy actually generates action, consumption-as-connection undoubtedly did. The ability to see everyday purchases as directly implicating buyers in the miseries of chattel slavery spurred the hundreds of thousands of British sugar boycotters who made up the first widespread grassroots abolitionist campaign in the late eighteenth century. It motivated even larger numbers of British sugar boycotters in the 1820s and the thousands of people in both the United States and Britain who continued to avoid the products of slavery and advocate for free labor goods until U.S. emancipation. Consumption-as-connection also drove a vast array of cultural production. From antislavery poems and pamphlets that focused on bloodstained sugar, to autobiographies and political speeches that lamented the cannibalistic nature of chattel slavery, to novels and paintings that depicted enslaved people at risk of being devoured by hungry animals, commentators throughout the Atlantic world sought to make sense of slavery's vast economic network and inhuman violence through metaphors of abject eating.

Even though the disgust at the heart of these formulations proved influential in inciting action, it was also a dangerous and unwieldy strategy in the fight against slavery. Sympathy may not have clearly led to direct action, but its affective gesture was one of rapprochement, of drawing fellow humans closer. Disgust more obviously inspired action, but it did so through an impulsive pushing away that often produced anti-Black racism as opposed to interracial solidarity. Eve Kosofsky Sedgwick's description of shame as a sort of free radical is also apt for disgust, which easily detached from its intended target (slavery) and attached instead to people of African descent.[5] This was especially true of white abolitionist constructions that frequently sought to trigger antislavery action by capitalizing on the presumed repulsion of white readers suddenly brought into close contact with Black bodies. In fact, disgust so reliably catalyzed anti-Black racism that it also infused consumption-as-connection tropes that were entirely outside an abolitionist context. Throughout blackface minstrelsy, the horrors of consumption-as-connection served to bolster racist humor and white working-class identity formation rather than to condemn slavery. Despite free produce advocates' confidence that recognizing the truth of consumer implication would galvanize action, many white supremacists saw this truth as a source of fun, with the only action galvanized being further attempts to create distance from Black people.

Black abolitionists throughout the Atlantic world nevertheless continued to deploy consumption-as-connection in the struggle for Black freedom. Many Black antislavery activists reworked consumption-as-connection in ways that suggested they recognized its potential harms but decided it was powerful enough to be worth the risk. Olaudah Equiano turned to cannibalism—the Ur-metaphor of consumption-as-connection—in a way that emphasized his own humanity. Hannah Crafts and Harriet Jacobs used depictions of hungry animals to insist that critiques of slavery must target both economics and irrational appetites. Other Black abolitionists used more conventional disgust-focused consumption-as-connection formulations. In prioritizing disgust's ability to prompt action, these abolitionists anticipated Sianne Ngai's defense of disgust as a political tactic despite past hateful uses: "The fact that the political right has more visibly and unhesitatingly instrumentalized its disgust throughout history does not mean, however, that the left lacks or should suppress its own—particularly if the harmful and contaminating qualities it identifies as intolerable are those of racism, misogyny, or the militarism of a political administration."[6] Many antislavery activists refused to relinquish the power of disgust just because it was so often weaponized against people of African descent, asserting instead that slavery as an institution remained a valid target of righteous revulsion.

In the hands of Black abolitionists, consumption-as-connection offers a story of pragmatism—of using the imperfect tools afforded by white supremacist Atlantic world institutions to attack those very institutions. When Henry Highland Garnet's British speaking tour was announced, Frederick Douglass derided Garnet's promotion of free produce as a position of convenience rather than deeply held principles, sneering that Garnet was a "practical man" willing to advocate any movement that was convenient.[7] In a fiery response, Garnet retorted that his trip was in support of both free produce and "the cause of freedom generally."[8] Garnet vigorously defended himself against Douglass's charge that he did not believe in using moral suasion by declaring that, in fact, he embraced moral, political, *and* physical tactics in the battle against slavery. In this way, he tacitly reclaimed Douglass's would-be slander of "practicality"; Garnet unapologetically advocated freedom by any means necessary.[9]

Garnet's support for free produce epitomized his emphasis on efficacy over abolitionist dogma. As Carol Faulkner puts it, "[F]or Garnet, it did not matter how slavery ended, only that it ended."[10] Garnet was optimistic that, when it came to capitalists and free labor cotton, less-than-honorable motivations could nevertheless be harnessed for the antislavery cause: "Allowing their motives to be purely commercial, yet the effect of their movement will be the same upon slavery, and will do the thing that those benevolent people desire who base their efforts upon humane and moral principles."[11] In his commitment to results rather than purity of principles, Garnet joined many other Black abolitionists in forging practical and shifting alliances instead of strictly adhering to a single abolitionist philosophy.[12] Even Douglass eventually followed suit. Within just a few years, he would break with Garrisonian orthodoxy to embrace a combination of political, moral, and even violent means to fight slavery.

The philosopher Alexis Shotwell has argued that ethical living necessitates adopting this kind of imperfect pragmatism rather than aiming for an idealized moral purity. She contends that living in the world means being "inescapably entwined and entangled with others," always complicit in "complex webs of suffering" even if we do not mean to be.[13] The "knottiness and tangle of entanglement" that she describes echoes the grievous entanglement on which my book has focused: the recognition that even apparently innocuous acts of consumption directly connected people to the global system of slavery and its depredations.[14] Shotwell condemns "purity politics" that react to the seeming inexorability of such entanglement by seeking to withdraw from connection. In Shotwell's view, such initiatives ignore the fact that personal purity is both impossible and inadequate to solving vast and complicated problems. Instead, Shotwell advocates "acting from where we are," acknowledging complicity yet still seeking an imperfect way forward through, rather than in spite of, interconnection.[15] The antislavery activism inspired by consumption-as-connection might seem to embody the purity politics that Shotwell criticizes. From early visionaries like John Woolman to the British sugar abstention campaign and the transatlantic free produce movement, consumer activists sought to purify their bodies and households from the immoral taint of slavery. The ways in which many Black abolitionists used consumption-as-connection nevertheless exemplify Shotwell's admonition to "act from where we are," embracing a doctrine of consumer purity in ways that were innovatively impure, unorthodox, and deeply pragmatic.

Although this study has focused on the eighteenth and nineteenth centuries, the ethical dimensions of consumption continue to shape both artistic production and personal action in the twenty-first century. In 2014 the U.S. artist Kara Walker captured the complexities of consumption-as-connection on a monumental scale. In a building that had formerly housed the Domino Sugar factory in Brooklyn, she created the installation *A Subtlety, or the Marvelous Sugar Baby, an Homage to the unpaid and overworked Artisans who have refined our Sweet tastes from the cane fields to the Kitchens of the New World on the Occasion of the demolition of the Domino Sugar Refining Plant*.[16] Featuring what Walker calls a "New World sphinx," an enormous sculpture of a Black woman seemingly made of white sugar, *A Subtlety* defamiliarizes an everyday commodity to link quotidian tastes with vast histories of oppression.[17] Along with the smaller sugar sculptures of Black children that surround it, the sphinx defetishizes the commodity by evoking the enslaved Black people whose labor originally transformed sugar from a rarified luxury to an everyday necessity for consumers in Europe and the United States. The figures sculpted in sugar embody the economic logic that used the fungibility of Black bodies to drive global trade. Like the eighteenth- and nineteenth-century abolitionists who embraced consumption-as-connection, Walker highlights the painful history lurking beneath the surface of sweetness, explaining that she "wanted to make something that would contain [the] sweat and labor in the histories of the totality of sugar production."[18] Her evocation of bodily fluid recalls the centrality of disgust to consumption-as-connection. The industrial location of the installation furthered the sense of disgust: The space oozed with molasses, which dripped from the walls and ceiling and emitted a strong and even nauseating odor.[19] Just as blood-sugar metaphors strove to render slavery viscerally immediate despite geographic distance, the overwhelming sights and smells of this New York art installation stressed that, in Duncan Faherty's words, "enslavement and other forms of labor exploitation were never just local issues."[20]

While *A Subtlety* defetishizes the commodity by insisting that modern tastes were forged in a global system inextricable from coerced labor, the installation simultaneously *re*-fetishizes the commodity by exposing a sexualized desire for Black bodies that is coterminous with extractive economies dependent on Black labor. Naked except for a headscarf, Walker's sphinx features enormous breasts, buttocks, and vulva. Although some commentators fretted over the many visitors who posted jokily sexualized photographs with the female figure, Walker oriented such reactions within the fundamental logic of the installation: "[H]uman behavior is so mucky and violent and messed-up and inappropriate. And I think my work draws on that."[21] The unsettling relish with which some viewers approached *A Subtlety* underscores a larger point. As we have seen throughout this study, the recognition of the enslaved labor behind a product sometimes led to consumer activism, but it also frequently fueled white desire for depictions of Black bodies as available for consumption. As when blackface minstrel performers gleefully staged enslaved people as products, Walker reminds us that histories of white supremacist oppression are often neither as hidden nor as aversive as some might like to think.

The British artist Lubaina Himid's 2002 installation *Cotton.com* shares Walker's commitment to plumbing the fraught history of a familiar commodity but offers a different vision of connection. According to Anna Arabindan-Kesson, Himid is one of multiple contemporary artists who have turned to cotton in its material form to "use the culture of the commodity . . . to comment on the legacies of colonial and transnational histories in the present."[22] Originally installed in a Manchester art gallery that was once a cotton mill, *Cotton.com* includes one hundred small canvases with abstract patterns painted in black and white. These paintings emphasize exchange. As Arabindan-Kesson notes, the paintings on the canvases (themselves made of cotton) evoke the patterns on the cotton textiles that circulated globally, but they also imaginatively stage the connection between the U.S. enslaved laborers who grew cotton and the British laborers who spun it into cloth. Inspired by British factory operatives who urged Abraham Lincoln to end slavery despite dire disruptions to the textile industry, Himid created the patterns as a visual representation of the conversations that might have occurred between cotton workers on both sides of the Atlantic.[23] Remarkably, Himid's concept originally stemmed from a scene of bodily contact straight out of consumer activist abolitionism: "This set of work imagined the cotton workers taking the cotton off the barges that had come up the ship canal and finding little bits of fabric, perhaps finding a bit of cloth, or a bit of hair, some kind of thing that had accidentally found its way from the cotton picker's body or clothes or field or whatever into these bales and managed to find its way back across the Atlantic."[24]

Whereas the prospect of finding bodily substances from enslaved laborers in a commodity had provided the primary source of disgust in consumption-as-connection formulations, Himid instead sees it as the basis for radical solidarity. In Himid's view, these bodily substances would have offered factory operatives the opportunity to imagine "how that other person lived their life," an opening that in turn allowed her to envision what a conversation between factory operatives and enslaved people might have entailed.[25] Rather than aversion, in other words, this imagined moment of proximity promoted empathy; rather than portraying enslaved people as voiceless sufferers, it enabled a two-way dialogue. As Himid conjures it, the discussion between enslaved people and factory operatives might have gone something like, "[D]o you see the situation we are in . . . we're all being done over here, stitched up here: perhaps we could try to communicate here, try to undercut, undermine this in some way."[26] Like many Black antislavery activists in the eighteenth and nineteenth centuries, Himid adopts tropes familiar from consumption-as-connection, but revises them to dismantle their deleterious tendencies. Here, bodily contact through a commodity facilitates what we might call production-as-connection, in which laborers recognize their shared exploitation and thereby lay the groundwork for revolutionary collaboration.

In many ways, the most obvious reverberation of consumption-as-connection in the twenty-first century is not contemporary art, but the pursuit of ethical relations between consumers and laborers through living wages and fair-trade products. Like their eighteenth- and nineteenth-century forbears, twenty-first-century advocates seek to render visible the hidden human tolls of everyday products to inspire consumers to disentangle themselves from exploitative networks. I wish to suggest another key lesson, however. Consumption-as-connection also illuminates what inspires people to act against vast and often apparently intractable crises like systemic racism and climate change. Although appeals to logic or sympathy represent the most familiar rhetorical strategies in these cases, this study reminds us that less noble affects like disgust and fear of contamination may be even more successful in producing action, despite potential pernicious side effects. Just as Black abolitionists continued to deploy consumption-as-connection while reworking its problematic aspects, contemporary activists might aim for efficacy over perfection while nevertheless striving to make both their rhetoric and their world ever more just.

NOTES

INTRODUCTION

1. Throughout this book I capitalize "Black" in reference to people of African descent, both to denote the cultural significance of shared experiences (Crenshaw, "Race, Reform, and Retrenchment," 1332) and as a mark of respect in opposition to historical belittlement (Du Bois, "Letter," 390). Because this book examines how ideas about race combined with ideas about consumption to shape responses to slavery, it frequently examines racist material. I believe that developing a nuanced understanding of consumption in relation to slavery requires close consideration of even upsetting texts, as they form a significant vein in the larger cultural pattern. Nevertheless, I recognize and respect the reasons other scholars have chosen not to reproduce such material (see Rusert, *Fugitive Science*, 25–26, on the decision not to reproduce racist images; Fielder, *Relative Races*, 247n28, on the decision not to print the N-word in quotations, and Mitchell, "Teaching and the N-Word," on approaches to the N-word in teaching and professional settings). I acknowledge that such material impacts different readers differently. In writing about harmful racialization, there is the risk of amplifying its underlying fallacies. In writing about painful subjects, there is the risk of causing more pain. I hope that deeper understanding of this conceptual framework, as well

as the ways Black commentators used it while challenging its problematic tendencies, will nevertheless prove worthwhile.

2. Woolman, *Journal and Major Essays*, 162.
3. Andrew White notes that the strange animal also serves as a fitting image for colonialism more broadly ("'Consuming' Oppression," 12).
4. Davis, *Problem of Slavery*, 485, 489–90.
5. Woolman, *Journal and Major Essays*, 156–58. Scholars continue to refine language in an attempt to avoid replicating the dehumanization of slavery. To disaggregate the person from the condition of enslavement, I avoid the term "slave" in reference to people. When I refer to the overarching system or to the provenance of certain crops, I often use terms like "slavery" or "slave-grown," since these refer to categories and classifications rather than people. For a nuanced discussion of the choice to use older terminology in certain situations, see Miles, *All That She Carried*, 287–89.
6. Woolman, *Journal and Major Essays*, 96, 185.
7. For estimated numbers of enslaved people transported across the Atlantic, see Eltis, "Transatlantic Slave Trade," 43, table 1. On the "consumer revolution" in England, see McKendrick et al., *Birth of a Consumer Society*, introduction and chapter 1; in America, see Breen, "'Baubles of Britain.'"
8. On the centrality of sugar, see Mintz, *Sweetness and Power* (esp. 45, 63–67), and Austen and Smith, "Private Tooth Decay." While there is far less information about sugar consumption in British colonial America than in Britain, available information suggests that, by 1770, the thirteen colonies imported less sugar per capita than Britain but much more rum and molasses, resulting in a higher overall per capita consumption of sugar products (Shammas, "English and Anglo-American Consumption," 183).
9. Mintz, *Sweetness and Power*, 175.
10. On sympathy and moral philosophers, see Festa, *Sentimental Figures*, 22–36; Todd, *Sensibility*, 24–28; and Merish, *Sentimental Materialism*, 48–54. On the rise of sentimental literature and its relation to sensibility, see Todd, *Sensibility*; McGann, *Poetics of Sensibility*; and M. Ellis, *Politics of Sensibility*.
11. According to Janet Todd, moral philosophy and literature worked together to make "sentimental theory and art . . . extremely widespread in England, touching the perceptions of most literate and semi-literate people" (*Sensibility*, 3–4). Sarah Knott, in *Sensibility and the American Revolution*, argues that sensibility was central to American independence.
12. M. Ellis, *Politics of Sensibility*, 3.
13. On "commercial humanism," see Pocock, *Virtue, Commerce, and History*. On the relationship between sentiment and capitalism, see M. Ellis, *Politics of*

Sensibility, and Gould, *Barbaric Traffic*. Eric Williams first advanced the argument that abolitionism and capitalism were closely related. For a discussion of Williams's highly influential work, see C. Brown, *Moral Capital*, 12–16.
14. Haskell, "Part 2," 551; "Part 1," 360; "Part 2," 566n42. For challenges to Haskell's thesis, see Bender, *Antislavery Debate*, and Boulukos, "Capitalism and Slavery."
15. Glickman, *Buying Power*, xi, 7.
16. Williams, *Keywords*, 42.
17. Ibid.
18. Cooper, *Letters on the Slave Trade*, 25. We can conclude that the "consumption" here represents the economic sense (rather than the sense of destruction) for two reasons. First, earlier on the same page, Cooper refers to an "average annual consumption" of 100,000 people, which corresponds to his earlier statement that "[t]he average import of slaves into the European colonies may be 100,000" (ibid., 24), indicating the consumption here describes importation. Second, Cooper's source text, the Abbé Raynal's *A Philosophical and Political History of the Settlements and Trade of the Europeans in the East and West Indies* (vol. 4), uses this figure in terms of transport rather than destruction: "eight or nine millions of slaves that have been conveyed there [the New World]" (Raynal, *Philosophical and Political History*, 4:117). While he doesn't use the terminology of consumption, the prominent English abolitionist Thomas Clarkson explicitly evokes sales in his citation of the same figures from Raynal: "[S]ince the slave-trade began, *nine millions* of men have been torn from their dearest connections, and sold into slavery" (*Essay on the Slavery and Commerce*, 76–77, italics original).
19. *Slavery and the Internal Slave Trade*, 25, emphasis original. Published in London and featuring responses by the American Anti-Slavery Society to questions posed by the British and Foreign Anti-Slavery Society, this text emphasizes the transatlantic nature of this discourse.
20. Cooper, *Letters on the Slave Trade*, 25.
21. Douglass, "What to the Slave Is the Fourth of July?," 120.
22. The historian Seymour Drescher has confirmed as reasonable contemporary estimates that 300,000 families participated in the British Sugar Abstention Campaign in 1791–92 (*Capitalism and Antislavery*, 78–79). In contrast to antislavery petitions, the "anti-saccharite" movement radically expanded abolitionist membership to include women and children (Drescher, "Public Opinion," 55). Because my study focuses on those geographically distant to slavery who may not have otherwise understood themselves as directly connected to slavery, I refer to organized antislavery campaigns in Britain and,

later, in the northern United States rather than to the sustained antislavery resistance practiced by enslaved people in the Caribbean and United States.
23. Sheller, *Consuming the Caribbean*, 72.
24. K. Tompkins, *Racial Indigestion*, 92.
25. In general, my project takes a similar approach to that described by Mimi Sheller, whose transhistorical investigation of the Caribbean in relation to Europe and North America seeks "to bring together within one analytic framework an analysis of both economic relations and symbolic relations of consumption" (*Consuming the Caribbean*, 4). Where my study diverges is in uncovering the relationship between economics, symbols, and the underlying logic of chattel slavery, and in investigating how that relationship enabled both antislavery action and anti-Black racism.
26. K. Tompkins, *Racial Indigestion*, 103; Woodard, *Delectable Negro*, 18. See also Piersen, *Black Legacy*, 12.
27. Vincent Woodard (*Delectable Negro*, passim) and Kyla Wazana Tompkins (*Racial Indigestion*, 93–103) argue that cannibalism metaphors express the violent desires of white supremacy, while Charlotte Sussman (*Consuming Anxieties*, 115–17) and Mimi Sheller (*Consuming the Caribbean*, 107–10, 143–73) relate cannibalism metaphors to sugar as a commodity and specific historical discourse about the Caribbean.
28. Lawrence B. Glickman notes that proslavery proponents used similar consumer activist techniques to encourage Southerners to avoid buying Northern products, but his examples demonstrate that the mechanics worked differently than in the antislavery "Free Produce" version, focusing on harming an adversary by refusing financial support (and thereby taking inspiration from revolutionary boycott [*Buying Power*, 95]) rather than on the intimate connection between the bodies of producers and consumers (ibid., 115–16).
29. Baptist, *Half Has Never Been Told*, 89; Beckert, *Empire of Cotton*, 98–120.
30. Sinha, *Slave's Cause*, 104.
31. Holcomb, *Moral Commerce*, 36–38.
32. Ibid., 90, 107.
33. Lynn Festa echoes Thomas Haskell's thesis of market-based remote consequences while arguing that sentimentalism was a vehicle by which such consequences could be grasped (*Sentimental Figures*, 8).
34. See Barnes, "Affecting Relations"; Dobson, "Reclaiming Sentimental Literature"; Sánchez-Eppler, *Touching Liberty*; Greyser, *On Sympathetic Grounds*; and Moody, *Sentimental Confessions*. Of course, the phrase "imaginative connections" evokes Benedict Anderson's "imagined communities," but what interests me here isn't a sense of broad belonging in a geographically dispersed community—though sentimental literature can certainly serve that function

as well—but rather a sense of intimate connection between individuals through consumption practices.
35. Sánchez-Eppler, *Touching Liberty*, 27.
36. The rise of sentimental literature in the eighteenth century corresponded with an explosion in book publishing (Campbell, *Romantic Ethic*, 26–27). The paradigmatic work of American sentimental literature, *Uncle Tom's Cabin*, also inspired a flood of mass-market merchandise, including commemorative plates, sheet music, figurines, and card games (Hirsch, "Uncle Tomitudes," 311–20). On the relationship between sentimentalism and consumerism, see A. Douglas, *Feminization of American Culture*; Berlant, *Female Complaint*; Merish, *Sentimental Materialism*; and G. Brown, *Domestic Individualism*.
37. Sarah Mesle ("Sentimentalism's Nation"), Joycelyn Moody (*Sentimental Confessions*), Brycchan Carey (*British Abolitionism and the Rhetoric of Sensibility*), and Cindy Weinstein (*Family, Kinship, and Sympathy*) all point out that there is nothing "inherently antislavery" (Moody, *Sentimental Confessions*, 10) about sentimentalism, but rather that it was deployed by people with varying ideological investments.
38. Greyser, *On Sympathetic Grounds*, 3.
39. Even scholars who have sought to complicate typical understandings of sympathy have underlined sentimentalism's focus on love. Cindy Weinstein has argued that nineteenth-century sentimental fictions deployed complex varieties of sympathy to reconfigure families based on love rather than consanguinity. Marianne Noble maintains that sympathy does not mean an erasure of difference but nevertheless centers on "caring non-knowing" (*Rethinking Sympathy*, 3). Kevin Pelletier seeks to unsettle the critical focus on love alone in relation to sentimental literature by introducing the centrality of terror, but he nevertheless argues that fear serves to "bolster[] love when love falters" (*Apocalyptic Sentimentalism*, 3).
40. Dobson, "Reclaiming Sentimental Literature," 267.
41. Ibid., 268.
42. Miller, *Anatomy of Disgust*, xii, 9.
43. Ngai, *Ugly Feelings*, 35; Miller, *Anatomy of Disgust*, 194.
44. Miller, *Anatomy of Disgust*, 194, 202; Ngai, *Ugly Feelings*, 354.
45. As Teresa A. Goddu has argued in *Gothic America*, the American gothic works to reveal what might otherwise remain hidden in U.S. national mythology.
46. There is a risk of reducing critical debates about sentimentalism to an oversimplified list of proponents and opponents. While an extended discussion of various scholarly positions is beyond the scope of this introduction, I note the many scholars who have approached the topic of sentimentality with attention to both its opportunities and potential harms, including Greyser, *On*

Sympathetic Grounds; Wanzo, *Suffering*; Moody, *Sentimental Confessions*; Noble, *Masochistic Pleasures*; Foreman, *Activist Sentiments*; and Jay, *White Writers, Race Matters*.

47. On the positive transformative aspects of sentimentalism, see Fisher. *Hard Facts*; J. Tompkins, *Sensational Designs*; and Weinstein, *Family, Kinship, and Sympathy*. On uneven power dynamics, see Yao, *Disaffected*; Schuller, *Biopolitics of Feeling*; Sánchez-Eppler, *Touching Liberty*; and E. Sedgwick, *Epistemology*, 150–51. On the dubious pleasures of sentimentalism, see Baldwin, "Everybody's Protest Novel"; Noble, *Masochistic Pleasures*; and Chow, *Sentimental Fabulations*. On the displacement of the experiences of those actually suffering, see Hartman, *Scenes of Subjection*, and Berlant, *Female Complaint*.

48. Jean Fagan Yellin asserts that, despite its spiritually focused attack on patriarchal institutions, *Uncle Tom's Cabin* ultimately "counter[s] the practical measures urged by the black and white activists" ("Doing It Herself," 102). See also Berlant, *Female Complaint*; Baldwin, "Everybody's Protest Novel"; and A. Douglas, *Feminization of American Culture*.

49. Both Marianne Noble (*Masochistic Pleasures*, 145) and Cindy Weinstein (*Family, Kinship, and Sympathy*, 6) passionately assert the ability of sentiment to spur real action, especially against slavery. Most scholars offer a somewhat more mixed assessment, emphasizing sentimentalism as paving the way for (rather than directly instigating) political action. Philip Fisher, for instance, calls sentimentalism a "politically radical technique" (*Hard Facts*, 17) that "arouses and excites action" (ibid., 18), but he also characterizes its immediate effects as interior (ibid., 20) and acknowledges a tendency to cultivate a sense of helplessness with certain conventions (ibid., 110). This ambivalence echoes Jane Tompkins, whose strident defense of sentimentalism's cultural impact depends on redefining that impact in distinction to typical understandings of political efficacy (*Sensational Designs*, 128). Even Rebecca Wanzo, who reminds us that political impact need not be perfect to be present (*Suffering*, 27), adopts the language of sentimentalism as the unseen foundation of subsequent action rather than necessarily a direct call itself (ibid., 13).

50. Baldwin, "Everybody's Protest Novel," 12.

51. Similarly, Angus Connell Brown has argued that close reading can bridge "the diverging methods of formalist criticism and cultural studies" ("Cultural Studies and Close Reading," 1192).

52. Goldsby, *Spectacular Secret*, 4; Coviello, *Intimacy in America*, 18.

53. I am, like Stephen Greenblatt, ultimately interested in how both literary and nonliterary texts can reveal the "imaginative universe" ("Touch of the Real," 27) that facilitated them.

54. Black, *Models and Metaphors*, 40.

55. Ricœur, "Metaphorical Process," 147. Ricœur's insistence that the new proximity facilitated by metaphors is "'felt' as well as 'seen.'" (ibid., 156) is particularly germane to consumption-as-connection, which attempts to engender intimate and even physical sensations as it proposes its intentionally horrifying new proximities.
56. Ibid., 153, 154.

1. BLOOD-SUGAR METAPHORS IN BRITISH ABOLITIONISM

1. Coleridge, "On the Slave Trade," in *Slavery, Abolition, and Emancipation*, 2:218. Coleridge delivered his "Lecture on the Slave-Trade" in Bristol in 1795 before publishing it the following year in his periodical *The Watchman*.
2. Coleridge, "On the Slave Trade," in *Slavery, Abolition, and Emancipation*, 2:219.
3. Gikandi, *Slavery and the Culture of Taste*, 109.
4. The term "boycott" is anachronistic and actually dates to 1880, when James Redpath and John O'Malley coined it in reference to Irish tenants who refused rent payments to Charles Cunningham Boycott (Glickman, *Buying Power*, 115–16). As Charlotte Sussman notes, "Antisaccharite" consumers in the late eighteenth century thought of themselves as participating in an abstention movement (*Consuming Anxieties*, 1). On numbers of abstention participants, see Drescher, *Capitalism and Antislavery*, 78–79.
5. Fox, *Address*, 2; Merry, "Slaves," 102. The blood-sugar metaphor also appears in writings about the Hispanophone and Francophone Caribbean: The historian Robert Paquette takes the title of his book about a planned Cuban uprising from the common planter saying "'*Con sangre se hace azúcar*'—'Sugar is made with blood'" (Paquette, *Sugar*, 56); the French philosopher Claude Adrien Helvétius describes the many ways people die in all parts of the slave trade and slavery in Saint Domingue before observing, "[O]ne will acknowledge that not a single barrel of sugar arrives in Europe that isn't stained with human blood" ["on conviendra qu'il n'arrive point de barrique de sucre en Europe qui ne soit teinte de sang humain"] (*De L'esprit*, 25 [my translation].) Nonetheless, the British abstention movement was unique in generating widespread popular support, and its use of blood-sugar metaphors is particularly significant in that those metaphors captured the imagination of a significant segment of the population. For figures on reprintings of Fox's pamphlet, see Whelan, "William Fox, Martha Gurney," 402.

6. Sussman, *Consuming Anxieties*, 116. See also Coleman, "Conspicuous Consumption," 349.
7. Morton, *Poetics of Spice*, 172–73.
8. Coleman, "Conspicuous Consumption," 358–59.
9. In addition to Coleman, "Conspicuous Consumption," see Sussman, *Consuming Anxieties*, 15–17, and Sheller, "Bleeding Humanity."
10. William Fox's pamphlet was published in the United States as well (Holcomb, *Moral Commerce*, 43). There was also a U.S. movement to replace cane sugar with maple sugar. On the maple sugar movement as an intersection of abolitionism, economic nationalism, and (eventually) racist fears stoked by the Haitian Revolution, see Faherty, *Haitian Revolution*, 84–114.
11. For rare examinations of these sonnets, see Morton, *Poetics of Spice*, 195–204, and Kitson, "Slave Resistance and Revolt," 112–18.
12. Coleridge, "On the Slave Trade," in *Slavery, Abolition, and Emancipation*, 2:218.
13. Marx, *Capital*, 165.
14. Pietz, "Problem of the Fetish, I," 7.
15. Best, *Fugitive's Properties*, 17.
16. Part of sugar's growing popularity was based on its ability to preserve food. In light of Coleridge's anti-commodity fetishism, the sense of preservation already implied with "conserves" may also apply to his vision of a commodity that visibly conserves and maintains the human labor that created it. See Mintz, *Sweetness and Power*, 123, 125.
17. Coleridge, "On the Slave Trade," in *Slavery, Abolition, and Emancipation*, 2:218.
18. At the time of his lecture, Coleridge was a Unitarian, but he had been raised in Church of England orthodoxy. In his extended examination of Coleridge's religious beliefs after his later return to Trinitarian Christianity, J. Robert Barth notes that Coleridge maintained his opposition to transubstantiation (*Coleridge and Christian Doctrine*, 175).
19. Kilgour, *From Communion to Cannibalism*, 83.
20. Coleridge, "Lecture on the Slave-Trade," in *Collected Works*, 2:248.
21. Milton, *Complete Prose Works*, 6:560. Earlier in the chapter Milton makes the cannibal connection explicit, lamenting how such "monstrous doctrines . . . practically turn[] the Lord's Supper into a cannibal feast" (6:554).
22. Winthrop D. Jordan argues that this effect was particularly pronounced in England (*White over Black*, 7).
23. Coleridge, "On the Slave Trade," in *Slavery, Abolition, and Emancipation*, 2:218–19.
24. Hartman, *Scenes of Subjection*, 94.
25. Ricœur, "Metaphorical Process," 147.

26. Sánchez-Eppler, *Touching Liberty*, 3. The examples in this section participate in what Cristin Ellis has called the biologically racist "attempt to quarantine privileged populations from the illiberal taint of their own materiality" (*Antebellum Posthuman*, 5).
27. Cowper, *Poems*, 3:13.
28. Kilner, *Rotchfords*, 2:105.
29. As Toni Morrison observes of white-authored American texts, "[T]he subject of the dream is the dreamer," in which portrayals of people of African descent represent a "powerful exploration of the fears and desires that reside in the writerly conscious" (*Playing*, 17). Dorothy Kilner's depiction captures the white drive to conjure imagined Black figures out of long-standing racist ideas like the association between Blackness and dirt (Jordan, *White over Black*, 7).
30. Kilner, *Rotchfords*, 2:105.
31. Ibid., 2:110.
32. Ibid.
33. Birkett, "Poem on the African Slave Trade," 211.
34. Ibid., 201, 215.
35. Ibid., 202–3.
36. Ibid., 208.
37. Falconbridge, *Account of the Slave Trade*, 32.
38. *Furibond*, 288.
39. Fox, *Address*, 156; 159; 156.
40. Ibid., 156.
41. Ibid.
42. Burn, *Second Address*, 3.
43. According to Charlotte Sussman, "[T]he insistence on the literal possibility of consuming the bodily fluids of slaves we find in the 'Second Address' is unusual, if not unique, in antislavery rhetoric" (*Consuming Anxieties*, 121). Carl Plasa writes that "such literalization puts [Burn's text] significantly out of step with the trends of its time" ("Stained with Spots," 227).
44. Burn, *Second Address*, 2.
45. Ibid.
46. Ibid.
47. Ibid., 6.
48. Ibid., 7.
49. Fittingly for someone who insists upon physical reality, Burn's pamphlet is dominated by the language of visuality—he writes based on "ocular demonstration" about these "plain matters of fact," which are "as clear as the noonday Sun" (ibid). This is not the realm of imagination and metaphors; it is the

realm of the visible real. Indeed, his argument's dependence on bodily fluids seems predicated on various eruptions of visibility, of bringing into the open what had previously been hidden.

50. Ibid.
51. Ibid.
52. Ibid., 8. Burn's biblical reference contributes to the underlying sense of excess (after God met Gideon's challenge by imbuing the fleece with dew while leaving the surrounding ground dry, Gideon was able to squeeze a bowlful of water from it [see Judges 6:37–38]) while also indulging in racial stereotyping. Next to Burn's earlier epithetic description of the enslaved man's "woolly head," the reference parallels the Black man's body and domestic livestock.
53. Ibid.
54. Ibid., 9.
55. Ibid.
56. Ibid., 8.
57. On "impregnated" as raising the specter of miscegenation, see Plasa, "Stained with Spots," 238. On blood-sugar metaphors as encoding white fears of miscegenation more broadly, see Coleman, "Conspicuous Consumption," 356–59.
58. See Sussman, *Consuming Anxieties*, 111.
59. Burn, *Second Address*, 12. According to Cowper's "Epigram," "No Nostrum, Planters say, is half so good / To make fine sugar, as a *Negro*'s blood" (*Poems*, 3:183). Like Coleridge's antislavery lecture, Cowper's poem combines imagery of cannibalistic consumption with divine sacrifice by satirically equating the practice of putting lamb's blood into wine with enhancing sugar with the blood of enslaved people. On Christian overtones of the lamb, see Tong, "'Pity,'" 137.
60. Burn, *Second Address*, 12.
61. Southey, *Poems*, 35.
62. Ibid., 33.
63. Ibid.
64. Ibid., 35.
65. Ibid., 37.
66. Ibid., 38.
67. Ibid., 35.
68. Mimi Sheller makes a similar point when discussing the inescapable "distinctions and hierarchies" that mark the visual emblems of the abolition movement ("Bleeding Humanity," 175).
69. Southey, *Poems*, 38.
70. Ibid., 36, 33.
71. See Piersen, *Black Legacy*, 5–12; Thornton, "Cannibals," 273–75; and Woodard, *Delectable Negro*, 56–57.

72. Equiano, *Interesting Narrative*, 55.
73. On Equiano's strategic depiction of naïveté, see Smith, *Self-Discovery and Authority*, 15–20; Stein, "Who's Afraid of Cannibals?," 98; and Rice, "Who's Eating Whom," 113.
74. Equiano, *Interesting Narrative*, 56.
75. Ibid., 57.
76. Ibid., 60.
77. Ibid., 60–61.
78. Prince, *History of Mary Prince*, 62.
79. Ibid., 63.
80. Ibid., 71.
81. Ibid., 94.
82. See Hoermann, "'Very Hell of Horrors,'" and Clavin, "Race, Rebellion, and the Gothic."
83. Hoermann, "'Very Hell of Horrors,'" 191.
84. Qtd. in Geggus, "Haitian Revolution," 47.
85. The zombie represents yet another nexus between cannibalism and slavery, especially in relation to Haiti. As Sarah Juliet Lauro argues, the zombie serves as a figure of both enslavement and resistance, even though its association with cannibalism developed after the Haitian Revolution (*Transatlantic Zombie*).

2. AMBIVALENT CONNECTIONS IN FREE PRODUCE ABOLITIONISM

1. Harper, *Brighter Coming Day*, 45.
2. Ibid.
3. See "Eliza Harris" (Harper, *Poems*, 9–11) and "Eva's Farewell" (ibid., 32).
4. Glickman, *Buying Power*, 64.
5. Kett, "Quaker Women," 140. The idea of ethically sourced produce did not originate with nineteenth-century free produce advocates, however. Even Fox's widely reproduced eighteenth-century sugar abstention pamphlet mentions the possibility of free labor sugar (*Address*, 161).
6. There was nevertheless still a strong theme of moral purification and asceticism that dominated Quaker approaches to free produce (Holcomb, *Moral Commerce*, 34).
7. Faulkner, "Root of the Evil," 383–85; Robertson, *Hearts Beating for Liberty*, 84; Kett, "Quaker Women," 142; Glickman, *Buying Power*, 69, 71; Philadelphia Free Produce Association of Friends, *Address to the Members*, 13.

8. Holcomb, *Moral Commerce*, 89–90, 94.
9. Heyrick, *Immediate, Not Gradual Abolition*, 15.
10. Faulkner, "Root of the Evil," 380. As Manisha Sinha notes, the Anglo-American turn to immediatism was directly inspired by the uprisings and advocacy of free and enslaved Black activists (*Slave's Cause*, 196–97).
11. Midgley, *Feminism and Empire*, 63.
12. Holcomb, *Moral Commerce*, 107.
13. BERA, "Ladies' Department," 134; "Consumers," 169–70; William Garrison, "Products of Slavery," 66.
14. "How Do We Know?," 37, italics original.
15. Ibid.
16. Chandler, *Essays*, 61.
17. Holcomb, *Moral Commerce*, 121.
18. McKnight, *Frances E. W. Harper*, 18.
19. In contrast to the hundreds of thousands of British sugar abstainers in the 1790s and 1820s, free produce practitioners in the United States numbered below an estimated 10,000 at the height of the movement (Holcomb, *Moral Commerce*, 189).
20. To some extent, suspicion about the ethics of consumption also put the free produce movement at odds with widely adopted strategies of the antebellum abolitionist movement. On the consumer culture of antislavery fairs, see Goddu, *Selling Antislavery*, 85–107.
21. William Garrison, "Products of Slave Labor," 38.
22. Wendell Garrison, "Free Produce," 492; Walker, "Products of Slave Labor," 39.
23. Wilkinson, "Philadelphia Free Produce Attack," 307–8.
24. Holcomb, *Moral Commerce*, 190.
25. See Holcomb, *Moral Commerce*; McDonald, "Consuming with a Conscience"; and Conrad, "'Polluted Luxuries.'"
26. Conrad, "'Polluted Luxuries,'" 11.
27. Ibid., 11, 2.
28. Thoreau, "Resistance," 17.
29. Ibid., 7.
30. That is not to say that Thoreau's withdrawal was apolitical, of course. As Alda Balthrop-Lewis has argued, Thoreau's asceticism was personal *and* political—designed to simplify his life and alter the capitalist conditions of his world (*Thoreau's Religion*, 96–97).
31. Ibid., 97.
32. Thoreau, *Walden*, 26.
33. Balthrop-Lewis, *Thoreau's Religion*, 99.
34. Thoreau, *Walden*, 116.

35. Ibid.
36. Thoreau does express concern for the well-being of those transporting goods as well as condemnation of the consumer appetite for superfluous luxuries in a lecture he began giving in the same year he published *Walden* (later published as the posthumous essay "Life Without Principle"). He incredulously muses on "[a] commerce that whitens every sea in quest of nuts and raisins, and makes slaves of its sailors for this purpose!" and on the fact that many sailors drown as a result of the trade ("Life Without Principle," 364). His constructions do not focus on the materiality of the commodities themselves, however.
37. See the introduction for a more extensive discussion of critiques of sentimentalism. On nineteenth-century critiques of sentimentalism, see Brady, "Theorizing a Reading Public," 723.
38. J. Tompkins, *Sensational Designs*, 145.
39. Merish, *Sentimental Materialism*, 4.
40. On the revolutionary free produce insight that markets could be exploited for good, see Glickman, *Buying Power*, 77–78.
41. Stowe, *Uncle Tom's Cabin*, 404.
42. Stowe, *Key to "Uncle Tom's Cabin,"* 501–2.
43. Stowe, *Uncle Tom's Cabin*, 65.
44. Stowe, *Key to "Uncle Tom's Cabin,"* 497.
45. Michaels, *Gold Standard*, 104.
46. Schermerhorn, *Business of Slavery*, 3–4.
47. Stowe, *Uncle Tom's Cabin*, 297–98.
48. Ibid., 300.
49. Ibid., 130.
50. Ibid.
51. Ibid.
52. Schoolman, *Abolitionist Geographies*, 129.
53. Stowe, *Uncle Tom's Cabin*, 121. The only scholarly reference I've found to *Uncle Tom's Cabin* in the context of the free produce movement refers to this passage alone (Glickman, *Buying Power*, 75, 329n19).
54. Stowe, *Uncle Tom's Cabin*, 128.
55. See Ammons, "Stowe's Dream," 168; Moers, *Harriet Beecher Stowe*, 25; and G. Brown, *Domestic Individualism*, 25, 32.
56. Stowe, *Uncle Tom's Cabin*, 121.
57. The Quaker antislavery activist and merchant James Mott (husband of Lucretia Mott) initially sold free labor cotton, but within a year had switched entirely to wool (Faulkner, "Root of the Evil," 389). In 1850 a free produce newspaper approvingly noted a "Wool League" started in England: "In advocating the

substitution of wool for cotton, the champions of the League avail themselves of the incontrovertible argument . . . against the use of cotton cultivated and ginned by slave labor" ("'Wool League,'" 205).

58. On the Halliday home as idealized separation from the market, see J. Tompkins, *Sensational Designs*, 141; G. Brown, *Domestic Individualism*, 25; and Logan, "Conventional Nineteenth-Century," 50.
59. Gallagher, "Bagging Factory," 179; Stowe, *Uncle Tom's Cabin*, 122, 175.
60. David Reynolds has identified Catherine and Levi Coffin as the sole inspirations for Rachel and Simeon Halliday (*Mightier Than the Sword*, 100), an assumption that Coffin himself did not deny in his memoirs (*Reminiscences*, 147). In *The Key to "Uncle Tom's Cabin,"* Stowe was more evasive: "The character of Rachel Halliday was a real one, but she has passed away to her reward" (a fact that, if true, would rule out Catherine Coffin, who died in 1881). "Simeon Halliday, calmly risking fine and imprisonment for his love to God and man, has had in this country many counterparts among the sect" (98).
61. Coffin, *Reminiscences*, 274, 293.
62. Ibid., 274.
63. "Letter from Mrs. Stowe"; Wilkinson, "Philadelphia Free Produce Attack," 309.
64. Stowe, *Uncle Tom's Cabin*, 404, italics original. That is not to say that Stowe's admonition, which appears in the novel's final chapter, represents the whole of sentimentalism, of course. As Marianne Noble trenchantly reminds us, "Sympathy is more complex than the first few pages of *The Theory of Moral Sentiments* and the last few pages of *Uncle Tom's Cabin*" (*Rethinking Sympathy*, 4).
65. *Who Are the Slaveholders?*, 10.
66. Harper, *Brighter Coming Day*, 101. That the speech originally happened at the anniversary meeting can be gathered from the larger context of the May 23, 1857, *National Anti-Slavery Standard*, in which it was reprinted.
67. In addition to dramatically increasing the circulation of *Punch*, the magazine in which it originally appeared, "The Song of the Shirt" proliferated through multiple periodicals, songs, consumer objects, and even paintings and illustrations (Edelstein, "They Sang 'The Song of the Shirt,'" 184).
68. Hood, "The Song of the Shirt," 260.
69. Ibid.
70. Ibid.
71. Ibid.
72. Chandler, *Essays*, 87–88. Chandler's essay originally appeared in the December 1831 edition of the *Genius of Universal Emancipation* newspaper.
73. Conrad, "'Polluted Luxuries,'" 14.

74. Chandler, *Essays*, 88.
75. Ibid.
76. Chandler, *Poetical Works*, 111. The poem originally appeared in the July 1831 edition of the *Genius of Universal Emancipation*.
77. Ibid.
78. Harper, "Free Labor Movement," 3.
79. Chandler, *Essays*, 88.
80. Miller, *Anatomy of Disgust*, 90.
81. Harper, "Free Labor Movement," 2.
82. Chandler, *Poetical Works*, 109.
83. Harper, *Poems*, 35.
84. Schuller, *Biopolitics of Feeling*, 74.
85. Harper, *Poems*, 35–36.
86. Ibid., 35.
87. Ibid., 36.
88. Melville, *Moby-Dick*, 391.
89. Ibid., 395.
90. Ibid.
91. Ibid., 224. Geoffrey Kirsch has argued that what is most significant in this line is not personal guilt, but the sense of shared responsibility for worker injuries that anticipates the move toward workers' compensation ("Loss Without Remedy," 49).
92. Melville, *Typee*, 220.
93. Ibid.
94. Cottom, *Cannibals and Philosophers*, 153.
95. Melville, *Moby-Dick*, 288.
96. Ibid., 299.
97. On Melville's cannibalism imagery, see Bohrer, "Melville's New Witness," 80; and Pettey, "Cannibalism." For analysis of the supposed actual cannibalism of characters like Queequeg or the Taipi, see Herbert, *Marquesan Encounters*; Breitwieser, "False Sympathy"; Sanborn, *Sign of the Cannibal*; Hoffman, *Form and Fable*; and Zoellner, *Salt-Sea Mastodon*.
98. Melville, *Moby-Dick*, 319.
99. Hartman, *Scenes of Subjection*, 21.
100. Melville, *Moby-Dick*, 325.
101. Ibid., 324. Josh Doty also notes the intertwined significance of sharks, cannibalism, and eating in *Moby-Dick*, but argues that Melville depicts ungovernable appetites to critique nineteenth-century dietetic reform and express the unlikelihood of truly controlling base urges (*Perfecting of Nature*, 64–70).
102. Melville, *Moby-Dick*, 299.

3. BLACKFACE MINSTRELSY AND THE DISAVOWAL OF CONSUMPTION'S CONNECTIONS

1. Mahar, *Behind the Burnt Cork Mask*, 21.
2. Winans, "Early Minstrel Show Music," 151.
3. Ibid.
4. I assume that the speaker of the song is Black because of the use of dialect and the fact that he plans to marry an enslaved woman, but it is worth noting that neither dialect nor blackface makeup necessarily provides a sure indicator of a character's racial identity (Mahar, *Behind the Burnt Cork Mask*, 100).
5. Nathan, "Performance of the Virginia Minstrels," 42n17, 40; Lott, *Love and Theft*, 136, 52.
6. Lott, *Love and Theft*.
7. On blackface minstrelsy in Britain and beyond, see Meer, *Uncle Tom Mania*; Thelwell, *Exporting Jim Crow*; and Pickering, "Blackface Songster in Britain."
8. The extent to which blackface minstrelsy is racist has been the source of much scholarly debate. See Toll, *Blacking Up*; Lott, *Love and Theft*; Cockrell, *Demons of Disorder*; Lhamon Jr., *Raising Cain*; and Jones, *Captive Stage*.
9. *Christy's*, 41.
10. Ibid., 42.
11. Deyle, *Carry Me Back*, 60.
12. "Virginia Slave Crop," 1.
13. *Christy's Ram's Horn*, 22; *Negro Singer's*, 219; *Christy's*, 204.
14. *Negro Singer's*, 306; *Christy's*, 90.
15. Lhamon Jr., *Raising Cain*, 188.
16. "The Old Pee Dee" (*Negro Forget-Me-Not*, 235–36), "Ring de Hoop an' Blow de Horn" (*Christy's*, 75–77), and "Latest Version of Going Ober de Mountain" (*Deacon Snowball's Negro Melodies*) all feature variations on the final verse, which here is quoted from *The Negro Forget-Me-Not*, 235–37. "De Nigger's Possum Hunt" proclaims, "In Jarsey dar de niggers breed, / If you only sow his wool for seed" (*De Shiney Eye*). "Away to de Sugar Cane Field" (ibid.) includes a more pedestrian reference to a deceased body simply helping to fertilize sugar cane.
17. *Christy's*, 166.
18. Lott, *Love and Theft*, 150. Michael Pickering sees such instances in British minstrel songsters as prefigurations of late nineteenth-century commodity

racism and exemplary of the British fascination with puns ("Blackface Songster in Britain," 189–90).
19. Lott, *Love and Theft*, 151.
20. The *Tobacco Dictionary* includes several entries for such tobacco products (Jahn, *Tobacco Dictionary*, 111, 113).
21. "Cannibalism."
22. Freedgood, *Ideas in Things*, 83. Freedgood argues that Dickens's references to the tobacco encode the genocide of Indigenous people in Australia.
23. *Frank Brower's*, 31.
24. There were white working-class abolitionists, but they were in the minority. See Cockrell, *Demons of Disorder*, 191n68.
25. Roediger, *Wages of Whiteness*, 65–77.
26. Blackface minstrel fantasies of self-perpetuating labor provide an interesting parallel to fantasies about coral in the same period. As Michele Currie Navakas has shown, antebellum Americans justified extractive labor in part by imagining coral reefs as the result of "'coral insects,' whose labor is inexhaustible because it meets all their needs, while fusing them so fully to the reef that the body becomes inseparable from the labor product" (*Coral Lives*, 55).
27. *Christy's*, 42.
28. His willingness to be hung up anticipates early twentieth-century depictions of hanging Raggedy Ann, which, as Robin Bernstein has demonstrated, mimics lynching but replaces it with a cheerfully complacent minstrel figure, fully available to accept abuse at the hands of her owners (*Racial Innocence*, 189–93). Although Jim's death also features elements that would become familiar in lynching (not least, the removal of bodily souvenirs), the song is careful to place responsibility for his death on Jim alone and responsibility for consuming him on a fellow enslaved person.
29. *Christy's*, 42.
30. Robert, *Tobacco Kingdom*, 222–24.
31. *Christy's*, 166–67.
32. Ibid., 41.
33. While the so-called cigar store Indian was the most popular icon, tobacco store signs included a wide range of figures, including Black people (Robert, *Story of Tobacco*, 98). The post–Civil War advertising boom offered a disquieting cultural afterlife to slavery: Well into the twentieth century, images of enslaved people were used to push products from pancake mix to soap to stove polish. See Manring, *Slave in a Box*, and Kern-Foxworth, *Aunt Jemima, Uncle Ben, and Rastus*.
34. *De Shiney Eye*.

35. *Christy's*, 167.
36. Ibid., 156.
37. *De Shiney Eye*.
38. Ibid.
39. Ibid.
40. *Christy's*, 42, 167; *De Shiney Eye*.
41. Roberts, *Blackface Nation*, 167.
42. *Negro Forget-Me-Not*, 117.
43. In 1857 three enslaved people convicted of murdering an overseer in Mississippi were hanged publicly. The *Mississippi Free Trader* described the spot's being chosen because it was "the most proper, where the slaves on all the neighboring plantations can witness the certain vengeance of the law" (Wayne, *Death of an Overseer*, 36). Frederick Law Olmsted describes the similarly gruesome spectacle that served to punish an enslaved man who killed his enslaver (*Cotton Kingdom*, 573).
44. As Roediger notes, striking white laborers often explicitly adopted the imagery of freedom-seeking revolutionaries (*Wages of Whiteness*, 67–69).
45. See, for example, Toll, *Blacking Up*, 66.
46. Black drivers appear frequently in minstrel songs. See "The Old Pee Dee," "Ring de Hoop an' Blow de Horn," "Gib Us Chaw Tobacco," and "Away to de Sugar Cane Field."
47. On the importance enslavers placed on Black drivers, see Owens, *This Species of Property*, 121.
48. It is worth considering how the other prominent figure of plantation management—the overseer—might represent a related displacement of responsibility, though this time onto a member of a different class rather than race.
49. *From Slave Cabin to the Pulpit*, 212–13.
50. Roediger, *Wages of Whiteness*, 97–114.
51. *Christy's*, 156.
52. *Negro Singer's*, 306, 65. The song "Cotton-Eyed Joe" is the exception to this rule. Notably, it was a song sung by enslaved people rather than a blackface minstrel song (the formerly enslaved William M. Adams recalled enslaved people singing it when he was interviewed as a part of the Federal Writers' Project, for instance ["William M. Adams (Interview)," 15]). As the rest of this section will argue, the cotton comparison made white workers nervous for reasons that would not have been relevant for people who had already been enslaved. I am grateful to Robin Bernstein for asking how this song fit into the larger pattern.
53. "Wool (*n.*)," def. 2a. *OED Online*. Oxford UP.

54. *Christy's*, 155.; *Negro Singer's*, 248. Charles Ball's slave narrative describes "picking" cotton wool: "A man can plant and cultivate more cotton plants, than he is afterwards able to pick the wool from, if the season is good" (*Slavery in the United States*, 210).
55. "He Had No Wool." The linking of Black hair and cotton became prominent in post–Civil War trade cards as well; many show Black women as if their hair were an enormous cotton boll. Even though these trade cards would have been targeted primarily to Northern consumers, their post-emancipation context would have mitigated the anxieties I will argue prevented antebellum minstrel songs from making the same connection.
56. Burton, *Rise and Fall of King Cotton*, 97; Yafa, *Big Cotton*, 130.
57. The white abolitionist Wendell Phillips referred to cotton as the "fibre that bound Massachusetts and Carolina together" (qtd. in Wirzbicki, *Fighting for the Higher Law*, 105).
58. Qtd. in Blewett, *Men, Women, and Work*, 128.
59. Qtd. in Commons and Phillips, *Documentary History*, 317–18.
60. Robinson, *Loom and Spindle*, 84.
61. Qtd. in Sinha, *Slave's Cause*, 351.
62. Robert, *Story of Tobacco*, 78. Even though Northeastern cities had cornered the domestic manufacture of cigars, they were still no match for the tobacco industry of the South, since the primary means of consuming tobacco in the first half of the nineteenth century was chewing (ibid., 97, 102), and in 1860 cigar manufacturing represented only $9 million to the $21 million non-cigar tobacco industries (Heimann, *Tobacco and Americans*, 191).
63. Albion, *Rise of New York Port*, 95–97, 59, 63–64.
64. Although my chapter focuses on at-home performances, there is also evidence that these songs helped workers pass the time. The musicologist Nicholas E. Tawa cites an antebellum observer who describes farm workers near Boston singing minstrel songs: "Hector marched at their head singing a negro melody. . . . Arriving at the edge of the field, the men rested their scythes upon the ground and began to whet them, having first wiped them with wisps of grass. The cheerful ring of the stone upon the metal beat a measured accompaniment to Hector's singing" (*High-Minded*, 272).
65. Other songster prefaces are less modest in their imagined audiences. *Christy's Plantation Melodies No. 4* waxes poetic in its assertion of universal usage: "In the drawing-room, counting-house, cottage, and camp—in the plantation and palace—in the street, saloon, and sabbath-school—[Christy's] airs are the preludes or finales to all operations" (Cohen, "American Secular Songsters," 24).
66. Watt, "Prefaces to Songsters," 42–43.

67. Mahar cites two 1840s minstrel show advertisements that list the price of admission at twenty-five cents, though he notes elsewhere that matinees could often be attended at half that price (*Behind the Burnt Cork Mask*, 12, 32). Cockrell also refers to twenty-five cents as "common for pit admission" (*Demons of Disorder*, 180n111).
68. As the editor Richard Storr Willis sniffed of Stephen Foster in 1853, "Much of his music is now excellent, but being wedded to negro idioms it is, of course, discarded by many who would otherwise gladly welcome it to their pianos" (qtd. in Tawa, *Sweet Songs*, 98).
69. Although, as Norm Cohen explains, songsters from the late 1820s through 1850s could be bound in leather or board, I have found extremely few minstrel songsters in anything other than wrappers ("American Secular Songsters," 20). Elizabeth Watts Pope at the American Antiquarian Society was instrumental in explaining both general printing techniques and the characteristics of this songster in particular. She also located the advertisement in which this songster's price was listed.
70. Bushman, *Refinement of America*, 283; C. Sedgwick, *Home*, 8.
71. Elizabeth Watts Pope at the American Antiquarian Society pointed out the similarities to Strong's children's books.
72. In his book on parlor songs, Tawa argues that they were popular in large part because "music was a necessary accomplishment and a mark of gentility" (*Sweet Songs*, 34).
73. Bernstein, *Racial Innocence*, 71–72.
74. Tawa, *Sweet Songs*, 39.
75. Jones, *Captive Stage*, 53.
76. Lhamon Jr., *Raising Cain*, 6.
77. Mahar, *Behind the Burnt Cork Mask*, 347–48.
78. Roberts, *Blackface Nation*, 169.
79. On the way Black dandy figures both mock white cultural elites and demean Black people, see Toll, *Blacking Up*, 68–69; Lott, *Love and Theft*, 111–12; Cockrell, *Demons of Disorder*, 94; and Roberts, *Blackface Nation*, 168.
80. Mahar, *Behind the Burnt Cork Mask*, 227.
81. Halttunen, *Confidence Men and Painted Women*, xvi.
82. *Christy's*, 81.
83. Ibid., 154. William J. Mahar offers a side-by-side comparison of the lyrics of the well-known aria and its popular minstrel parody (*Behind the Burnt Cork Mask*, 149–53.). The source of the original, *The Bohemian Girl*, was also a story of true origins shining through—in this case, an aristocratic woman kidnapped as a child and raised by people below her class.

84. As Barbara Lewis writes, "The dandy, symbolizing the unholy aspirations of this emergent group, was the favored target, the effigy of their unauthorized progress" ("Daddy Blue," 264). Brian Roberts argues that the Black dandy stereotype "made uplift a white privilege, denying it as a possibility for African Americans" (*Blackface Nation*, 168).
85. Jacobson, *Whiteness of a Different Color*, 119–22.
86. This understanding ignores the way minstrelsy had always worked differently when performed outside of formal theatrical settings. See Tawa, *Sweet Songs* 97; Cockrell, *Demons of Disorder*, 146–54; Lhamon Jr., *Raising Cain*, 45; and Mahar, *Behind the Burnt Cork Mask*, 26–27. Roberts, significantly, argues that minstrel audiences had always been more mixed in class than scholars tend to allow (*Blackface Nation*, 18).
87. Meer, *Uncle Tom Mania*.
88. Karen Halttunen has argued that the middle class in this period became less invested in sincerity and more comfortable with the "theatricality" of everyday life, which included parlor theatricals in blackface makeup (*Confidence Men and Painted Women*, 172–78).
89. Tawa, *High-Minded*, 150, and *Sweet Songs*, 89.
90. O'Connell, *Life and Songs of Stephen Foster*, 43.
91. Richards et al., *Julia Ward Howe*, 116–17. In his memoir of nineteenth-century New York, Charles Haswell supports the sense that minstrel songs were sung even by those with the most refined music taste: "New 'negro songs' were sent out almost daily from the publishers' presses and were sung all over the land.... [T]he use of them was almost universal. Households that had amused themselves with singing English opera (which had been greatly in fashion) and English glees and part-songs, turned to the new melodies" (*Reminiscences of New York*, 447).
92. In her analysis of the "domestication of blackface minstrelsy," Stephanie Dunson similarly observes that the preponderance of blackface minstrel sheet music suggests its popularity among those with the resources to purchase both sheet music and a piano on which to play it. My argument that we must consider songsters separate from theatrical contexts is indebted to the similar intervention Dunson makes about sheet music, though her analysis focuses on middle-class practitioners as opposed to the typically working-class consumers of minstrel songsters ("Minstrel in the Parlor," 242–43).
93. Douglas A. Jones argues that minstrelsy's obsessive staging of enslaved people fulfilled white audience desires for Black captivity, making the form "a kind of aesthetic surrogate for the loss of slavery in the north" (*Captive Stage*, 56).

4. FEEDING THE BODY POLITIC

1. Baptist, *Half Has Never Been Told*, 33.
2. On the essential role of Black activists in leading the fight against slavery, see Sinha, *Slave's Cause*.
3. K. Tompkins, *Racial Indigestion*, 92.
4. Woodard, *Delectable Negro*, 18; K. Tompkins, *Racial Indigestion*, 103.
5. Although this chapter focuses on metaphors of cannibalism, Vincent Woodard (*Delectable Negro*) and Mimi Sheller (*Consuming the Caribbean*, 148) remind us that these metaphors were rooted in literal forms of violence (eating-related and otherwise) experienced by enslaved people.
6. Even in ancient Greece and Rome, accusations of cannibalism denoted Others—they tended to be people who lived far away or were carefully distinguished from the storytellers (Cueva, "Cannibalism," 67).
7. Columbus, *Voyages*, 180.
8. Peter Hulme argues that the phrase "who are recorded to have been" allows the *OED* to conceal the fraught history of labeling ethnic Others as cannibals "beneath its blandness" (*Colonial Encounters*, 16), opting instead for the appearance of impartial observation.
9. See Hulme, *Colonial Encounters*, 21–22; and Lestringant, *Cannibals*, 17–19.
10. Although at the time "cannibal" was most likely still understood as primarily an ethnic designation, the decree repeatedly mentions the fact that these so-called cannibals were in the habit of apprehending other indigenous people friendly to the Spaniards in order to eat them. See Palencia-Roth, "Cannibal Law of 1503."
11. Daniel Cottom points out that early critics like Las Casas in 1559 and John Atkins in 1735 cast doubt on the veracity of claims of cannibalism, arguing instead that they were used as cover for European plunder (*Cannibals and Philosophers*, 138).
12. Montaigne, *Essays*, 113.
13. Ibid., 105, 106. The avarice that drives global conquest is not shared by the Brazilians, who Montaigne claims "do not strive for conquest of new territories.... They are still at the happy stage of desiring no more than their simple appetites demand" (ibid., 114).
14. Watson, *Insatiable Appetites*, 2.
15. Booth, "Metaphor as Rhetoric," 52.
16. Ibid., 54–55.
17. "Modest Proposal," 296–97. An earlier mournful reference to impoverished Irish children forced to "sell themselves to the *Barbadoes*" (ibid., 295)

explicitly refers to indentured servitude but also raises the specter of the many people of African descent enslaved and sold there. Charlotte Sussman notes that some of Swift's other tracts from this era evoke the commodification and sale of Irish people (*Consuming Anxieties*, 73–74).

18. Swift, "Modest Proposal," 300.
19. Ibid., 297–98.
20. Ibid., 301.
21. Barker, *African Link*, 120–21, 128–35.
22. Hegel, *Philosophy of History*, 95.
23. Wilson, "Letter," 1.
24. "Cannibal Slavery," 100.
25. Ibid.
26. American Colonization Society, *Fifteenth Annual Report*, 26.
27. Scientific racism became a dominant mode in white racialist thought over just a few decades starting in the 1820s (Bay, *White Image*, 14).
28. "History of Slavery," 7.
29. Priest, *Slavery, As It Relates to the Negro*, 191.
30. Fanon, *Black Skin*, 112–15, 203.
31. Emerson, *Journals*, 11:354.
32. Ibid.
33. Ibid., 11:355.
34. Two years before the Compromise of 1850, the antislavery representative Joshua Reed Giddings gave a speech that anticipates Emerson's evocation of cannibalism as a threat to overall national identity. Woodard cites this speech as an example of political rhetoric suggesting that America was at risk of becoming a "cannibal nation" (*Delectable Negro*, 65), but while he rightly notes fears of being tainted by slavery, he does not examine the deeper significance of cannibalism other than as a marker of depravity.
35. Kilgour, *From Communion to Cannibalism*, 7.
36. Ricœur, "Metaphorical Process," 148.
37. Douglas, *Purity and Danger*, 3–4.
38. "Too Black a Dose."
39. Jacobson, *Whiteness of a Different Color*, 41, 42–44.
40. Qtd. in Albanese, *King Crockett*, 238.
41. This anecdote also suggests territorial expansionism, or what Lori Merish has called "explicit imagery of imperial cannibalism" (*Sentimental Materialism*, 292). See also Norton, *Republic of Signs*, 203–18.
42. Jefferson, *Notes on the State of Virginia*, 138.
43. This sentiment is famously echoed in Lincoln's 1858 "House Divided" speech: "It will become *all* one thing, or *all* the other. Either the *opponents* of slavery,

will arrest the further spread of it ... or its *advocates* will push it forward, till it shall become alike lawful in *all* the states, *old* as well as *new—North* as well as *South*" ("'House Divided' Speech," 131).

44. Nearly seventy years after U.S. emancipation, the white historian and Southern Agrarian Frank Lawrence Owsley demonstrated the lingering influence of these ideas among white supremacists, giving voice to the cannibalistic echoes that may have played around Jefferson's fears of extermination: "For the negroes were cannibals and barbarians, and therefore dangerous. No white man who had any contact with slavery was willing to free the slaves and allow them to dwell among the whites.... Even if no race wars occurred, there was dread of being submerged and absorbed by the black race" ("Irrepressible Conflict," 77). For white supremacists, the danger of incorporating Black Americans is that they will figuratively swallow up white identity instead.
45. Emerson, "American Slavery," 3.
46. In this way, the lecture echoes Emerson's older optimism in human progress, which was shattered by the enforcement of the Fugitive Slave Law of 1850 (Gougeon, *Virtue's Hero*, 142–51).
47. Gilliland, "Burke, William."
48. "Kanzas and Nebraska," 104.
49. "Northern Cannibalism," 4.
50. Currier and Magee, *Dish of "Black Turtle."* For the original source of the phrase, see Blair and Rives, *Appendix*, 652.
51. Going, *David Wilmot, Free-Soiler*, 174.
52. McBride, *Impossible Witnesses*, 71.
53. Emerson, "Seventh of March," 339.
54. Thoreau, "Slavery in Massachusetts," 337.
55. Ibid., 337.
56. Barney, *Oxford Encyclopedia of the Civil War*, 270–71; Ruffin, *Essay on Calcareous Manures*, 199.
57. "Sketch," 381.
58. Tocqueville, *Journey to America*, 159.
59. Beaumont, *Marie*, 45.
60. Ibid., 46.
61. As Manisha Sinha has demonstrated, many abolitionists strongly critiqued capitalism, and Black abolitionists were particularly incisive in condemning the capitalist foundations of slavery (*Slave's Cause*, 151, 351–52).
62. Douglass, *Narrative*, 73; William Garrison, "Address," 70.
63. Douglass, *My Bondage*, 311. On Douglass's extensive elaboration of his experience of slavery in *My Bondage and My Freedom* compared to the *Narrative*,

see W. Andrews, *To Tell a Free Story*, 217–18. See also Sundquist, *To Wake the Nations*, 83–134.
64. Douglass, *My Bondage*, 374.
65. Ibid., 373, italics original.
66. "Kentucky Slaves," 1.
67. "Bell Everett Movement," 3.
68. Fitzhugh, *Cannibals All!*, 118.
69. Marx, *Capital*, 342. As Jerry Phillips has demonstrated, Karl Marx repeatedly turned to metaphors of cannibalistic bloodthirst to capture the workings of capital ("Cannibalism qua Capitalism").
70. Fitzhugh, *Cannibals All!*, 17.
71. "Modern Cannibal," 3.
72. On Hawthorne's own racism and skepticism about reform movements, see Yellin, "Hawthorne and the Slavery Question."
73. Hawthorne, *House of the Seven Gables*, 38.
74. Ibid., 43, 50, 60.
75. Ibid., 83.
76. Ibid., 38.
77. K. Tompkins, *Racial Indigestion*, 95.
78. Ibid.
79. Hawthorne, *House of the Seven Gables*, 39.
80. Anthony, "Class, Culture," 253–57.
81. G. Brown, *Domestic Individualism*, 25.
82. Kyla Wazana Tompkins notes that the stain on Hepzibah's palm echoes abolitionist rhetoric about guilt in relation to sugar, suggesting that we can consider the ingredients of this cookie and its negative impacts as another example of consumption-as-connection (*Racial Indigestion*, 97–98).
83. On Hawthorne's suggestions that Salem's wealth is ignominiously stained by slavery, see Matthews, *Hidden in Plain Sight*, 44.
84. Judge Pyncheon's bachelor uncle, having the rare capacity for recognizing and confronting the family guilt, imagines that their figurative bloodstains have permeated the house itself (Hawthorne, *House of the Seven Gables*, 18). For images of bloodstains on white objects, see ibid., 13, 147, 194, 198.
85. Ibid., 7.
86. Ibid., 17.
87. Ibid., 194.
88. "Ogre (*n.*)." *OED Online*. Oxford UP. Marina Warner observes that fairytale ogres tend to have different features depending on the gender of the protagonist: For male protagonists, ogres are often rich, powerful, and unintelligent;

for female protagonists, they embody the threats of sex or pregnancy ("Fee Fie Fo Fum," 164–65). Perhaps because *The House of the Seven Gables* features both male and female protagonists in Hepzibah, Clifford, and Phoebe, Judge Pyncheon displays features of both kinds of ogres. The narrator implies that Judge Pyncheon had committed sexual transgressions similar to those of his progenitor, who "had worn out three wives" (Hawthorne, *House of the Seven Gables*, 88). While he certainly isn't dumb, his greed, power, and appetite recall the qualities of ogres faced by male characters.

89. Hawthorne, *House of the Seven Gables*, 84.
90. Ibid., 88.
91. Ibid., 117.
92. Gilmore, *American Romanticism*, 103; Anthony, "Class, Culture," 254.
93. Hawthorne, *House of the Seven Gables*, 84.
94. Ibid., 21, 5.
95. Ibid., 85, 198.
96. Ibid., 44.
97. Ibid., 195. See, for example, Anthony, "Class, Culture," 263–64; and Matthews, *Hidden in Plain Sight*, 47.

5. CONSUMING MONSTERS

1. Douglass, *My Bondage*, 322.
2. On the range of human/dog relationships under slavery, see Fielder, "Black Dogs." On pets and abolitionist sympathy, see Fielder, "Animal Humanism." On animals and resistance in Stowe and Douglass, respectively, see Bolker, "Stowe's Birds," and Boggs, *Animalia Americana*.
3. T. Andrews, "Beasts of the Southern Wild," 46.
4. See Boggs, *Animalia Americana*, 81, 101; T. Andrews, "Beasts of the Southern Wild," 40; and Johnson, "'You Should Give Them Blacks to Eat,'" 69. Zakiyyah Iman Jackson, conversely, challenges the assumption that animalization means dehumanization, noting instead that "animalization is not incompatible with humanization: what is commonly deemed dehumanization is, in the main, more accurately interpreted as the violence of humanization or the burden of inclusion into a racially hierarchized universal humanity" (*Becoming Human*, 18). On the redemptive or revolutionary possibilities of thinking about Blackness through animals, see C. Ellis, *Antebellum Posthuman*; Bennett, *Being Property Once Myself*; Holland, *An Other*; and L. Johnson, *Race Matters, Animal Matters*.

5. Boisseron, *Afro-Dog*, 53.
6. K. Tompkins, *Racial Indigestion*, 90; Boisseron, *Afro-Dog*, 71–73.
7. Scholars working in animal studies and posthumanism have problematized the anthropocentrism of the human/nonhuman binary. See, for example, Wolfe, "Human, All Too Human," 569; and Peterson, *Bestial Traces*, 2–16. My analysis is not invested in overturning that binary, but rather in understanding how it structured the larger discourse on consumption, slavery, and resistance. In this way my work hews more closely to what Michael Lundblad has called "animality studies," which considers how animals in discourse illuminate larger questions about human history and politics (*Birth of a Jungle*).
8. Montgomery, "West Indies," 309; Southey, "Verses Spoken," 257.
9. Clarkson, *Slavery and Commerce*, 87.
10. See ibid., 100–101. Marcus Rediker notes that historical accounts of sharks following ships are supported by modern research on shark behavior ("History," 291–92).
11. Melville, *Moby-Dick*, 319.
12. Rediker has identified the broadside's author as the white Scottish activist James Tytler and notes that the broadside was published in Scotland and New York ("History," 294, 296n26). All broadside citations come from the reproduction printed in Rediker, "Slavery: A Shark's Perspective."
13. Equiano, *Interesting Narrative*, 172.
14. Crèvecœur, *Letters from an American Farmer*, 214–15.
15. Ibid., 216.
16. Ibid., 226.
17. Ibid., 233–34.
18. Goddu, *Gothic America*, 20.
19. Birkett, "Poem on the African Slave Trade," 201.
20. Lundblad, *Birth of a Jungle*, 4.
21. Hartman, *Scenes of Subjection*, 20.
22. Jackson, *Becoming Human*, 27.
23. Cutter, *Illustrated Slave*, 10.
24. Hartman, *Scenes of Subjection*, 21.
25. Kyla Wazana Tompkins discusses animals biting African Americans in late nineteenth-century trade cards (*Racial Indigestion*, 169–71) and the 1900 Thomas Edison Company silent film *The Gator and the Pickaninny* (ibid., 1); Tavia Nyong'o examines twentieth-century "racist kitsch" in general ("Racial Kitsch and Black Performance"), while Patricia Turner focuses on racist depictions of alligator encounters in her chapter "Alligator Bait" in *Ceramic Uncles and Celluloid Mammies* (31–40).

26. *Negro Singer's*, 89.
27. *Frank Brower's*, 43.
28. Wittke, *Tambo and Bones*, 159, 168.
29. *Negro Forget-Me-Not*, 129.
30. Ibid., 217–18.
31. Jones, *Captive Stage*, 14.
32. On Douglass's animalization of Covey in *My Bondage and My Freedom*, see Dorsey, "Becoming the Other," 440; and Boggs, *Animalia Americana*, 92–93.
33. Rohrbach, "'Silent Unobtrusive Way,'" 9. For discussions of how Crafts defied expectations by combining conventions from slave narratives and sentimental novels and borrowing and reworking other writing, see Gates and Robbins, *In Search of Hannah Crafts*, esp. chapters by Augusta Rohrbach, William L. Andrews, Hollis Robbins, Catherine Keyser, Jean Fagan Yellin, and Shelley Fisher Fishkin.
34. Crafts, *Bondwoman's Narrative*, 21.
35. Crèvecœur, *Letters from an American Farmer*, 216; Ross, *Slavery, Surveillance and Genre*, 114.
36. Crafts, *Bondwoman's Narrative*, 239.
37. Ibid., 65.
38. Ibid., 149.
39. Ibid., 112.
40. Douglass, *My Bondage*, 311.
41. Crafts, *Bondwoman's Narrative*, 53.
42. Northup, *Twelve Years a Slave*, 91.
43. Jacobs, *Incidents in the Life of a Slave Girl*, 113.
44. Ibid., 174.
45. Johnson, *River of Dark Dreams*, 235.
46. Bennett, *Being Property Once Myself*, 140–41.
47. S. Johnson, "'You Should Give Them Blacks to Eat,'" 69.
48. On the prevalent sense of slavery as "irrational non-economy," see Newbury, "Eaten Alive," 161. As I will argue, however, enslaved people used consumption to capture both anti-economic destruction and more obviously rational economic motives.
49. Jacobs, *Incidents in the Life of a Slave Girl*, 18.
50. Douglass, *My Bondage*, 175.
51. Northup, *Twelve Years a Slave*, 86, 87.
52. Johnson, *River of Dark Dreams*, 237–38.
53. Cutter, *Illustrated Slave*, 210. On Stowe's use of crows to embody smaller acts of enslaved resistance, see Bolker, "Stowe's Birds."

54. Northup, *Twelve Years a Slave*, 159.
55. As Stephen M. Best has written about the fundamental "emptiness" or "absence" at the heart of the visual archive of slavery in the Americas, "[S]laves are not the subject of the visual imagination, they are its object" ("Neither Lost nor Found," 151). For works that acknowledge the largely problematic tendencies of white abolitionist visual culture but still identify crucial interventions made by Black abolitionists, see Chaney, *Fugitive Vision*; Cutter, *Illustrated Slave*; Blackwood, "Fugitive Obscura"; and Goddu, *Selling Antislavery*.
56. Ruggles, *Unboxing of Henry Brown*, 88, 115, 152.
57. Greenspan, *William Wells Brown*, 289. For a reproduction of the broadside, see the plates in Greenspan, *William Wells Brown*.
58. Chaney, *Fugitive Vision*, 132.
59. Brooks, *Bodies in Dissent*, 68–69.
60. Ibid., 83.
61. Brooks includes a list of Henry "Box" Brown's scenes as they appeared in *The Liberator*, including "Henry Bibb, Escaping" and "Nubian Slaves Retaken" (ibid., 86–88). The former presumably showed Bibb escaping from wolves, as depicted in his slave narrative; the latter presumably drew on Charles C. Green's 1845 illustrated antislavery poem *The Nubian Slave*—a source identified by Jeffrey Ruggles—which prominently features pursuing dogs in the scene in which the fugitives are recaptured (*Unboxing of Henry Brown*, 94).
62. W. Brown, *Description of William Wells Brown's Original Panoramic Views*, 201–3.
63. Goddu notes that Bibb's narrative is the "most illustrated slave narrative in the canon" (*Selling Antislavery*, 183), and that while the majority of his illustrations were recycled from other American Anti-Slavery Society sources, the image of him fighting wolves seems to be one of the images Bibb commissioned specifically for the narrative (ibid., 183; 274n17). Even before the images were reused by other formerly enslaved abolitionists, then, this was a scene Bibb determined crucial to depict visually.
64. For the relationship between confrontations with wild animals and the frontier, see Allen, *Animals in American Literature*, 12; and Chaney, *Fugitive Vision*, 133, 136. For a reading of the visual logic of Bibb's escape as affirmation of manhood, see Goddu, *Selling Antislavery*, 187.
65. Ruggles, *Unboxing of Henry Brown*, 94.
66. Green, *Nubian Slave*, 8.
67. McInnis, *Slaves Waiting for Sale*, 207–9.
68. Cherry, *Beyond the Frame*, 132.
69. W. Andrews, *To Tell a Free Story*, xi.

70. In addition to previously cited work by Brooks (*Bodies in Dissent*), Dorsey ("Becoming the Other"), and multiple writers in *In Search of Hannah Crafts*, see Smith, *Self-Discovery and Authority*, 28–43.

CONCLUSION

1. Douglass, "Rev. Henry Highland Garnet."
2. Schor, *Henry Highland Garnet*, 117.
3. Garnet, "Henry Highland Garnet to Samuel Rhoads," 232.
4. "Free-Labour Movement," 15; "Anti-Slavery Demonstration."
5. E. Sedgwick, "Shame," 62.
6. Ngai, *Ugly Feelings*, 339.
7. Douglass, "Rev. Henry Highland Garnet."
8. Garnet, "'Calling Him Out,'" 2.
9. I use "by any means necessary" intentionally. It not only echoes Garnet's own advocacy of using "every means" to defeat slavery (Blackett, *Building an Antislavery Wall*, 121), it evokes the phrase's famous use by Frantz Fanon (*Alienation and Freedom*, 654) and by Malcolm X ("Founding Rally," 37). The context of violent resistance to colonial and racial oppression is appropriate, given Garnet's own embrace of Black Nationalism and his sense that violence was one important antislavery strategy.
10. Faulkner, "Root of the Evil," 400.
11. Garnet, "Henry Highland Garnet to Samuel Rhoads," 232.
12. On ideological pragmatism as a defining feature of Black American abolitionist activity in Britain, see Blackett, *Building an Antislavery Wall*, 119–23. On the Black abolitionist emphasis on practicality as opposed to the white abolitionist focus on personal purity in the Free Produce movement, see Faulkner, "Root of the Evil," 398–99.
13. Shotwell, *Against Purity*, 8, 5.
14. Ibid., 195.
15. Ibid., 4.
16. Creative Time, "About the Project."
17. Rooney, "Sonorous Subtlety."
18. Ibid.
19. Ibid.
20. Faherty, *Haitian Revolution*, 111.
21. Miranda, "Q&A." For essays critical of visitor behavior, see Powers, "Why I Yelled at the Kara Walker Exhibit," and Munro, "Offensive Instagram Pics."

22. Arabindan-Kesson, *Black Bodies, White Gold*, 5.
23. Rice, "Exploring Inside," 24.
24. Ibid.
25. Ibid.
26. Ibid.

WORKS CITED

Albanese, Catherine Louise. *King Crockett: Nature and Civility on the American Frontier.* Worcester, MA: American Antiquarian Society, 1979.
Albion, Robert Greenhalgh. *The Rise of New York Port, 1815–1860.* Boston: Northeastern UP; South Street Seaport Museum, 1984.
Allen, Mary. *Animals in American Literature.* Urbana: U of Illinois P, 1983.
American Colonization Society. *The Fifteenth Annual Report of the American Society for Colonizing the Free People of Colour of the United States.* Washington, DC: James C. Dunn, 1832.
Ammons, Elizabeth. "Stowe's Dream of the Mother-Savior: Uncle Tom's Cabin and American Women Writers Before the 1920s." In *New Essays on "Uncle Tom's Cabin,"* edited by Eric J. Sundquist, 155–95. The American Novel. Cambridge: Cambridge UP, 1986.
Anderson, Benedict. *Imagined Communities: Reflections on the Origin and Spread of Nationalism.* Rev. ed. London: Verso, 2016.
Andrews, Thomas G. "Beasts of the Southern Wild: Slaveholders, Slaves, and Other Animals in Charles Ball's Slavery in the United States." In *Rendering Nature: Animals, Bodies, Places, Politics,* edited by Marguerite S Shaffer and Phoebe S. K. Young, 21–47. Philadelphia: U of Pennsylvania P, 2015.
Andrews, William L. *To Tell a Free Story: The First Century of Afro-American Autobiography, 1760–1865.* Urbana: U of Illinois P, 1986.

Ansdell, Richard. *The Hunted Slaves*. Oil on canvas, 1862. National Museum of African American History & Culture.

Anthony, David. "Class, Culture, and the Trouble with White Skin in Hawthorne's *The House of the Seven Gables*." *Yale Journal of Criticism* 12, no. 2 (1999): 249–68.

"Anti-Slavery Demonstration." *North Star,* October 31, 1850.

Arabindan-Kesson, Anna. *Black Bodies, White Gold: Art, Cotton, and Commerce in the Atlantic World*. Durham, NC: Duke UP, 2021.

Austen, Ralph A., and Woodruff D. Smith. "Private Tooth Decay as Public Economic Virtue: The Slave-Sugar Triangle, Consumerism, and European Industrialization." In *The Atlantic Slave Trade: Effects on Economies, Societies, and Peoples in Africa, the Americas, and Europe,* edited by Joseph E. Inikori and Stanley L. Engerman, 183–203. Durham, NC: Duke UP, 1992.

Baldwin, James. "Everybody's Protest Novel." In *Collected Essays,* 11–18. New York: Library of America, 1998.

Ball, Charles. *Slavery in the United States: A Narrative of the Life and Adventures of Charles Ball, a Black Man*. Detroit: Negro History P, 1970.

Balthrop-Lewis, Alda. *Thoreau's Religion: Walden Woods, Social Justice, and the Politics of Asceticism*. New Cambridge Studies in Religion and Critical Thought. Cambridge: Cambridge UP, 2021.

Baptist, Edward E. *The Half Has Never Been Told: Slavery and the Making of American Capitalism*. Boulder, CO: Basic Books, 2012.

Barker, Anthony J. *The African Link: British Attitudes to the Negro in the Era of the Atlantic Slave Trade, 1550–1807*. London: Frank Cass, 1978.

Barnes, Elizabeth. "Affecting Relations: Pedagogy, Patriarchy, and the Politics of Sympathy." *American Literary History* 8, no. 4 (1996): 597–614.

Barney, William L. *The Oxford Encyclopedia of the Civil War*. New York: Oxford UP, 2011.

Barth, J. Robert. *Coleridge and Christian Doctrine*. Cambridge, MA: Harvard UP, 1969.

Bay, Mia. *The White Image in the Black Mind: African-American Ideas About White People, 1830–1925*. New York: Oxford UP, 2000.

Beaumont, Gustave de. *Marie, or Slavery in the United States: A Novel of Jacksonian America*. Translated by Barbara Chapman. Stanford, CA: Stanford UP, 1958.

Beckert, Sven. *Empire of Cotton: A Global History*. New York: Vintage, 2014.

"The Bell Everett Movement." *New York Herald,* October 5, 1860. America's Historical Newspapers.

Bender, Thomas, ed. *The Antislavery Debate: Capitalism and Abolitionism as a Problem in Historical Interpretation*. Berkeley: U of California P, 1992.

Bennett, Joshua. *Being Property Once Myself: Blackness and the End of Man*. Cambridge, MA: Harvard UP, 2020.

BERA. "Ladies' Department—Dialogue." *The Liberator*, August 25, 1832. Nineteenth Century U.S. Newspapers.

Berlant, Lauren. *The Female Complaint: The Unfinished Business of Sentimentality in American Culture*. Durham, NC: Duke UP, 2008.

Bernstein, Robin. *Racial Innocence: Performing American Childhood and Race from Slavery to Civil Rights*. New York: New York UP, 2012.

Best, Stephen M. *The Fugitive's Properties: Law and the Poetics of Possession*. Chicago: U of Chicago P, 2004.

———. "Neither Lost nor Found: Slavery and the Visual Archive." *Representations* 113, no. 1 (February 2011): 150–63.

Birkett, Mary. "A Poem on the African Slave Trade, Addressed to Her Own Sex." In *Slavery, Abolition, and Emancipation: Writings in the British Romantic Period*, vol. 4: *Verse*, edited by Alan Richardson, 196–217. London: Pickering & Chatto, 1999.

Black, Max. *Models and Metaphors: Studies in Language and Philosophy*. Ithaca, NY: Cornell UP, 1962.

Blackett, R. J. M. *Building an Antislavery Wall: Black Americans in the Atlantic Abolitionist Movement, 1830–1860*. Baton Rouge: Louisiana State UP, 2002.

Blackwood, Sarah. "Fugitive Obscura: Runaway Slave Portraiture and Early Photographic Technology." *American Literature* 81, no. 1 (2009): 93–125.

Blair, Francis P., and John C. Rives. *Appendix to "The Congressional Globe," for the First Session, Twenty-Ninth Congress: Containing Speeches and Important State Papers*. Washington, DC: Blair & Rives, 1846.

Blewett, Mary H. *Men, Women, and Work: Class, Gender, and Protest in the New England Shoe Industry, 1780–1910*. Urbana: U of Illinois P, 1988.

Boggs, Colleen Glenney. *Animalia Americana: Animal Representations and Biopolitical Subjectivity*. New York: Columbia UP, 2013.

Bohrer, Randall. "Melville's New Witness: Cannibalism and the Microcosm-Macrocosm Cosmology of *Moby-Dick*." *Studies in Romanticism* 22, no. 1 (1983): 65–91.

Boisseron, Bénédicte. *Afro-Dog: Blackness and the Animal Question*. New York: Columbia UP, 2018.

Bolker, Jamie M. "Stowe's Birds: Jim Crows and the Nature of Resistance in Dred." *J19: The Journal of Nineteenth-Century Americanists* 6, no. 2 (2018): 237–57.

Booth, Wayne C. "Metaphor as Rhetoric: The Problem of Evaluation." *Critical Inquiry* 5, no. 1 (1978): 49–72.

Boulukos, George. "Capitalism and Slavery, Once Again with Feeling." In *Affect and Abolition in the Anglo-Atlantic, 1770–1830*, edited by Stephen Ahern, 23–43. Surrey, UK: Ashgate, 2013.

Brady, Jennifer L. "Theorizing a Reading Public: Sentimentality and Advice about Novel Reading in the Antebellum United States." *American Literature* 83, no. 4 (December 1, 2011): 719–46.

Breen, T. H. "'Baubles of Britain': The American and Consumer Revolutions of the Eighteenth Century." *Past and Present*, no. 119 (1988): 73–104.

Breitwieser, Mitchell. "False Sympathy in Melville's *Typee*." *American Quarterly* 34, no. 4 (1982): 396–417.

Brooks, Daphne. *Bodies in Dissent: Spectacular Performances of Race and Freedom, 1850–1910*. Durham, NC: Duke UP, 2006.

Brown, Angus Connell. "Cultural Studies and Close Reading." *PMLA* 132, no. 5 (2017): 1187–93.

Brown, Christopher Leslie. *Moral Capital: Foundations of British Abolitionism*. Chapel Hill: U of North Carolina P, 2006.

Brown, Gillian. *Domestic Individualism: Imagining Self in Nineteenth-Century America*. The New Historicism. Berkeley: U of California P, 1990.

Brown, William Wells. *A Description of William Wells Brown's Original Panoramic Views of the Scenes in the Life of an American Slave, from His Birth in Slavery to His Death or His Escape to His First Home of Freedom on British Soil*. In *The Black Abolitionist Papers*, vol. 1: *The British Isles, 1830–1865*, edited by C. Peter Ripley, 190–224. Chapel Hill: U of North Carolina P, 1985.

Burn, Andrew. *A Second Address to the People of Great Britain: Containing a New, and Most Powerful Argument to Abstain from West India Sugar*. 2nd ed. London: M. Gurney, 1792.

Burton, Anthony. *The Rise and Fall of King Cotton*. London: A. Deutsch and British Broadcasting Corp., 1984.

Bushman, Richard L. *The Refinement of America: Persons, Houses, Cities*. First published by Alfred A. Knopf, 1992. New York: Vintage Books, 1993.

Campbell, Colin. *The Romantic Ethic and the Spirit of Modern Consumerism*. Ideas. Oxford: B. Blackwell, 1987.

"Cannibal Slavery." *The Liberator*, June 21, 1839. Nineteenth Century U.S. Newspapers.

"Cannibalism." *Daily Evening Bulletin* (San Francisco), August 14, 1862. Nineteenth Century U.S. Newspapers.

Carey, Brycchan. *British Abolitionism and the Rhetoric of Sensibility: Writing, Sentiment, and Slavery, 1760–1807*. Palgrave Studies in the Enlightenment, Romanticism and Cultures of Print. Houndmills, Basingstoke, Hampshire, UK: Palgrave MacMillan, 2005.

Chandler, Elizabeth Margaret. *Essays, Philanthropic and Moral, by Elizabeth Margaret Chandler, Principally Relating to the Abolition of Slavery in America*. Philadelphia: T. E. Chapman, 1845.

———. *The Poetical Works of Elizabeth Margaret Chandler: With a Memoir of Her Life and Character*, by Benjamin Lundy. Philadelphia: T. E. Chapman, 1845.

Chaney, Michael A. *Fugitive Vision: Slave Image and Black Identity in Antebellum Narrative.* Bloomington: Indiana UP, 2009.

Cherry, Deborah. *Beyond the Frame: Feminism and Visual Culture, Britain 1850–1900.* London: Routledge, 2000.

Chow, Rey. *Sentimental Fabulations, Contemporary Chinese Films: Attachment in the Age of Global Visibility.* Film and Culture Series. New York: Columbia UP, 2007.

Christy's Nigga Songster. New York: T. W. Strong, 1850.

Christy's Ram's Horn Nigga Songster: As Sung by White's, Christy's, Harmonist's, Sable Brothers', and Dumbleton's Bands of Nigger Minstrels. New York: Elton, 1849.

Clarkson, Thomas. *An Essay on the Slavery and Commerce of the Human Species.* 2nd ed. London: J. Phillips, 1788.

Clavin, Matt. "Race, Rebellion, and the Gothic: Inventing the Haitian Revolution." *Early American Studies* 5, no. 1 (2007): 1–29.

Cockrell, Dale. *Demons of Disorder: Early Blackface Minstrels and Their World.* Cambridge: Cambridge UP, 1997.

Coffin, Levi. *Reminiscences of Levi Coffin, the Reputed President of the Underground Railroad.* 2nd ed. Cincinnati, OH: Robert Clarke, 1880.

Cohen, Norm. "American Secular Songsters in the Nineteenth Century: An Overview." In *Cheap Print and Popular Song in the Nineteenth Century: A Cultural History of the Songster*, edited by Paul Watt, Derek Scott, and Patrick Spedding, 11–31. Cambridge: Cambridge UP, 2017.

Coleman, Deirdre. "Conspicuous Consumption: White Abolitionism and English Women's Protest Writing in the 1790's." *ELH* 61, no. 2 (1994): 341–62.

Coleridge, Samuel Taylor. "Lecture on the Slave-Trade." In *The Collected Works of Samuel Taylor Coleridge*, vol. 1: *Lectures, 1795: On Politics and Religion*, edited by Lewis Patton and Peter Mann, 231–51. London: Routledge, 1971.

———. "On the Slave Trade." In *Slavery, Abolition, and Emancipation: Writings in the British Romantic Period*, vol. 2: *The Abolition Debate*, edited by Peter J. Kitson, 209–20. London: Pickering & Chatto, 1999.

Columbus, Christopher. *The Voyages of Christopher Columbus, Being the Journals of His First and Third, and the Letters Concerning His First and Last Voyages, to Which Is Added the Account of His Second Voyage.* Translated by Lionel Cecil Jane. London: Argonaut P, 1930.

Commons, John R., and Ulrich B. Phillips, eds. *A Documentary History of American Industrial Society.* New York: Russell & Russell, 1958.

Conrad, Jessica. "'Polluted Luxuries': Consumer Resistance, the Senses of Horror, and Abolitionist Boycott Literature." *American Literature* 90, no. 1 (2018): 1–26.

"Consumers." *Genius of Universal Emancipation*, February 1831. ProQuest.

Cooper, Thomas. *Letters on the Slave Trade: First Published in "Wheeler's Manchester Chronicle"; and Since Re-Printed with Additions and Alterations*. Manchester, UK: C. Wheeler, 1787.

Cottom, Daniel. *Cannibals and Philosophers: Bodies of Enlightenment*. Baltimore: Johns Hopkins UP, 2001.

Coviello, Peter. *Intimacy in America: Dreams of Affiliation in Antebellum Literature*. Minneapolis: U of Minnesota P, 2005.

Cowper, William. *The Poems of William Cowper*. Edited by John D. Baird and Charles Ryskamp. Vol. 3. Oxford: Oxford UP, 1980.

Crafts, Hannah. *The Bondwoman's Narrative*. Edited by Henry Louis Gates Jr. New York: Grand Central Publishing, 2014.

Creative Time. "About the Project." n.d. https://creativetime.org/projects/karawalker/.

Crenshaw, Kimberlé Williams. "Race, Reform, and Retrenchment: Transformation and Legitimation in Antidiscrimination Law." *Harvard Law Review* 101, no. 7 (May 1988): 1331–87.

Crèvecœur, J. Hector St John de. *Letters from an American Farmer: Describing Certain Provincial Situations, Manners and Customs, Not Generally Known; and Conveying Some Idea of the Late and Present Interior Circumstances of the British Colonies in North America*. London: Thomas Davies and Lockyer Davis, 1783.

Cueva, Edmund P. "Cannibalism and the Ancient Novel Revisited." In *Interdisciplinary Essays on Cannibalism: Bites Here and There*, edited by Giulia Champion, 67–82. London: Routledge, 2023.

Currier, Nathaniel, and John L. Magee. *A Dish of "Black Turtle."* Lithograph on wove paper, 1852. American Cartoon Print Filing Series. Library of Congress.

Cutter, Martha J. *The Illustrated Slave: Empathy, Graphic Narrative, and the Visual Culture of the Transatlantic Abolition Movement, 1800–1852*. Athens: U of Georgia P, 2017.

Davis, David Brion. *The Problem of Slavery in Western Culture*. New York: Oxford UP, 1966.

De Shiney Eye, Crooked Shin, and, Oh, Susannah Songster. New York: Turner & Fisher, 1843.

Deacon Snowball's Negro Melodies. New York: Turner & Fisher, 1841.

Deyle, Steven. *Carry Me Back: The Domestic Slave Trade in American Life*. Oxford: Oxford UP, 2005.

Dobson, Joanne. "Reclaiming Sentimental Literature." *American Literature* 69, no. 2 (1997): 263–88.

Dorsey, Peter A. "Becoming the Other: The Mimesis of Metaphor in Douglass's *My Bondage and My Freedom*." *PMLA* 111, no. 3 (1996): 435–50.

Doty, Josh. *The Perfecting of Nature: Reforming Bodies in Antebellum Literature*. Chapel Hill: U of North Carolina P, 2020.

Douglas, Ann. *The Feminization of American Culture*. New York: Noonday Press/Farrar, Straus and Giroux, 1998.

Douglas, Mary. *Purity and Danger: An Analysis of Concepts of Pollution and Taboo*. New York: Frederick A. Praeger, 1966.

Douglass, Frederick. *My Bondage and My Freedom*. In *Autobiographies*, 103–452. New York: Library of America College Editions, 1996.

———. *Narrative of the Life of Frederick Douglass, An American Slave*. In *Autobiographies*, 1–102. New York: Library of America College Editions, 1996.

———. "Rev. Henry Highland Garnet." *North Star*, July 27, 1849. Accessible Archives.

———. "What to the Slave Is the Fourth of July?" In *The Oxford Frederick Douglass Reader*, edited by William L. Andrews, 108–30. New York: Oxford UP, 1996.

Drescher, Seymour. *Capitalism and Antislavery: British Mobilization in Comparative Perspective*. New York: Oxford UP, 1987.

———. "Public Opinion and Parliament in the Abolition of the British Slave Trade." In *The British Slave Trade: Abolition, Parliament and People: Including the Illustrated Catalogue of the Parliamentary Exhibition in Westminster Hall, 23 May–23 September 2007*, edited by Stephen Farrell, Melanie Unwin, and James Walvin, 42–65. Edinburgh: Edinburgh UP, 2007.

Du Bois, W. E. B. "Letter to Franklin Henry Hooper, 14 February 1929." In *The Correspondence of W. E. B. Du Bois*, vol. 1: *Selections, 1877–1934*, edited by Herbert Aptheker, 390. Amherst: U of Massachusetts P, 1973.

Dunson, Stephanie. "The Minstrel in the Parlor: Nineteenth-Century Sheet Music and the Domestication of Blackface Minstrelsy." *American Transcendental Quarterly* 16, no. 4 (2002): 241–55.

Edelstein, T. J. "They Sang 'The Song of the Shirt': The Visual Iconology of the Seamstress." *Victorian Studies* 23, no. 2 (1980): 183–210.

Ellis, Cristin. *Antebellum Posthuman: Race and Materiality in the Mid-Nineteenth Century*. New York: Fordham UP, 2018.

Ellis, Markman. *The Politics of Sensibility: Race, Gender and Commerce in the Sentimental Novel*. Cambridge Studies in Romanticism. Cambridge: Cambridge UP, 1996.

Eltis, David. "The Volume and Structure of the Transatlantic Slave Trade: A Reassessment." *William and Mary Quarterly* 58, no. 1 (2001): 17–46.

Emerson, Ralph Waldo. "'American Slavery' (25 January 1855)." In *The Later Lectures of Ralph Waldo Emerson, 1843–1871*, vol. 2: *1855–1871*, edited by Ronald A. Bosco and Joel Myerson, 1–14. Athens: U of Georgia P, 2001.

———. *The Journals and Miscellaneous Notebooks of Ralph Waldo Emerson*. Edited by William H. Gilman and A. W. Plumstead. Vol. 11. Cambridge, MA: Belknap P of Harvard UP, 1960.

———. "Seventh of March Speech on the Fugitive Slave Law, 7 March 1854." In *The Later Lectures of Ralph Waldo Emerson, 1843–1871*, vol. 1: 1843–1854, edited by Ronald A. Bosco and Joel Myerson, 333–47. Athens: U of Georgia P, 2001.

Equiano, Olaudah. *The Interesting Narrative of the Life of Olaudah Equiano, or Gustavus Vassa, the African, Written by Himself.* Edited by Vincent Carretta. New York: Penguin, 2003.

The Ethiopian Glee Book: A Collection of Popular Negro Melodies, Arranged for Quartett Clubs. Boston: Elias Howe, 1848.

Faherty, Duncan. *The Haitian Revolution in the Early Republic of Letters.* Oxford: Oxford UP, 2023.

Falconbridge, Alexander. *An Account of the Slave Trade on the Coast of Africa, by Alexander Falconbridge, Late Surgeon in the African Trade.* 2nd ed. London: James Phillips, 1788.

Fanon, Frantz. *Alienation and Freedom.* Edited by Jean Khalfa and Robert J. C. Young. Translated by Steve Corcoran. London: Bloomsbury Academic, 2018.

———. *Black Skin, White Masks.* New York: Grove P, 1967.

Faulkner, Carol. "The Root of the Evil: Free Produce and Radical Antislavery, 1820–1860." *Journal of the Early Republic* 27, no. 3 (2007): 377–405.

Festa, Lynn. *Sentimental Figures of Empire in Eighteenth-Century Britain and France.* Baltimore: Johns Hopkins UP, 2006.

Fielder, Brigitte. "Animal Humanism: Race, Species, and Affective Kinship in Nineteenth-Century Abolitionism." In "Species/Race/Sex," edited by Claire Jean Kim and Carla Freccero, special issue, *American Quarterly* 65, no. 3 (September 2013): 487–514.

———. "Black Dogs, Bloodhounds, and Best Friends: African Americans and Dogs in Nineteenth-Century Abolitionist Literature." In *American Beasts: Perspectives on Animals, Animality and U.S. Culture, 1776–1920*, edited by Dominik Ohrem, 153–73. Berlin: Neofelis Verlag, 2017.

———. *Relative Races: Genealogies of Interracial Kinship in Nineteenth-Century America.* Durham, NC: Duke UP, 2020.

Fisher, Philip. *Hard Facts: Setting and Form in the American Novel.* New York: Oxford UP, 1985.

Fitzhugh, George. *Cannibals All! or, Slaves Without Masters.* Cambridge, MA: Belknap P of Harvard UP, 1960.

Foreman, P. Gabrielle. *Activist Sentiments: Reading Black Women in the Nineteenth Century.* New Black Studies Series. Urbana: U of Illinois P, 2009.

Fox, William. *An Address to the People of Great Britain, on the Propriety of Abstaining from West India Sugar and Rum.* In *Slavery, Abolition, and Emancipation: Writings in the British Romantic Period*, vol. 2: *The Abolition Debate*, edited by Peter Kitson, 153–65. London: Pickering & Chatto, 1999.

Hegel, Georg Wilhelm Friedrich. *The Philosophy of History*. Translated by J. Sibree. New York: Colonial P, 1900.

Heimann, Robert K. *Tobacco and Americans*. New York: McGraw-Hill, 1960.

Helvétius, Claude Adrien. *De L'esprit*. Paris: Chez Durand, 1758.

Herbert, T. Walter. *Marquesan Encounters: Melville and the Meaning of Civilization*. Cambridge, MA: Harvard UP, 1980.

Heyrick, Elizabeth. *Immediate, Not Gradual Abolition, or An Inquiry into the Shortest, Safest, and Most Effectual Means of Getting Rid of West Indian Slavery*. London: Hatchard, 1824.

Hirsch, Stephen A. "Uncle Tomitudes: The Popular Reaction to *Uncle Tom's Cabin*." *Studies in the American Renaissance* (1978): 303–30.

"History of Slavery, White and Black—The Abolitionists the Enemies of the Negro Race." *New York Herald*, January 19, 1860. America's Historical Newspapers.

Hoermann, Raphael. "'A Very Hell of Horrors'? The Haitian Revolution and the Early Transatlantic Haitian Gothic." *Slavery and Abolition* 37, no. 1 (January 2, 2016): 183–205.

Hoffman, Daniel. *Form and Fable in American Fiction*. New York: Oxford UP, 1961.

Holcomb, Julie L. *Moral Commerce: Quakers and the Transatlantic Boycott of the Slave Labor Economy*. Ithaca, NY: Cornell UP, 2016.

Holland, Sharon Patricia. *An Other: A Black Feminist Consideration of Animal Life*. Durham, NC: Duke UP, 2023.

Hood, Thomas. "The Song of the Shirt." *Punch* 5 (1843): 260.

hooks, bell. "Eating the Other: Desire and Resistance." In *Black Looks: Race and Representation*, 21–39. New York: Routledge, 1992.

"How Do We Know?" *The Non-Slaveholder*, May 1853.

Hulme, Peter. *Colonial Encounters: Europe and the Native Caribbean, 1492–1797*. London: Routledge Kegan & Paul, 1987.

Jackson, Zakiyyah Iman. *Becoming Human: Matter and Meaning in an Antiblack World*. Sexual Cultures. New York: New York UP, 2020.

Jacobs, Harriet. *Incidents in the Life of a Slave Girl, Written by Herself*. Edited by Jean Fagan Yellin. Cambridge, MA: Harvard UP, 1987.

Jacobson, Matthew Frye. *Whiteness of a Different Color: European Immigrants and the Alchemy of Race*. Cambridge, MA: Harvard UP, 1998.

Jahn, Raymond. *Tobacco Dictionary*. Mid-Century Reference Library. New York: Philosophical Library, 1954.

Jay, Gregory S. *White Writers, Race Matters: Fictions of Racial Liberalism from Stowe to Stockett*. Oxford Studies in American Literary History. Oxford: Oxford UP, 2018.

Jefferson, Thomas. *Notes on the State of Virginia*. Edited by William Harwood Pede. Chapel Hill: U of North Carolina P, 1955.

Johnson, Lindgren. *Race Matters, Animal Matters: Fugitive Humanism in African America, 1840–1930*. London: Routledge, 2018.

Johnson, Sara E. "'You Should Give Them Blacks to Eat:' Waging Inter-American Wars of Torture and Terror." *American Quarterly* 61, no. 1 (March 2009): 65–92, 219.

Johnson, Walter. *River of Dark Dreams: Slavery and Empire in the Cotton Kingdom*. Cambridge, MA: Harvard UP, 2017.

Jones, Douglas A. *The Captive Stage: Performance and the Proslavery Imagination of the Antebellum North*. Ann Arbor: U of Michigan P, 2014.

Jordan, Winthrop D. *White over Black: American Attitudes Toward the Negro, 1550–1812*. Chapel Hill: U of North Carolina P, 1968.

"Kanzas and Nebraska." *North American Review*, January 1855.

"The Kentucky Slaves: The Slave Mother Indicted for Murder—Closing Argument of Mr. Jolliffe—Decision Reserved." *New York Daily Times*, February 12, 1856.

Kern-Foxworth, Marilyn. *Aunt Jemima, Uncle Ben, and Rastus: Blacks in Advertising, Yesterday, Today, and Tomorrow*. Westport, CT: Greenwood P, 1994.

Kett, Anna Vaughan. "Quaker Women and Anti-Slavery Activism: Eleanor Clark and the Free Labour Cotton Depot in Street." *Quaker Studies* 19, no. 1 (September 2014): 137–56.

Kilgour, Maggie. *From Communion to Cannibalism: An Anatomy of Metaphors of Incorporation*. Princeton, NJ: Princeton UP, 1990.

Kilner, Dorothy. *The Rotchfords; or, The Friendly Counsellor: Designed for the Instruction and Amusement of the Youth of Both Sexes. By M. P. in Two Volumes*. Vol. 2. London: John Marshall, 1786.

Kirsch, Geoffrey R. "Loss Without Remedy: *Moby-Dick* and the Laws of Compensation." *PMLA* 138, no. 1 (January 2023): 37–51.

Kitson, Peter J. "Fictions of Slave Resistance and Revolt: Robert Southey's *Poems on the Slave Trade* (1797) and Charlotte Smith's 'The Story of Henrietta' (1800)." In *Race, Romanticism, and the Atlantic*, edited by Paul Youngquist, 107–24. Surrey, UK: Ashgate, 2013.

Knott, Sarah. *Sensibility and the American Revolution*. Chapel Hill: U of North Carolina P, 2009.

Lauro, Sarah Juliet. *The Transatlantic Zombie: Slavery, Rebellion, and Living Death*. New Brunswick, NJ: Rutgers UP, 2015.

Lestringant, Frank. *Cannibals: The Discovery and Representation of the Cannibal from Columbus to Jules Verne*. Translated by Rosemary Morris. Berkeley: U of California P, 1997.

"Letter from Mrs. Stowe." *Frederick Douglass' Paper*, January 20, 1854. Accessible Archives.

Lewis, Barbara. "Daddy Blue: The Evolution of the Dark Dandy." In *Inside the Minstrel Mask: Readings in Nineteenth-Century Blackface Minstrelsy*, edited by

Annemarie Bean, James V. Hatch, and Brooks McNamara. Hanover, NH: Wesleyan UP, 1996.

Lhamon, W. T., Jr. *Raising Cain: Blackface Performance from Jim Crow to Hip Hop.* Cambridge, MA: Harvard UP, 2000.

Lincoln, Abraham. "'House Divided' Speech at Springfield, Illinois." In *Selected Speeches and Writings*, 131–39. New York: Library of America, 2009.

Logan, Lisa. "*Uncle Tom's Cabin* and Conventional Nineteenth-Century Domestic Ideology." In *Approaches to Teaching Stowe's "Uncle Tom's Cabin,"* edited by Elizabeth Ammons and Susan Belasco, 46–56. Approaches to Teaching World Literature. New York: Modern Language Association of America, 2000.

Lott, Eric. *Love and Theft: Blackface Minstrelsy and the American Working Class.* Oxford: Oxford UP, 1995.

Lundblad, Michael. *The Birth of a Jungle: Animality in Progressive-Era U.S. Literature and Culture.* New York: Oxford UP, 2015.

Magee, John L. *Forcing Slavery Down the Throat of a Freesoiler.* Lithograph on wove paper, 1856. Prints and Photographs Division. Library of Congress.

Mahar, William J. *Behind the Burnt Cork Mask: Early Blackface Minstrelsy and Antebellum American Popular Culture.* Urbana: U of Illinois P, 1999.

Manring, M. M. *Slave in a Box: The Strange Career of Aunt Jemima.* Charlottesville: UP of Virginia, 1998.

Marx, Karl. *Capital: Volume 1: A Critique of Political Economy.* Translated by Ben Fowkes. New York: Penguin, 1992.

Matt Peel's Banjo. New York: Robert M. De Witt, 1859.

Matthews, John T. *Hidden in Plain Sight: Slave Capitalism in Poe, Hawthorne, and Joel Chandler Harris.* Mercer University Lamar Memorial Lectures. Athens: U of Georgia P, 2020.

McBride, Dwight A. *Impossible Witnesses: Truth, Abolitionism, and Slave Testimony.* New York: New York UP, 2001.

McDonald, Michelle Craig. "Consuming with a Conscience: The Free Produce Movement in Early America." In *Shopping for Change: Consumer Activism and the Possibilities of Purchasing Power,* edited by Louis Hyman and Joseph Tohill, 17–27. Ithaca, NY: Cornell UP, 2017.

McGann, Jerome. *The Poetics of Sensibility: A Revolution in Literary Style.* Oxford: Clarendon P, 1996.

McInnis, Maurie D. *Slaves Waiting for Sale: Abolitionist Art and the American Slave Trade.* Chicago: U of Chicago P, 2013.

McKendrick, Neil, John Brewer, and J. H. Plumb. *The Birth of a Consumer Society: The Commercialization of Eighteenth-Century England.* Bloomington: Indiana UP, 1982.

McKnight, Utz. *Frances E. W. Harper: A Call to Conscience.* Black Lives Series. Cambridge: Polity P, 2021.

Meer, Sarah. *Uncle Tom Mania: Slavery, Minstrelsy, and Transatlantic Culture in the 1850s*. Athens: U of Georgia P, 2005.
Melville, Herman. *Moby-Dick; or, The Whale*. Rev. ed. New York: Penguin, 2003.
———. *Typee: Complete Text with Introduction, Historical Contexts, Critical Essays*. Edited by Geoffrey Sanborn. Boston: Houghton Mifflin, 2004.
Merish, Lori. *Sentimental Materialism: Gender, Commodity Culture, and Nineteenth-Century American Literature*. Durham, NC: Duke UP, 2000.
Merry, Robert. "The Slaves. An Elegy." In *Slavery, Abolition, and Emancipation: Writings in the British Romantic Period*, vol. 4: *Verse*, edited by Alan Richardson, 101–2. London: Pickering & Chatto, 1999.
Mesle, Sarah. "Sentimentalism's Nation: Maria J. McIntosh and the Antebellum Contexts of 'Southern' Fiction." *Studies in American Fiction* 40, no. 2 (2013): 203–30.
Michaels, Walter Benn. *The Gold Standard and the Logic of Naturalism*. Berkeley: U of California P, 1987.
Midgley, Clare. *Feminism and Empire: Women Activists in Imperial Britain, 1790–1865*. London: Routledge, 2007.
Miles, Tiya. *All That She Carried: The Journey of Ashley's Sack, a Black Family Keepsake*. New York: Random House, 2021.
Miller, William Ian. *The Anatomy of Disgust*. Cambridge, MA: Harvard UP, 1997.
Milton, John. *Complete Prose Works of John Milton*. Vol. 6. Edited by Maurice Kelley, Translated by John Carey. New Haven, CT: Yale UP, 1953.
Mintz, Sidney W. *Sweetness and Power: The Place of Sugar in Modern History*. New York: Viking, 1985.
Miranda, Carolina A. "Q&A: Kara Walker on the Bit of Sugar Sphinx She Saved, Video She's Making." *Los Angeles Times*, October 13, 2014, sec. Entertainment & Arts.
Mitchell, Koritha. "Teaching and the N-Word: Questions to Consider," March 23, 2018. https://www.korithamitchell.com/teaching-and-the-n-word/.
"A Modern Cannibal." *Cleveland Herald*, September 18, 1848. Nineteenth Century U.S. Newspapers.
Moers, Ellen. *Harriet Beecher Stowe and American Literature*. Hartford, CT: Stowe-Day Foundation, 1978.
Montaigne, Michel de. *Essays*. Translated by J. M. Cohen. Baltimore: Penguin, 1958.
Montgomery, James. "The West Indies." In *Slavery, Abolition, and Emancipation: Writings in the British Romantic Period*, vol. 4: *Verse*, edited by Alan Richardson, 279–332. London: Pickering & Chatto, 1999.
Moody, Joycelyn. *Sentimental Confessions: Spiritual Narratives of Nineteenth-Century African American Women*. Athens: U of Georgia P, 2001.

Moran, Thomas. *Slave Hunt, Dismal Swamp, Virginia*. Oil on canvas, 1862. Philbrook Museum of Art, Tulsa.
Morrison, Toni. *Playing in the Dark: Whiteness and the Literary Imagination*. First published by Harvard UP, 1992. New York: Vintage, 1993.
Morton, Timothy. *The Poetics of Spice: Romantic Consumerism and the Exotic*. Cambridge: Cambridge UP, 2000.
Munro, Cait. "Offensive Instagram Pics Plague Walker's Sphinx." *Artnet News*, May 30, 2014, sec. Art & Exhibitions. https://news.artnet.com/art-world/kara-walkers-sugar-sphinx-spawns-offensive-instagram-photos-29989.
Nathan, Hans. "The Performance of the Virginia Minstrels." In *Inside the Minstrel Mask: Readings in Nineteenth-Century Blackface Minstrelsy*, edited by Annemarie Bean, James V. Hatch, and Brooks McNamara, 35–42. Hanover, NH: Wesleyan UP, 1996.
Navakas, Michele Currie. *Coral Lives: Literature, Labor, and the Making of America*. Princeton, NJ: Princeton UP, 2023.
The Negro Forget-Me-Not Songster. Philadelphia: Fisher & Brother, 1857.
The Negro Singer's Own Book: Containing Every Negro Song That Has Ever Been Sung or Printed. Philadelphia: Turner & Fisher, 1846.
Newbury, Michael. "Eaten Alive: Slavery and Celebrity in Antebellum America." *ELH* 61, no. 1 (1994): 159–87.
Ngai, Sianne. *Ugly Feelings*. Cambridge, MA: Harvard UP, 2004.
Noble, Marianne. *The Masochistic Pleasures of Sentimental Literature*. Princeton, NJ: Princeton UP, 2000.
———. *Rethinking Sympathy and Human Contact in Nineteenth-Century American Literature: Hawthorne, Douglass, Stowe, Dickinson*. Cambridge: Cambridge UP, 2019.
"Northern Cannibalism." *New York Times*, December 22, 1859.
Northup, Solomon. *Twelve Years a Slave*. New York: Penguin, 2012.
Norton, Anne. *Republic of Signs: Liberal Theory and American Popular Culture*. Chicago: U of Chicago P, 1993.
Nyong'o, Tavia. "Racial Kitsch and Black Performance." *Yale Journal of Criticism* 15, no. 2 (Fall 2002): 371–91.
O'Connell, JoAnne. *The Life and Songs of Stephen Foster: A Revealing Portrait of the Forgotten Man Behind "Swanee River," "Beautiful Dreamer," and "My Old Kentucky Home."* Lanham, MD: Rowman & Littlefield, 2016.
Olmsted, Frederick Law. *The Cotton Kingdom: A Traveller's Observations on Cotton and Slavery in the American Slave States. Based upon Three Former Volumes of Journeys and Investigations by the Same Author*. New York: Knopf, 1953.
Owens, Leslie Howard. *This Species of Property: Slave Life and Culture in the Old South*. New York: Oxford UP, 1976.

Owsley, Frank Lawrence. "The Irrepressible Conflict." In *I'll Take My Stand: The South and the Agrarian Tradition*, 61–91. New York: Harper, 1962.

Palencia-Roth, Michael. "The Cannibal Law of 1503." In *Early Images of the Americas: Transfer and Invention*, edited by Jerry M. Williams and Robert E. Lewis, 21–64. Tucson: U of Arizona P, 1993.

Paquette, Robert L. *Sugar Is Made with Blood: The Conspiracy of La Escalera and the Conflict Between Empires over Slavery in Cuba*. Middletown, CT: Wesleyan UP, 1988.

Pelletier, Kevin. *Apocalyptic Sentimentalism: Love and Fear in U.S. Antebellum Literature*. Athens: U of Georgia P, 2015.

Peterson, Christopher. *Bestial Traces: Race, Sexuality, Animality*. New York: Fordham UP, 2013.

Pettey, Homer B. "Cannibalism, Slavery, and Self-Consumption in *Moby-Dick*." *Arizona Quarterly: A Journal of American Literature, Culture, and Theory* 59, no. 1 (2003): 31–58.

Philadelphia Free Produce Association of Friends. *An Address to the Members of the Religious Society of Friends on the Subject of Slavery and the Slave-Trade*. Philadelphia, 1849.

Phillips, Jerry. "Cannibalism qua Capitalism: The Metaphorics of Accumulation in Marx, Conrad, Shakespeare and Marlowe." In *Cannibalism and the Colonial World*, edited by Francis Barker, Peter Hulme, and Margaret Iversen, 183–203. Cambridge: Cambridge UP, 1998.

Pickering, Michael. "The Blackface Songster in Britain." In *Cheap Print and Popular Song in the Nineteenth Century: A Cultural History of the Songster*, edited by Paul Watt, Derek Scott, and Patrick Spedding, 184–204. Cambridge: Cambridge UP, 2017.

Piersen, William Dillon. *Black Legacy: America's Hidden Heritage*. Amherst: U of Massachusetts P, 1993.

Pietz, William. "The Problem of the Fetish, I." *Res: Anthropology and Aesthetics* 9 (1985): 5–17.

Plasa, Carl. "'Stained with Spots of Human Blood': Sugar, Abolition and Cannibalism." *Atlantic Studies* 4, no. 2 (2007): 225–43.

Pocock, J. G. A. *Virtue, Commerce, and History: Essays on Political Thought and History, Chiefly in the Eighteenth Century*. Ideas in Context. Cambridge: Cambridge UP, 1985.

Powers, Nicholas. "Why I Yelled at the Kara Walker Exhibit," June 30, 2014. https://indypendent.org/2014/06/why-i-yelled-at-the-kara-walker-exhibit/.

Priest, Josiah. *Slavery, As It Relates to the Negro, or African Race*. Albany, NY: C. Van Benthuysen, 1843.

Prince, Mary. *The History of Mary Prince: A West Indian Slave*. Edited by Moira Ferguson. Ann Arbor: U of Michigan P, 1997.
"Products of Slave Labor." *The Liberator*, March 5, 1847. Nineteenth Century U.S. Newspapers.
Randolph, Peter. *From Slave Cabin to the Pulpit: the Autobiography of Rev. Peter Randolph: The Southern Question Illustrated and Sketches of Slave Life*. Boston: James H. Earle, 1893.
Raynal, Abbé (Guillaume-Thomas-François). *A Philosophical and Political History of the Settlements and Trade of the Europeans in the East and West Indies* [. . .]. Translated by J. O. Justamond. Vol. 4. Dublin: John Exshaw, Grafton Street, and Luke White, Dame Street, 1784.
Rediker, Marcus. "History from Below the Water Line: Sharks and the Atlantic Slave Trade." *Atlantic Studies* 5, no. 2 (August 2008): 285–97.
———. "Slavery: A Shark's Perspective." *Boston Globe*, September 23, 2007, sec. Ideas.
Reynolds, David S. *Mightier Than the Sword: "Uncle Tom's Cabin" and the Battle for America*. New York: W. W. Norton, 2011.
Rice, Alan. "Exploring Inside the Invisible: An Interview with Lubaina Himid." *Wasafiri* 18, no. 40 (2003): 20–26.
———. "'Who's Eating Whom': The Discourse of Cannibalism in the Literature of the Black Atlantic from *Equiano's Travels* to Toni Morrison's *Beloved*." *Research in African Literatures* 29, no. 4 (Winter 1998): 106–21.
Richards, Laura Elizabeth Howe, Maud Howe Elliott, and Florence Howe Hall. *Julia Ward Howe, 1819–1910*. Boston: Houghton Mifflin, 1915.
Ricœur, Paul. "The Metaphorical Process as Cognition, Imagination, and Feeling." *Critical Inquiry* 5, no. 1 (Autumn 1978): 143–59.
Robert, Joseph C. *The Story of Tobacco in America*. Chapel Hill: U of North Carolina P, 1967.
———. *The Tobacco Kingdom: Plantation, Market, and Factory in Virginia and North Carolina, 1800–1860*. Gloucester, MA: P. Smith, 1965.
Roberts, Brian. *Blackface Nation: Race, Reform, and Identity in American Popular Music, 1812–1925*. Chicago: U of Chicago P, 2017.
Robertson, Stacey M. *Hearts Beating for Liberty*. Chapel Hill: U of North Carolina P, 2010.
Robinson, Harriet Jane Hanson. *Loom and Spindle: or, Life Among the Early Mill Girls. With a Sketch of "The Lowell Offering" and Some of Its Contributors*. New York: T. Y. Crowell, 1898.
Roediger, David R. *The Wages of Whiteness: Race and the Making of the American Working Class*. London: Verso, 1991.

Rohrbach, Augusta. "'A Silent Unobtrusive Way': Hannah Crafts and the Literary Marketplace." In *In Search of Hannah Crafts: Critical Essays on "The Bondwoman's Narrative,"* edited by Henry Louis Gates Jr. and Hollis Robbins, 3–15. New York: BasicCivitas, 2004.

Rooney, Kara L. "A Sonorous Subtlety: Kara Walker with Kara Rooney." *Brooklyn Rail*, May 2014. https://brooklynrail.org/2014/05/art/kara-walker-with-kara-rooney/.

Ross, Kelly. *Slavery, Surveillance and Genre in Antebellum United States Literature*. Oxford Studies in American Literary History. Oxford: Oxford UP, 2022.

Ruffin, Edmund. *An Essay on Calcareous Manures*. Petersburg, VA: J. W. Campbell, 1832.

Ruggles, Jeffrey. *The Unboxing of Henry Brown*. Richmond: Library of Virginia, 2003.

Rusert, Britt. *Fugitive Science: Empiricism and Freedom in Early African American Culture*. New York: New York UP, 2017.

Sanborn, Geoffrey. *The Sign of the Cannibal: Melville and the Making of a Postcolonial Reader*. Durham, NC: Duke UP, 1998.

Sánchez-Eppler, Karen. *Touching Liberty: Abolition, Feminism, and the Politics of the Body*. Berkeley: U of California P, 1993.

Schermerhorn, Calvin. *The Business of Slavery and the Rise of American Capitalism, 1815–1860*. New Haven, CT: Yale UP, 2015.

Schoolman, Martha. *Abolitionist Geographies*. Minneapolis: U of Minnesota P, 2014.

Schor, Joel. *Henry Highland Garnet: A Voice of Black Radicalism in the Nineteenth Century*. Westport, CT: Greenwood P, 1977.

Schuller, Kyla. *The Biopolitics of Feeling: Race, Sex, and Science in the Nineteenth Century*. Durham, NC: Duke UP, 2018.

Sedgwick, Catharine Maria. *Home*. Boston: James Munroe, 1850.

Sedgwick, Eve Kosofsky. *Epistemology of the Closet*. Berkeley: U of California P, 2008.

———. "Shame, Theatricality, and Queer Performativity: Henry James's *The Art of the Novel*." In *Touching Feeling: Affect, Pedagogy, Performativity*, 35–65. Series Q. Durham, NC: Duke UP, 2003.

Shammas, Carole. "Changes in English and Anglo-American Consumption from 1550 to 1800." In *Consumption and the World of Goods*, edited by John Brewer and Roy Porter, 177–205. Consumption and Culture in the 17th and 18th Centuries. London: Routledge, 1993.

Sheller, Mimi. "Bleeding Humanity and Gendered Embodiments: From Antislavery Sugar Boycotts to Ethical Consumers." *Humanity: An International Journal of Human Rights, Humanitarianism, and Development* 2, no. 2 (2011): 171–92.

———. *Consuming the Caribbean: From Arawaks to Zombies*. London: Routledge, 2003.

Shotwell, Alexis. *Against Purity: Living Ethically in Compromised Times.* U of Minnesota P, 2016.

Sinha, Manisha. *The Slave's Cause: A History of Abolition.* New Haven, CT: Yale UP, 2016.

"Sketch of a Few of the Horrors of Slavery." *Weekly Aurora,* January 18, 1819. America's Historical Newspapers.

Slavery and the Internal Slave Trade in the United States of North America: Being Replies to Questions Transmitted by the Committee of the British and Foreign Anti-Slavery Society for the Abolition of Slavery and the Slave Trade Throughout the World, Presented to the General Anti-Slavery Convention Held in London, June 1840. London: Thomas Ward, 1841.

Smith, Valerie. *Self-Discovery and Authority in Afro-American Narrative.* Cambridge, MA: Harvard UP, 1987.

Songs of the Congo Melodists. Sheet Music Lithograph, 1844. American Antiquarian Society.

Southey, Robert. *Poems.* Bristol, UK: N. Biggs, for Joseph Cottle, 1797.

———. "Verses Spoken in the Theatre at Oxford upon the Installation of Lord Grenville." In *Slavery, Abolition, and Emancipation: Writings in the British Romantic Period,* vol. 4: *Verse,* edited by Alan Richardson, 255–58. London: Pickering & Chatto, 1999.

Stein, Mark. "Who's Afraid of Cannibals? Some Uses of the Cannibalism Trope in Olaudah Equiano's Interesting Narrative." In *Discourses of Slavery and Abolition: Britain and Its Colonies, 1760–1838,* edited by Brycchan Carey, Markman Ellis, and Sara Salih. Houndmills, Basingstoke, Hampshire, UK: Palgrave Macmillan, 2004.

Stowe, Harriet Beecher. *The Key to Uncle Tom's Cabin.* Salem, NH: Ayer, 1987.

———. *Uncle Tom's Cabin.* Edited by Elizabeth Ammons. 2nd ed. Norton Critical Edition. New York: W. W. Norton, 2010.

Sundquist, Eric J. *To Wake the Nations.* Cambridge, MA: Belknap P of Harvard UP, 1993. http://archive.org/details/towakenationsracoosund.

Sussman, Charlotte. *Consuming Anxieties: Consumer Protest, Gender, and British Slavery, 1713–1833.* Stanford: Stanford UP, 2000.

Swift, Jonathan. "A Modest Proposal." In *The Essential Writings of Jonathan Swift,* edited by Claude Julien Rawson and Ian Higgins, 295–301. New York: W. W. Norton, 2007.

Tawa, Nicholas E. *High-Minded and Low-Down: Music in the Lives of Americans, 1800–1861.* Boston: Northeastern UP, 2000.

———. *Sweet Songs for Gentle Americans.* Bowling Green, OH: Bowling Green U Popular P, 1980.

Thelwell, Chinua. *Exporting Jim Crow: Blackface Minstrelsy in South Africa and Beyond*. Amherst: U of Massachusetts P, 2020.
Thoreau, Henry David. "Life Without Principle." In *Collected Essays and Poems*, 348–66. New York: Library of America, 2001.
———. "Resistance to Civil Government." In *Thoreau: Political Writings*, edited by Nancy L. Rosenblum, 1–21. Cambridge: Cambridge UP, 1996.
———. "Slavery in Massachusetts." In *Collected Essays and Poems*, 333–47. New York: Library of America, 2001.
———. *Walden: A Fully Annotated Edition*. Edited by Jeffrey S. Cramer. New Haven, CT: Yale UP, 2004.
Thornton, John. "Cannibals, Witches, and Slave Traders in the Atlantic World." *William and Mary Quarterly* 60, no. 2 (April 2003): 273–94.
Tocqueville, Alexis de. *Journey to America*. Edited by J. P. Mayer. Translated by George Lawrence. New Haven, CT: Yale UP, 1960.
Todd, Janet. *Sensibility: An Introduction*. London: Methuen, 1986.
Toll, Robert C. *Blacking Up: The Minstrel Show in Nineteenth Century America*. New York: Oxford UP, 1974.
Tompkins, Jane. *Sensational Designs: The Cultural Work of American Fiction, 1790–1860*. New York: Oxford UP, 1985.
Tompkins, Kyla Wazana. *Racial Indigestion: Eating Bodies in the 19th Century*. New York: New York UP, 2012.
Tong, Joanne. "'Pity for the Poor Africans': William Cowper and the Limits of Abolitionist Affect." In *Affect and Abolition in the Anglo-Atlantic, 1770–1830*, edited by Stephen Ahern, 129–50. Surrey, UK: Ashgate, 2013.
"Too Black a Dose." *Frank Leslie's Illustrated Newspaper*, November 23, 1867.
Turner, Patricia A. *Ceramic Uncles and Celluloid Mammies: Black Images and Their Influence on Culture*. Charlottesville: UP of Virginia, 1994.
"The Virginia Slave Crop." *Frederick Douglass' Paper*, February 25, 1853.
Wanzo, Rebecca. *The Suffering Will Not Be Televised: African American Women and Sentimental Political Storytelling*. New York: State U of New York P, 2009.
Warner, Marina. "Fee Fie Fo Fum: The Child in the Jaws of the Story." In *Cannibalism and the Colonial World*, edited by Francis Barker, Peter Hulme, and Margaret Iversen, 158–82. Cambridge: Cambridge UP, 1998.
Watson, Kelly L. *Insatiable Appetites: Imperial Encounters with Cannibals in the North Atlantic World*. Early American Places. New York: New York UP, 2015.
Watt, Paul. "The Prefaces to Songsters: The Law, Aesthetics, Performers and Their Reputations." In *Cheap Print and Popular Song in the Nineteenth Century: A Cultural History of the Songster*, edited by Paul Watt, Derek Scott, and Patrick Spedding, 32–46. Cambridge: Cambridge UP, 2017.

Walker, Jonathan. "Products of Slave Labor." *The Liberator*, March 5, 1847. Nineteenth Century U.S. Newspapers.

Wayne, Michael. *Death of an Overseer: Reopening a Murder Investigation from the Plantation South*. Oxford: Oxford UP, 2001.

Weinstein, Cindy. *Family, Kinship, and Sympathy in Nineteenth-Century American Literature*. Cambridge Studies in American Literature and Culture. Cambridge: Cambridge UP, 2004.

Whelan, Timothy. "William Fox, Martha Gurney, and Radical Discourse of the 1790s." *Eighteenth-Century Studies* 42, no. 3 (2009): 397–411.

White, Andrew. "A 'Consuming' Oppression: Sugar, Cannibalism and John Woolman's 1770 Slave Dream." *Quaker History* 96, no. 2 (2007): 1–27.

Who Are the Slaveholders? A Moral Drawn from "Uncle Tom's Cabin," Respectfully Submitted to the Readers of That Work. Newcastle-on-Tyne: Selkirk and Rhago, Printers, [18–?].

Wilkinson, Norman B. "The Philadelphia Free Produce Attack upon Slavery." *Pennsylvania Magazine of History and Biography* 66, no. 3 (1942): 294–313.

"William M. Adams (Interview)." In *Federal Writers' Project: Slave Narrative Project, Vol. 16, Texas, Part 1, Adams-Duhon*. n.d. http://hdl.loc.gov/loc.mss/mesn.161.

Williams, Raymond. *Keywords: A Vocabulary of Culture and Society*. Oxford: Oxford UP, 2014.

Wilson, James C. "Letter of Rev. James C. Wilson." *Texas State Gazette*, September 24, 1859. America's Historical Newspapers.

Winans, Robert B. "Early Minstrel Show Music, 1843–1852." In *Inside the Minstrel Mask: Readings in Nineteenth-Century Blackface Minstrelsy*, edited by Annemarie Bean, James V. Hatch, and Brooks McNamara, 141–62. Hanover, NH: Wesleyan UP, 1996.

Wirzbicki, Peter. *Fighting for the Higher Law: Black and White Transcendentalists Against Slavery*. Philadelphia: U of Pennsylvania P, 2021.

Wittke, Carl Frederick. *Tambo and Bones: A History of the American Minstrel Stage*. Durham, NC: Duke UP, 1930.

Wolfe, Cary. "Human, All Too Human: 'Animal Studies' and the Humanities." *PMLA* 124, no. 2 (March 2009): 564–75.

Woodard, Vincent. *The Delectable Negro: Human Consumption and Homoeroticism Within U.S. Slave Culture*. New York: New York UP, 2014.

"The 'Wool League.'" *The Non-Slaveholder*, September 2, 1850. Slavery and Anti-Slavery.

Woolman, John. *The Journal and Major Essays of John Woolman*. Edited by Phillips P. Moulton. New York: Oxford UP, 1971.

X, Malcolm. "Founding Rally of the OAAU (New York, June 28, 1964)." In *By Any Means Necessary*, 33–67. New York: Pathfinder P, 1970.

Yafa, Stephen H. *Big Cotton: How a Humble Fiber Created Fortunes, Wrecked Civilizations, and Put America on the Map*. New York: Viking, 2005.

Yao, Xine. *Disaffected: The Cultural Politics of Unfeeling in Nineteenth-Century America*. Durham, NC: Duke UP, 2021.

Yellin, Jean Fagan. "Doing It Herself: *Uncle Tom's Cabin* and Woman's Role in the Slavery Crisis." In *New Essays on "Uncle Tom's Cabin,"* edited by Eric J. Sundquist, 85–105. The American Novel. Cambridge: Cambridge UP, 1986.

———. "Hawthorne and the Slavery Question." In *A Historical Guide to Nathaniel Hawthorne*, edited by Larry J. Reynolds, 135–64. Historical Guides to American Authors. Oxford: Oxford UP, 2001.

Zoellner, Robert. *The Salt-Sea Mastodon: A Reading of "Moby-Dick."* Berkeley: U of California P, 1973.

INDEX

abolitionism, 1–2, 5–6, 11–12, 71, 161n22; cannibalism metaphors and, 19–21, 24–27, 35–36, 38–41, 43, 47, 67, 100, 113–14, 119, 124–25, 127; capitalism and, 3–4, 160n13, 182n61; connection and, 5–6, 8–11, 13–14, 16, 22, 45–50, 52, 59–62, 64–65, 71, 73–75, 77–80, 94–95, 109–10, 116–18, 126–27, 151–57; disgust and, 21–22, 24, 32–36, 40–41, 47–50, 62–65, 71, 73–75, 109–10, 125–27, 151–53; hungry animal tropes and, 127–30, 132–39, 141–49; physicality and, 21–22, 25–31, 33–34, 36, 39–41, 43, 49–50; racism and, 6–7, 13, 15–16, 20–21, 24–28, 33–36, 40–41, 43, 126–27, 132–34, 148; sentimentalism and, 8–9, 13–14, 19–20, 45–50, 52–53, 55–58, 61–66, 71; stoic slave figure and, 30; as transatlantic, 7–8, 12, 15–16, 45–47; violent resistance and, 46, 141–49, 161n22. *See also* free produce (free labor) movement

abstention, 7–8, 12, 20, 22, 45–49, 154–55, 162n28, 165nn4–5, 169n5. *See also* free produce (free labor) movement; sugar: abstention campaign

action, 3–4, 15–16; versus emotion, 9–11, 13–14, 16, 19–23, 40–41, 45, 48–50, 52–54, 57–58, 61–66, 152–53, 157, 164n49

activism, 2–14, 16, 21–22, 43, 44–47, 54, 56–58, 61–62, 77–79, 100, 121, 125, 151–57, 162n28, 170n10, 180n2; disgust and, 8–11, 21, 47, 151–53; sentimentalism and, 8. *See also* abstention; free produce (free labor) movement; *and under* consumption

affect. *See* emotion

alligators, 133–36, 185n25. *See also* animals, animality

American Colonization Society, 106
Andrews, William L., 148–49
animals, animality, 12, 15–16, 68, 99, 126–49, 152–53, 184n2, 184n4, 185n7, 185n25, 187n61. *See also individual animals by name*
Ansdell, Richard, *Hunted Slaves*, 146–48
Anthony, David, 122, 124
anthropophagi. *See* cannibalism
anti-Blackness. *See* racism
appetite. *See* consumption
Arabindan-Kesson, Anna, 156
Arawak people, 101–2
aversion. *See* disgust

Baldwin, James, 10
Ball, Charles, 141–42; *Slavery in the United States*, 127–28
Balthrop-Lewis, Alda, 51, 170n30
Baptist, Edward E., 100
Barrow, Washington, 119–20
Beaumont, Gustave de, *Marie, or Slavery in the United States*, 118
Beckert, Sven, 47–48
Bennett, Joshua, 132, 140
Bernstein, Robin, 91–92, 175n28, 176n52
Best, Stephen M., 23, 187n55
Bibb, Henry, 141–44, 187n61, 187n63
Birkett, Mary, "A Poem on the African Slave Trade, Addressed to Her Own Sex," 28–30, 132
blackface. *See* minstrelsy, blackface
blood, 8–9, 11–14, 19–43, 44–49, 59–67, 122–23, 131–32, 151–52, 155, 165n5, 168n57, 168n59, 183n84. *See also under* sugar
bloodhounds. *See* dogs

body: commodity and, 6, 8, 14, 20–25, 61–64, 68–70, 72–74, 76–82, 85–89, 116–19, 127–28, 134–35, 143, 156–57; consumption and, 31–36, 39–40, 43, 77–78, 80–81, 86–87, 101, 109–10, 119, 121–22, 131, 133–36, 155–57; fluids of, 20–22, 30–31, 33–35, 44–45, 47–49, 61–63, 131–32, 155, 167n49; labor and, 60–61; physicality and, 24–31, 35, 39–40; race and, 6, 24–25, 27–36, 39–40, 43, 101, 124, 127–28, 155–56, 168n52, 177n55
Boggs, Colleen Glenney, 127–28
Boisseron, Bénédicte, 127–28
Bolker, Jamie, 127–28
Booth, Wayne C., 103–4
boycott. *See* abstention; activism
Brooks, Daphne A., 143
Brown, Clara, 87–88
Brown, Gillian, 53, 122–23
Brown, Henry "Box," *Mirror of Slavery*, 142–45, 148–49, 187n61
Brown, William Wells, 136–37; "Hunting the Slave with the Negro Dogs," 143; *Original Panoramic Views of the Scenes in the Life of an American Slave*, 142–44
Buchanan, James, 115–16
Burke, William, 113
Burn, Andrew, 22, 35–36, 167n49, 168n52; *A Second Address to the People of Great Britain*, 32–35

cannibalism, 168n59, 173n97, 173n101, 180nn5–6, 180n8, 183n69; colonialism and, 102–6, 124–25, 180nn10–11; communion and, 22–25, 166n21; disgust and, 20–21, 24–25, 33, 43;

national identity and, 14–15, 100–101, 107–16, 121, 181n34; proximity and, 20–21, 26–27, 34, 109–10; race and, 105–16, 119–25, 127–28, 169n85, 180n10, 182n44; slavery and, 6, 12–13, 20–27, 32–36, 38–43, 44–46, 67–70, 78, 100–122, 124–25, 126–28, 138, 152, 162n27, 169n85

capitalism, 53–55, 120, 182n61, 183n69; abolitionism and, 3–4, 160n13

Chandler, Elizabeth Margaret, 13–14, 46–47, 49–50; "Oh Press Me Not to Taste Again," 64; "Slave Luxuries," 61–63; "Slave Produce," 61–62

Chaney, Michael A., 143

Clarkson, Thomas, 129, 133, 161n18

class: consumption and, 78–79, 86–88, 91–95; identity and, 75–76, 89–90, 92–94, 152–53; minstrelsy and, 14, 75–76, 78–80, 86–95, 152–53, 179n88, 179n92; race and, 5–6, 73–76, 79–80, 83–84, 86–88, 91–95, 122; respectability and, 75–76, 89, 91–95; sentimental literature and, 3; slavery and, 11–12, 14, 75–76, 83, 86–88

close reading, 11

coffee, 77–78, 85–87

Coffin, Catherine, 57, 172n60

Coffin, Levi, 57, 172n60

Coleman, Deirdre, 21

Coleridge, Samuel Taylor, 13, 19–20, 36, 47, 166n18; "On the Slave Trade," 22–25

colonialism, 102–6, 109, 124–25, 180n11

Columbus, Christopher, 101–2

commodity, commodification: body and, 6, 8, 14, 20–25, 61–64, 68–70, 72–74, 76–82, 85–89, 116–19, 127–28, 134–35, 143, 156–57; defetishizing, 11–14, 22–23, 35–36, 46–47, 50–51, 59, 70, 73, 78, 155–56; human as, 20, 26–27, 59–61, 69–70, 72–74, 76–83, 99, 101, 104, 119, 148; labor and, 13–15, 22–23, 35–36, 38–39, 52, 59–61, 63–64, 71, 77–78, 85, 88–89, 155–56; as luxury, 2–3, 22–23, 44–45, 51, 131, 171n36; materiality of, 2–3, 23, 27, 40, 59, 61–66, 73, 99, 156, 171n36; networks of, 13–14, 49–53, 56–59, 65–66, 70; proximity and, 46–47, 49, 157; race and, 72–73, 85, 88–89, 94–95, 101, 117–18, 127–28; suffering and, 1–2, 5–6, 19–20, 22–23, 26, 44–45, 49–50, 55–56, 59, 62–68, 70, 83; willing, 79–85, 94–95. *See also* consumption; fetish

communion, 23–27

connection. *See* consumption-as-connection

Conrad, Jessica, 49, 61

Constitutional Unionist Party, 119–20

consumer activism. *See* activism

consumption, 4–5, 161n18, 162n25; activism and, 3–8, 10–13, 21–22, 45–47, 56–58, 61–62, 77–79, 151–51, 154–56, 162n28; animality and, 126–29, 131–39, 141–48, 152–53, 185n7; body and, 31–36, 39–40, 43, 77–78, 80–81, 86–87, 101, 109–10, 119, 121–22, 131, 133–36, 155–57; class and, 78–79, 86–88, 91–95; desire and, 6, 74–75, 134–35, 155–56; disgust and, 13–14, 73–74, 78, 151–53, 155, 157; domesticity and, 53, 56–58; ethics of, 3–4, 9, 11–12, 24, 28–29, 44–47, 49–53, 56–59, 64–65, 74–75,

consumption (*continued*)
78, 107–8, 111–12, 119, 121–23, 132, 138, 141, 151–55, 157, 169nn5–6, 170n20; gender and, 52–53, 56–57, 93–94; materiality of, 6, 11–12, 51, 99; metaphors of, 5–6, 8, 11–16, 20–22, 24–27, 33–36, 40–43, 68–69, 99–112, 116–17, 119–31, 133, 139–42, 148–49, 152, 162n27, 165n5, 168n57, 180n5, 183n69; multivalence of, 4–7, 99, 101; networks of, 6–7, 13–14, 49–50, 58, 74–75, 152, 157; passive victims of, 15–16, 127, 133–36, 148; of performance, 14, 71, 75–76; proximity and, 20–21, 26–27, 34, 109–10; race and, 6, 14–15, 73–89, 93–95, 100–103, 108–11, 114–15, 121–25, 127–29, 132–35, 159n1; resistance and, 142–48; slavery and, 1–16, 19–20, 31–32, 36–50, 59–60, 68, 72–75, 78–80, 82–83, 86–89, 99, 108, 117–19, 126–32, 135–38, 141–43, 148–49, 151–52, 154–56, 159n1, 161n18, 162n25; violence of, 1–2, 6, 19–20, 33, 36–38, 66, 68–70, 83, 101, 115–16, 120, 125–27, 129, 131–33, 137–41. *See also* animals, animality; cannibalism; commodity, commodification

consumption-as-connection, 5–16, 40–41, 44–50, 52, 58–62, 71, 73–80, 126–27, 162n34, 165n55, 183n82; action and, 13–14, 44–50, 153–55, 157; animals and, 99–100, 126–27; cannibalism and, 20–22, 24, 26–27, 31–32, 44–45, 68–69, 99–100, 108–10, 116–18, 121, 126–27, 133–34, 153; disgust and, 9–10, 13–14, 21, 24, 26–27, 44–45, 48–50, 61–62, 64–66, 108–10, 151–53; minstrelsy and, 14, 73–75, 78, 94–95, 152–53; sentimentalism and, 8–11, 44–45, 49–50

contamination. *See* disgust

Cooper, Thomas, *Letters on the Slave Trade*, 4–5, 161n18

corn, 72, 77, 85

Cottom, Daniel, 67, 180n11

cotton, 4–5, 7–8, 11–12, 44–45, 47–48, 57, 61–64, 75–76, 79–80, 85–89, 99, 117–18, 156, 171n57, 176n52, 177n55

Coviello, Peter, 11

Cowper, William, "Negro's Complaint," 27

Crafts, Hannah, 136–37, 153, 186n33; *The Bondwoman's Narrative*, 137–40, 148–49

Crèvecœur, J. Hector St. John de, *Letters from an American Farmer*, 131, 133, 135–38

Cutter, Martha J., 133, 141–42

dandy, 93–94, 178n79, 179n84

Davis, David Brion, 2

defetishization. *See* commodity, commodification: defetishizing

Dessalines, Jean-Jacques, 43

Dickens, Charles, *Great Expectations*, 78

disgust: cannibalism and, 20–21, 24–25, 33, 43; consumption and, 8–11, 13–16, 19–21, 24–25, 27–28, 33–36, 40–41, 43–45, 47–50, 58, 61–66, 74–75, 78–80, 109–10, 121–23, 125, 126–27, 151–53, 155, 157, 173n91, 183n82; political efficacy of, 9, 71; racism and, 9, 13–16, 20–21, 27–28, 33–36, 40–41, 43, 71, 74–75, 78, 109–10, 121–22, 125, 126–27, 152–53

Dish of "Black Turtle," A, 114–15

Dobson, Joanne, 8–9

dogs, 1–2, 138–48, 184n2, 187n61
Domino Sugar, 155
Douglas, Mary, 109–10
Douglas, Stephen, 115–16
Douglass, Frederick, 14–15, 153–54; *My Bondage and My Freedom*, 118–19, 126, 136–39, 141, 148–49; *Narrative of the Life of Frederick Douglass*, 118–19; "What to the Slave Is the Fourth of July?," 4–5
drivers, 84, 176nn46–47

eating. *See* consumption
economics: consumption and, 116–31, 133–36, 138, 148; ethics and, 7–8, 11–12, 49, 51; of slavery, 4, 6–8, 11–16, 20, 46, 51–58, 65–66, 68–70, 74–75, 80, 87–88, 99–101, 116–21, 126–31, 133–38, 141, 148–49, 152–53, 155–56, 161n18, 162n25
Ellis, Markman, 3
Emerson, Ralph Waldo, 14–15, 107–8, 111–13, 116–17
emotion: action and, 9–11, 13–14, 16, 19–23, 40–41, 45, 48–50, 52–54, 57–58, 61–66, 152–53, 157, 164n49; consumption and, 8–10, 22–23, 32, 47, 62–64, 101, 126–27, 152–53, 155. *See also* disgust; sympathy
entanglement, 2, 5–7, 12, 47–48, 50–51, 54–55, 57–58, 78–79, 154–55
Equiano, Olaudah, 13, 22, 40–43, 118–19, 131, 153

Faherty, Duncan, 155
Falconbridge, Alexander, *Account of the Slave Trade on the Coast of Africa*, 30–31

Fanon, Frantz, 106–7, 188n9
Faulkner, Carol, 154
fetish, 22–23, 51–52, 70, 78. *See also* commodity, commodification
Fielder, Brigitte, 127–28
Fitzhugh, George, *Cannibals All!*, 120
Foster, Stephen, 94; "Uncle Ned," 85–86
Fox, William, 20, 47, 166n10; *An Address to the People of Great Britain*, 31–32
Franklin, Benjamin, 32
Freedgood, Elaine, 78
free produce (free labor) movement, 13–14, 44–50, 53–58, 60–66, 71, 151–55, 162n28, 169nn5–6, 170nn19–20, 171n57. *See also* abstention
Free Soil Party, 115–16
Fugitive Slave Law, 23, 107–9, 113–17, 181n34
Furibond; or, Harlequin Negro, 30–31

Garner, Margaret, 119
Garnet, Henry Highland, 151–54
Garrison, William Lloyd, 46–48, 118–19
gender: consumption and, 53, 56–57, 93–94, 141; race and, 93–94, 155–56; sentimental literature and, 3
Gikandi, Simon, 19–20
Gilmore, Michael T., 124
Glickman, Lawrence B., 3–4, 6, 162n28
Goddu, Teresa A., 131–32, 163n45, 187n63
Goldsby, Jacqueline, 11
Green, Charles C., *The Nubian Slave*, 144–45, 187n61
Green, J. D., 141–42
Greyser, Naomi, 8

Haitian Revolution, 43, 166n10, 169n85
Halttunen, Karen, 93, 179n88
Harper, Frances Ellen Watkins, 13–14, 44–45, 49–50, 59–60, 62–63; "Free Labor," 47, 64–65; "The Free Labor Movement," 63–64; *Poems on Miscellaneous Subjects*, 47
Hartman, Saidiya, 25, 69–70, 132–33
Haskell, Thomas, 3–4, 162n33
Hawthorne, Nathaniel, *The House of the Seven Gables*, 100–101, 121–22, 124–25
Hegel, Georg Wilhelm Friedrich, *Philosophy of History*, 105–6
Herodotus, *Histories*, 101–2
Heyrick, Elizabeth, *Immediate, Not Gradual Abolition*, 7–8, 46–47
Himid, Lubaina, *Cotton.com*, 156–57
Hoermann, Raphael, 43
Holcomb, Julie L., 48–49
Hood, Thomas, "The Song of the Shirt," 60–61
hooks, bell, 109–10
Howe, Julia Ward, "The Battle Hymn of the Republic," 94
humanitarianism, 3–7, 13, 21, 23–24, 26–27
Hume, David, 3

identity: class and, 75–76, 89–90, 92–94, 152–53; difference and, 14–15, 112–13, 120; national, 14–15, 101, 108–14, 181n34
immigration, 93–94, 110–11
Indigenous people, 101–3, 105–6, 180n10
irony, 103–5
Isabella, Queen, 101–2

Jackson, Zakiyyah Iman, 132–33, 184n4
Jacobs, Harriet, 136–37, 153; *Incidents in the Life of a Slave Girl*, 139–41, 148–49
Jacobson, Matthew Frye, 110–11
Jefferson, Thomas, *Notes on the State of Virginia*, 111–12
"Jim Jawbone," 76–77, 80–81, 83, 89–91, 94–95. *See also* minstrelsy, blackface
Johnson, Sara E., 140–41
Johnson, Walter, 141–42
Jolliffe, John, 119
Jones, Douglas A., 92, 94–95, 179n93

Kansas-Nebraska Act, 108–9, 113, 115–16
Kilgour, Maggie, 24, 108–9
Kilner, Dorothy, 167n29; *The Rotchfords*, 27–28
kinship: difference and, 22, 25–30, 39–40, 43; disgust and, 13–14, 33, 43; sentimentalism and, 8–11, 52–53

Lay, Benjamin, 20
Lewis, Matthew, 131
Lhamon, W. T., Jr., 92
Lincoln, Abraham, 156
London Committee of the Society for Effecting the Abolition of the Slave Trade, "Am I Not a Man and a Brother?" 25
Lott, Eric, 74, 77–78, 134–35
Lundy, Benjamin, 46–47

magic lantern slides, 136–37, 143
Mahar, William J., 92–93

Marx, Karl, 22–23, 120, 183n69
McBride, Dwight A., 116–17
Melville, Herman, 12, 49–50, 74; *Moby-Dick*, 13–14, 47, 65–71, 129, 173n101; *Typee*, 67
Merish, Lori, 53, 181n41
Merry, Robert, 20
metaphor: consumption and, 5–6, 8, 11–16, 20–22, 24–27, 33–36, 40–43, 68–69, 99–112, 116–17, 119–31, 133, 139–42, 148–49, 152, 162n27, 165n5, 168n57, 180n5, 183n69; proximity and, 11, 20–21, 165n55; weapon, 103–5, 119–20. *See also* animals, animality; cannibalism
metonymy, 78, 81–82, 85–86
Mexican-American War, 50
Michaels, Walter Benn, 54–55
Middle Passage, 36, 129, 148
Miller, William Ian, 9, 62–63
Milton, John, *On Christian Doctrine*, 24–25
minstrelsy, blackface, 5–6, 11–12, 14, 71–76, 122, 124, 155–56, 174n18, 176n52, 179n93; class and, 14, 75–76, 78–80, 86–95, 152–53, 179n88, 179n92; disgust and, 73–76; domestic performance and, 89–95; examples of songs, 72–73, 76–77, 80–86, 89–91, 93–95, 133–36; hungry animal tropes in, 128–29, 133–36; indistinguishability between enslaved person and product, 76–79, 85–89; willing commodification and, 79–85, 94–95. *See also* songsters
Mintz, Sidney, 2–3
Montaigne, Michel de, "On Cannibals," 102–4

Montgomery, James, "The West Indies," 129
morality: animals and, 132, 138; consumption and, 3–4, 9, 11–12, 24, 28–29, 44–47, 49–53, 56–59, 64–65, 74–75, 78, 107–8, 111–12, 119, 121–23, 132, 138, 141, 151–55, 157, 169nn5–6, 170n20; sympathy and, 3–4, 10, 160nn10–11
Moran, Thomas, *The Slave Hunt*, 146–48
Morrison, Toni, 167n29; *Beloved*, 119
Morton, Timothy, 20–21

nation: difference and, 108–14; identity and, 14–15, 101, 108–14, 181n34; race and, 14–15, 100–101, 109–12, 116; slavery and, 14–15, 108–15
Newcastle Antislavery Society, 58
New York City Anti-Slavery Society, 59
Ngai, Sianne, 9, 153
noble savage, 102–3
Northup, Solomon, *Twelve Years a Slave*, 139–42

panoramas, 136–37, 142–44
performance: consumption of, 14, 71, 75–76; domestic, 89–95; public, 136–37
"Petition of the Sharks of Africa, The," 130
physicality, 21–22, 24–31, 33–36, 39–43, 49–50, 63–66. *See also under* abolitionism; body; race
Pierce, Franklin, 115–16
Pietz, William, 23
Polack, Joel Samuel, 106

pragmatism, 153–55
Priest, Josiah, *Slavery, As It Relates to the Negro, or African Race*, 106–7
Prince, Mary, 13, 22, 40–43

race: animality and, 123–24, 127–28, 132–37, 141–42, 148, 184n4, 185n7, 185n25; body and, 6, 24–25, 27–36, 39–40, 43, 101, 124, 127–28, 155–56, 168n52, 177n55; cannibalism and, 105–16, 119–25, 127–28, 169n85, 180n10, 182n44; class and, 5–6, 73–76, 79–80, 83–84, 86–88, 91–95, 122; commodification and, 72–73, 85, 88–89, 94–95, 101, 117–18, 127–28; consumption and, 6, 14–15, 73–89, 93–95, 100–103, 108–11, 114–15, 121–25, 127–29, 132–35, 159n1; difference and, 21, 27–28, 39–41, 43, 99–101, 108–12, 121–22, 132–33; gender and, 93–94, 155–56; nation and, 14–15, 100–101, 109–12, 116; passivity and, 133–36, 148; physicality and, 13–14, 24–25, 27–31, 39–41, 43
racism, 5–6, 71, 91–95, 109–10, 152–53, 159n1, 167n29; abolitionism and, 6–7, 13, 15–16, 20–21, 24–28, 33–36, 40–41, 43, 126–27, 132–34, 148; connection and, 87–88; disgust and, 9, 13–16, 20–21, 27–28, 33–36, 40–41, 43, 71, 74–75, 78, 109–10, 121–22, 125, 126–27, 152–53; of hungry animal tropes, 133–34; scientific, 106–7, 123, 181n27
Randolph, Peter, 84
Remond, Sarah Parker, 87–88
resistance, 15–16, 83–84, 116–17, 127–29, 133, 136–37, 139–49, 154, 188n9

revulsion. *See* disgust
Rhoads, Samuel, 151–52
Ricœur, Paul, 11, 26, 109, 165n55
Roberts, Brian, 83, 92
Roediger, David R., 79–80
Ross, Kelly, 137–38
Ruffin, Edmund, 117–18
Ruggles, Jeffrey, 144–45, 187n61
rum, 35–36, 160n8. *See also* sugar

Sánchez-Eppler, Karen, 8, 27
satire, 103–5
Schoolman, Martha, 55–56
Schuller, Kyla, 64
Scott, Winfield, 114–15
Sedgwick, Catharine Maria, *Home*, 91
Sedgwick, Eve Kosofsky, 152–53
sensationalism, 49
sentimentalism, 3, 8–11, 34, 44–45, 152, 160n11, 160n13, 162nn33–34, 163nn36–37, 163n39, 163n46, 164n49, 172n64, 186n33; abolitionism and, 8–9, 13–14, 19–20, 45–50, 52–53, 55–58, 61–66, 71; disgust and, 49, 62–66, 71; political efficacy of, 10, 164n49. *See also* sympathy
sharks, 129–30, 173n101, 185n10
Sheller, Mimi, 3–4, 6, 162n25, 162n27, 168n68, 180n5
Shotwell, Alexis, 154–55
sighs, 44–47, 55–56, 60–65
slave narratives, 15–16, 127–28, 141–43, 177n54, 186n33, 187n61, 187n63
slavery, 160n5; animals and, 126–28, 136–45, 148–49, 184n2, 187n61; body and, 25–35, 69–70; cannibalism and, 6, 12–13, 20–27, 32–36, 38–43, 44–46, 67–70, 78, 100–122, 124–25, 126–28,

138, 152, 162n27, 169n85; class and, 11–12, 14, 75–76, 83, 86–88; commodity fetish and, 23; consumption and, 1–16, 19–20, 31–32, 36–50, 59–60, 68, 72–75, 78–80, 82–83, 86–89, 99, 108, 117–19, 126–32, 135–38, 141–43, 148–49, 151–52, 154–56, 159n1, 161n18, 162n25; economics of, 4, 6–8, 11–16, 20, 46, 51–58, 65–66, 68–70, 74–75, 80, 87–88, 99–101, 116–21, 126–31, 133–38, 141, 148–49, 152–53, 155–56, 161n18, 162n25; entanglement and, 2, 6–7, 12, 47–48, 50–51, 54–55, 57–58, 78–79, 154–55; financial networks of, 13–14, 49–50, 54–60; nation and, 14–15, 108–15; passivity and, 133–36, 148; violence of, 37–40, 83–84, 101, 106, 110–11, 116–20, 126–27, 129, 131–33, 137–42, 152, 180n5; "wage slavery," 59–60, 79–80, 87–88; as willing, 79–85, 94–95
Smith, Adam, 3
Smith, James C. A., 142–43
songsters, 75–76, 89–95, 174n18, 178n69. *See also* minstrelsy, blackface
sonnet form, 38–39
Southey, Robert, 22, 36–40, 129
Stevens, Thaddeus, 110–11
Stowe, Calvin Ellis, 57–58
Stowe, Harriet Beecher, 49–50; *The Key to "Uncle Tom's Cabin,"* 54–55; *Uncle Tom's Cabin,* 13–14, 44–45, 47, 52–58, 94, 163n36
subjectivity, 43, 127, 136–37, 148–49
sugar, 2–6, 8–9, 11–12, 14, 37–39, 57, 64, 73, 77, 79–80, 99, 117–18, 160n8, 162n27, 183n82; abstention campaign, 7–8, 13–14, 20–22, 33–34, 45–49, 62–63, 152, 154–55, 161n22, 165nn4–5, 166n10, 169n5, 170n19; blood and, 8–9, 11–14, 19–43, 44–49, 59–67, 131–32, 151–52, 155, 165n5, 168n57, 168n59
Sumner, Charles, 110–11
Sussman, Charlotte, 3–4, 6, 20–21, 162n27, 165n4, 180n17
Swift, Jonathan, "A Modest Proposal," 103–5, 180n17
sympathy, 3–4, 6–9, 13–14, 47–50, 62–63, 71, 152, 163n39; action and, 19–21, 44–45, 52–53, 57–58, 152–53, 157; animals and, 127–28; power dynamics of, 10. *See also* sentimentalism

Tawa, Nicholas E., 91–92, 94
tears, 8, 11–13, 22–24, 30–31, 44–47, 55–56, 60–65, 131–32, 151–52
Thistlewood, Thomas, 131
Thoreau, Henry David, 49–50, 58, 170n30, 171n36; "Resistance to Civil Government," 50–51; "Slavery in Massachusetts," 116–17; *Walden*, 13–14, 47, 51–52
tobacco, 8, 11–12, 14, 73, 75–83, 85–89, 99, 177n62
tobacco signs, 81–83, 175n33
Tocqueville, Alexis de, 118
Tompkins, Jane, 52–53, 164n49
Tompkins, Kyla Wazana, 6, 101, 122, 127–28, 162n27, 183n82, 185n25
"Too Black a Dose," 110–11
transatlantic slave trade, 2–8, 13, 19–31, 36–38, 41–43, 45–46, 68–70, 105–6, 118–19, 129–31, 160n7, 161n18. *See also* slavery

transubstantiation. *See* communion
travel narratives, 106
Turner, J. M. W., 146–48

violence: of colonialism, 102–3; of consumption, 1–2, 6, 19–20, 33, 36–38, 66, 68–70, 83, 101, 115–16, 120, 125–27, 129, 131–33, 137–41; erotics of, 101; resistance and, 141–49, 188n9; of slavery, 37–40, 83–84, 101, 106, 110–11, 116–20, 126–27, 129, 131–33, 137–42, 152, 180n5
Virginia Minstrels, 73
Wade, Benjamin F., 113–14

Walker, Kara, *A Subtlety, or the Marvelous Sugar Baby*, 155–56
Watson, Kelly L., 102–3

Watt, Paul, 89–90
Wedgwood, Josiah, 25
whaling, 65–70
white supremacy, 5–7, 11–12, 100, 110–11, 116, 125, 127–28, 152–53, 155–56; cannibalism and, 162n27, 182n44; hungry animal tropes and, 133–35, 143
Williams, Raymond, 4
Wilmot, David, 116
Wilmot Proviso, 116
Wilson, James C., 105–6
wolves, 143–44, 187n61. *See also* dogs
Woodard, Vincent, 6, 101, 127–28, 162n27, 180n5
wool, 56, 85–86, 168n52, 171n57. *See also* cotton
Woolfolk, Austin, 118
Woolman, John, 1–3, 7–8, 20, 154–55
Wordsworth, William, 36

RECENT BOOKS IN
THE CARTER G. WOODSON INSTITUTE SERIES
Black Studies at Work in the World

Unleashing Black Power: Grassroots Organizing in Harlem and the Advent of the Long, Hot Summers
PETER D. BLACKMER

The Evolution of a Rural Free Black Community: Goochland County, Virginia, 1728–1832
REGINALD D. BUTLER, EDITED BY PETER S. ONUF

Roses in December: Black Life in Hanover County from Civil War to Civil Rights
JODY LYNN ALLEN

The Struggle for Change: Race and the Politics of Reconciliation in Modern Richmond
MARVIN T. CHILES

A Little Child Shall Lead Them: A Documentary Account of the Struggle for School Desegregation in Prince Edward County, Virginia
BRIAN J. DAUGHERITY AND BRIAN GROGAN, EDITORS

We Face the Dawn: Oliver Hill, Spottswood Robinson, and the Legal Team That Dismantled Jim Crow
MARGARET EDDS

Keep On Keeping On: The NAACP and the Implementation of Brown v. Board of Education *in Virginia*
BRIAN J. DAUGHERITY

Schooling Jim Crow: The Fight for Atlanta's Booker T. Washington High School and the Roots of Black Protest Politics
JAY WINSTON DRISKELL JR.

The Punitive Turn: New Approaches to Race and Incarceration
DEBORAH E. MCDOWELL, CLAUDRENA N. HAROLD,
AND JUAN BATTLE, EDITORS

Freedom Has a Face: Race, Identity, and Community in Jefferson's Virginia
KIRT VON DAACKE

Gabriel's Conspiracy: A Documentary History
PHILIP J. SCHWARZ, EDITOR

Rambles of a Runaway from Southern Slavery
HENRY GOINGS, EDITED BY CALVIN SCHERMERHORN,
MICHAEL PLUNKETT, AND EDWARD GAYNOR

Whispers of Rebellion: Narrating Gabriel's Conspiracy
MICHAEL L. NICHOLLS

*Word, Like Fire: Maria Stewart, the Bible, and the Rights
of African Americans*
VALERIE C. COOPER

*Strategies for Survival: Recollections of Bondage
in Antebellum Virginia*
WILLIAM DUSINBERRE

*Criminal Injustice: Slaves and Free Blacks in Georgia's
Criminal Justice System*
GLENN MCNAIR

Segregation's Science: Eugenics and Society in Virginia
GREGORY MICHAEL DORR

*The Segregated Scholars: Black Social Scientists and the
Creation of Black Labor Studies, 1890–1950*
FRANCILLE RUSAN WILSON

*Bitter Fruits of Bondage: The Demise of Slavery and the
Collapse of the Confederacy, 1861–1865*
ARMSTEAD L. ROBINSON

www.ingramcontent.com/pod-product-compliance
Lightning Source LLC
Chambersburg PA
CBHW070315240426
43661CB00057B/2649